CASES IN FINANCIAL MANAGEMENT

IQBAL MATHUR
SOUTHERN ILLINOIS UNIVERSITY,
CARBONDALE

FREDERICK C. SCHERR
WEST VIRGINIA UNIVERSITY

Macmillan Publishing Co., Inc.
New York

Collier Macmillan Publishing
London

**To
Jennifer
and
Susan**

Macmillan Publishing Co., Inc.
866 Third Avenue, New York, N.Y. 10022

Collier Macmillan Canada, Ltd.

Library of Congress Cataloging in Publication Data

Mathur, Iqbal.
  Cases in financial management.

  1. Corporations—Finance—Case studies.
2. Business enterprises—Finance—Case studies.
I. Scherr, Frederick C., joint author. II. Title.
HG4026.M366   658.1'5   78-8925
ISBN 0-02-377260-3

Printing: 1 2 3 4 5 6 7 8   Year: 9 0 1 2 3 4 5

PREFACE

The successful financial manager often needs to relate one abstract financial notion to another to solve problems on hand. Sometimes the problems and the related alternatives are obvious. At other times neither the central issues nor the spectrum of relevant alternatives is easily comprehended. The successful financial manager systematically looks at the available evidence and, using his or her analytical and intuitive skills, makes a decision and proceeds to implement it. The purpose of this casebook is to let the student apply financial concepts and techniques to real-life situations. The book provides a broad spectrum of financial situations as viewed from the decision-maker's or analyst's standpoint. In solving these cases the student not only becomes familiar with typical issues in finance and with applying financial methodology but also, we hope, develops intuitive skills in problem identification and solution.

The cases we have brought together vary in the complexity of their concepts and in the amount of time needed for their solution. The cases can be used both in the classroom for illustrative purposes and for assignments to students. We have used these cases in both modes and at the introductory and intermediate levels at a variety of institutions. Our experience has shown that some cases lend themselves to the introductory level with great success. Still others require a certain background before a student can tackle them and probably are more appropriate at intermediate levels. The majority of them have proved effective at both the introductory and intermediate levels.

In developing the cases we made a special effort to try to capture and preserve the business and decision-making environment. Also to the extent possible, we had a number of former students who are now in managerial positions look over the cases and solutions to

ensure that we are dealing with situations involving commonly en-
countered problems and with solutions consistent with widely
accepted managerial practices.

We express our gratitude to the many executives without whose
cooperation this casebook would not have been possible. We are
grateful for the valuable comments of William Beranek, University of
Georgia, Z. Lew Melnyk, University of Cincinnati, Coral Snodgrass,
Marshall University, Alex O. Williams, University of Virginia, and
Mark Yogman on many of the cases. We thank our colleagues at
Southern Illinois University and West Virginia University for their
helpful discussions of various financial issues. Maureen Jenkins de-
serves our thanks for typing many of the cases. We thank Kenneth
MacLeod at Macmillan for making the completion of the book a very
pleasant task. Our special thanks go to our students who provided us
valuable feedback on earlier drafts of the cases.

We realize that in any project of this nature there is always room
for improvement. We would greatly appreciate comments and suggestions.

I.M.

F.C.S.

CONTENTS

PART I

Financial
Statements
and Financial
Analysis

Case 1

MOXIE MOLDERS

FINANCIAL STATEMENTS

Mr. George, credit manager of Plastics Supplier, Inc., sat at his desk reviewing his credit file on Moxie Molders, a firm located in California. He had visited there five months previously, and had recently received a new six-month financial statement dated May 31, 1973. He had just completed a conversation with Dan Roberts, president, part owner, and plant manager for Moxie.

"I know our statement isn't audited, Bob, but you know how it is in a small business," Roberts had said. "We aren't as sophisticated as you are. Take that May 31, 1973 financial statement that I gave the salesman to send to you. We've written off $27,000 in accounts receivable to bad debts during the past year, but we still have $12,300 over 60-days old; $1,500 is in the courts. Our accounts are slow but good, and this slows down our cash flow. Our biggest customer, Quark Manufacturing, pays us in 45 days; they're 40 percent of our total receivables. That 'other accounts receivable' is a personal loan I took out for my car. I'm good for that. One-third of our raw-materials inventories are not being utilized; we bought this material in advance because we thought the price was going up; we may use it later in the year. We've got good profit possibilities in that power-tool-housing job; that should keep us running and making money until the end of the fiscal year on November 30, 1973. That other asset—that mold—we built that for a guy who never picked it up. It's a one-of-a-kind job. The termination claim for breach of contract is in the courts. That accrued liability is a note we owe another supplier for material which we purchased last year. The SBA has agreed to defer this year's $37,500 payment until next year. We want to use your material, but we've got to have open credit; our cash flow is too slow for COD. Go along with us and we'll push 250,000 pounds of volume your way at $1.00 per pound for the power-tool-housing job. If you don't, we'll have to buy the material elsewhere."

From visiting the firm and reading trade reports, Mr. George knew a lot about Moxie Molders' line of business and about Dan Roberts' background. Moxie Molders is a mold manufacturer and injection molder of plastic products, with sales volumes running

40 percent from the former and 60 percent from the latter. There is a very large number of such firms in the United States. Plastic molders buy raw plastic from a plastic producer, normally a large chemical firm, and reform this plastic, using a relatively simple process, into parts required by assemblers and large manufacturers. The molds used in this operation are usually owned by the manufacturer, who lends them to the molder for the parts production run after a contract has been signed. Some firms, like Moxie, also build molds, although this is usually done as more of a service to customers than as a profit-making operation. Because of the large number of molders and the relatively low number of manufacturers, plastic molding is a very competitive, marginally profitable venture. Most plastic molders have cash flow problems, and commonly pay in 50 days; terms of sale for raw plastic are 30 days. Moxie Molders shows a sporadic payment record in the industry, paying suppliers in anywhere from 50 to 150 days. During the last year, Moxie bought $6,700 from Plastic Supplier, Inc., and paid in 120 days. The majority of materials used by Moxie Molders, in the past, was provided for the firm by manufacturers who bought it, directly, from plastic makers. This is a common arrangement in the business, since manufacturers use many molders and can obtain quantity discounts by buying for all of the molders at once.

Dan Roberts is 36-years old. He joined the Marine Corps after graduating from high school, and served four years. He has worked in the plastics molding business since 1959, in various capacities. He has a college degree (obtained at night) from a small California school. He has been the plant manager of two other firms. The regional sales manager for Plastics Supplier, Inc., has visited Moxie Molders, and believes Roberts to be honest but doubts his business ability.

The sales department of Plastics Supplier, Inc., has advised Mr. George that they are very interested in selling to the account. Profit margins are 20 percent on the product that Moxie wants to buy. Recently, several accounts, to which Mr. George elected not to grant credit, have gone to competitors and have not defaulted. The salesman, John Richards, has meet with Roberts, and considers Moxie a good customer. "Sure they pay slow," Richards commented, "but so does everyone else in the industry. I know Roberts; he's a good guy. He'll pay up eventually."

EXHIBIT 1

May 31, 1973 Six-Month, Unaudited Financial Statement of Moxie Molders, Inc.

Current assets			
Cash in bank		$ 3,241	
Accounts receivable			
Trade (pledged)	119,284		
Other	10,110		
Total accounts receivable		129,394	
Inventories			
Raw materials	99,990		
Tooling	37,800		
Finished parts	81,642		
Total inventories		219,432	
Total current assets			352,067
Other assets			
Termination claim		45,645	
Mold		27,424	
Total other assets			73,069
Fixed assets			
Equipment less depreciation		315,985	
Total fixed assets			315,985
Total assets			$741,121
Current liabilities			
Notes payable (secured)		$ 92,398	
Accounts payable		112,309	
Accrued liabilities		45,668	
Current portion of S.B.A. loan		37,500	
Total current liabilities			287,875
Other liabilities			
Customer deposits		48,750	
Total other liabilities			48,750
Long-term liabilities			
S.B.A. loan (secured by fixed assets)		314,948	
Total long-term liabilities			314,948
Owners equity			
Capital stock		27,000	
Retained earnings		62,548	
Total owners' equity			89,548
Total liabilities and owners' equity			$741,121

EXHIBIT 2

November 30, 1972 Unaudited Fiscal Income Statement of Moxie Molders, Inc.

Sales	$584,652
Cost of goods sold	482,718
Gross margin on sales	101,934
Selling and administrative expenses	51,060
Interest expense	13,839
Profit before taxes	$ 37,035

Questions

1. Restate the May 31, 1973 balance sheet for Moxie Molders based on Roberts' conversation with Mr. George. Use your best judgement regarding the validity and location on the balance sheet of assets. State your assumptions.

2. To go with your *proforma* balance sheet for Question 1, comput a *proforma* income statement for the six months ending May 31, 1973 and the year ending November 30, 1973. Assume that the power-tool-housing job represents an additional $400,000 in sales volume and that everything else remains the same, including rate of sales external to this job.

3. Compute the following ratios, using the May 31, 1973 statement submitted by Roberts and your *proforma* balance sheet and income statement:
   1. Current ratio
   2. Accounts payable turnover ratio (based on CGS)
   3. Accounts receivable turnover ratio (based on sales)
   4. Quick (acid test) ratio (use cash and accounts receivable)
   5. Debt to net worth ratio

4. The industry median ratios are 1.5, 10.8, 8.8, 0.8, and 1.9 for companies of Moxie's class size in this industry. If you were Mr. George, and your only options were open credit or COD, how would you handle orders from Moxie Molders?

5. What do you think of Moxie's chances for survival as a going concern?

Case 2

VOPAL PLASTICS

FINANCIAL RATIO ANALYSIS

On January 7, 1976, Dick Smith, the assistant credit manager of Gymbal Plastic Resins, had just finished a meeting with his boss, Bob Little. Mr. Little had received a call the previous day from Gymbal's salesman for Michigan regarding Vopal Plastics, a firm located in Muskegon. Vopal had been a customer in 1971 and 1972, but had not purchased anything from Gymbal for the past three years.

"I haven't looked at the Vopal file, Dick," Little had said. "You weren't here then, but when we were selling to them in 1972, they were slow-payers. The salesman tells me that they lost money in 1974 and 1975; things are probably pretty grim there now from a financial standpoint. However, the salesman says that they are using a lot of materials that are competitive with ours. We could make some money if we could sell some plastic there, and payments aren't too far beyond our terms of sale. We might sell them as much as $50,000 per month. Check it out and get back to me."

Gymbal had maintained a running credit file on Vopal Plastics. This file contained credit agency reports and trade clearances (lists of Vopal's suppliers that report the highest balance owed to them, amounts owing, amounts past due, terms of sale, and payment patterns). Stock in Vopal was publically traded on a local stock exchange; audited financial statements from annual reports had been reproduced in credit agency presentations. Since the auditor was a major accounting firm, and since the auditor's opinion contained no disclaimer, Smith felt that he could use the statements in analysis with a high degree of confidence.

From reading the credit agency reports, Dick ascertained that Vopal's recent history had contained some high- and low-points. The firm had been founded in the late 1940's, and was one of the oldest plastic-molding firms in the Muskegon area. Sales volumes had grown steadily in the 1969–1974 period, but had suffered a severe decline in 1975. In a mid-1975 message to stockholders, Vopal's president had attributed the cause of this decline to customers' caution in responding to the economic upturn.

Profits, too, had declined recently. The years 1971 to 1973 had been profitable, but 1974 and 1975 had been loss years. The losses in these years had been attributed by Vopal's management to several causes. Profits in 1974 were good through three quarters, but significant losses were incurred in the fourth quarter due to diminished demand, rising raw-material costs, customer resistance to price increases, rises in indirect costs, and a write-down of some assets. The latter factor, alone, increased net loss by $130,000. In 1975, selling and administrative expenses were reduced significantly; an unprofitable operation was closed, resulting in a non-recurring item which reduced income by $126,000. However, operations still resulted in a small net loss due to decreased sales volumes. See Exhibit 1 and 2 for a presentation of Vopal's financial statements from 1971 to 1975.

Vopal's negotiations with banks had always been satisfactory, according to bankers' comments. Vopal had consolidated a number of loans granted by various banks into a medium-length, secured term loan in 1969. In 1973, this had been paid off and replaced with an unsecured term loan, and revolving credit arrangements in which three local banks participated. The covenants of this loan agreement had been given in Vopal's annual report, and they included restrictions on net worth, working capital, cash dividends, and capital spending.

Finally, Dick Smith noted that the raw materials purchased by Vopal were not sold on cash-discount terms. Vopal had always had a reputation in the trade as a slow-paying account. Vopal's management had always had some excuse for this condition. Dick Smith used his credit file's trade clearances to make a table of Vopal's payment pattern over time and the reasons they gave for this slowness (see Exhibit 3, page 10).

EXHIBIT 1

Vopal Plastics

Balance Sheets, December 31, 1971 to 1975

(rounded thousands of dollars)

	12/31/71	12/31/72	12/31/73	12/31/74	12/31/75
Cash	$ 48	$ 90	$ 90	$ 184	$ 319
Accounts receivable	630	766	939	1,090	896
Inventories	888	725	958	1,261	785
Prepaid expenses	40	52	61	60	47
Other current assets	19	19	21	114	17
Total current assets	1,625	1,652	2,069	2,709	2,064

EXHIBIT 1 (Cont'd)

Property, plant, equipment less depreciation	1,288	1,311	1,298	1,796	1,591
Other fixed assets	259	121	78	43	22
Total fixed assets	1,547	1,432	1,376	1,839	1,613
Total assets	3,172	3,084	3,445	4,548	3,677
Accounts payable	722	390	510	706	366
Current portion long-term debt	218	210	404	373	352
Accruals	80	110	124	229	248
Other current liabilities	73	156	99	52	22
Total current liabilities	1,093	866	1,137	1,360	988
Long-term debt	596	634	596	1,620	1,257
Stock	96	96	93	93	90
Additional paid-in capital	440	440	440	440	440
Retained earnings	947	1,048	1,179	1,038	902
Total equity	1,483	1,584	1,712	1,571	1,432
Total liabilities & owner equity	$3,172	$3,084	$3,445	$4,548	$3,677

EXHIBIT 2

Vopal Plastics

Income Statements for Years Ending
December 31, 1971 to December 31, 1975

(rounded thousands of dollars)

	12/31/71	12/31/72	12/31/73	12/31/74	12/31/75
Sales	$4,639	$5,850	$7,184	$8,282	$6,207
Cost of goods sold	3,842	4,899	6,084	7,148	5,115
Gross margin on sales	797	951	1,100	1,134	1,092
Selling and administrative expenses *	739	724	970	1,373	1,105
Operating income	58	227	130	(239)	(13)
Extraordinary profit & loss	(5)	(28)	84	0	(126)
Net income before tax	53	199	214	(239)	(139)
Income taxes	(12)	98	86	(98)	0
Net profit after tax	$ 65	$ 101	$ 128	$(141)	$(139)

* Includes interest expense

EXHIBIT 3

Vopal Plastics

Summary of Trade Payments and Management Comments, 1971 to 1975

Year	Trade Payment Habit	Reasons Given for Slowness
1971	Generally pays 30 days beyond terms. Some suppliers paid promptly.	"Surplus" cash was invested in treasury bills.
1972	Generally pays 60 days beyond terms.	Lack of working capital.
1973	Generally pays promptly; some minor slowness of up to 20 days beyond terms.	Funds being used for expansion.
1974	Generally pays promptly; some minor slowness up to 20 days beyond terms.	Increases in cost of raw materials.
1975	Some prompt payment; some slowness up to 10 days beyond terms.	Slow moving inventory.

Questions

1. Compute the following liquidity ratios for Vopal for 1971 to 1975:

    1. Current ratio
    2. Acid-test ratio (use year-end cash and receivables only in the numerator.)

   Do these ratios, in general, coincide with the payment pattern of Vopal shown in Exhibit 3? In your opinion, is there any reason exhibited in the 1975 ratios for Vopal's slowness? How do these ratios compare to the 1975 industry medians of 1.5 and 0.8?

2. Compute the following coverage and debt ratios for 1971 to 1975. These ratios are used by analysts to assess the firm's financial risk.

    1. Total debt to net worth
    2. Total debt to total assets
    3. Interest coverage (annual earnings, before interest and taxes, divided by interest payments. Assume interest was on long-term debt, only, computed on year-end long-term balances, and was 6 percent for 1971 and 1972, and 8 percent thereafter.)

The industry medians for the first two of these ratios in 1975 were approximately 1.5 and .64. Given the three ratios computed above, Vopal's cost of goods sold, and Vopal's level of net worth, does the $50,000 sales per month mentioned in case (on net 30-day terms) seem to be a relatively safe, credit exposure? What information about Gymbal's product line and customers would assist you in this assessment?

3. In 1972, Vopal's management claimed that slow payments to suppliers were due to an abnormally low, working capital position. Do the current and quick ratios bear this out?

4. In 1975, Vopal's management claimed that slow payments were due to abnormally slow-moving inventory. Compute Vopal's inventory turnover ratio for 1971–1975 (use end-of-year cost of goods sold in the numerator). Does this ratio bear out management's contentions?

5. Compute Vopal's percent gross margin on sales. Among other things, this ratio gives some indication of the marginal profitability of the firm's sales. Has this measure been relatively stable over time? If the industry median for this measure is 25.6, how would you judge Vopal's profit potential in relation to other participants? Does this ratio contain information not in the "bottom line" (profit after taxes) entry on the financial statement?

6. Compute the following turnover ratios for 1975. Such ratios are used by analysts to rate the efficiency with which firms manage certain assets.
   1. Fixed-assets turnover (annual sales divided by year-end, net fixed assets)
   2. Total-assets turnover (annual sales divided by year-end, total assets)
   3. Average collection period (in days; year-end accounts receivable, divided by annual sales, times 365)

The industry medians for these ratios as of 1975 were approximately 5.67, 2.37, and 42.9. Does it appear that Vopal is managing fixed assets, total assets, and receivables in line with industry standards?

7. If you were Dick Smith, what would you report to Bob Little regarding Vopal's relative credit worthiness for the amounts discussed?

Case 3

GYRE MANUFACTURING DIVISION
FINANCIAL FORECASTING

The return flight from Denver to New York was a long one, but John Pens had much to do. This rushed and unexpected trip, from the corporate headquarters to the division headquarters and back, had not gone smoothly. The results had to be compiled and made ready for presentation to the financial vice president by the next morning.

John's employer, Bemish Corporation, had acquired Gyre Manufacturing almost by accident. Bemish Corporation was basically a major manufacturer of industrial chemicals. In the early 1960's, Gyre Manufacturing (then a privately held firm) had been one of Bemish's bigger customers, although they accounted for only 5 percent of Bemish's sales volume. Gyre used Bemish's products to make a line of consumer goods which were sold through distributors. Due to eroding profit margins, Gyre has experienced financial difficulty and, in 1965, bankruptcy was declared. Bemish was the major creditor. Bemish did not want to lose this outlet for their product, so they bought the assets from the court and had been operating Gyre as a division.

In an effort to make Gyre a profitable operation, a new, modern, high-capacity plant had recently been constructed, adjacent to the old, fully-depreciated plant in Denver. Most of the prebankruptcy Gyre personnel had left and had been replaced by Bemish people. Despite the investment of money and personnel, the operation was only marginally profitable. There were several other producers of products similar to Gyre's in the immediate area, and price competition was rampant. Since Bemish also sold products to the other competitors, it was felt that the Gyre Division should not instill any hostility in these firms by pricing too aggressively. Consequently, Gyre was a price-follower, always lagging in price reductions, and thus, suffering lower-than-potential sales volumes.

Further, not much attention had been paid by the corporate finance people to Gyre's problems. There were several causes for this. The Bemish Corporation had traditionally de-emphasized the finance function in favor of the sales department, and the finance department consequently was understaffed. Gyre's assets and sales were a very small part of the total corporation. The people at

Bemish's corporate headquarters were unfamiliar with the markets and operations of Gyre, and did not feel equipped to question Gyre people on financial topics. Gyre was physically separated from other Bemish facilities; aside from Gyre, Bemish had no plants west of St. Louis. Finally, because of their hectic marketplace, the management at Gyre was continually "putting out fires" and had little time to familiarize the corporate people with their operation.

Matters had come to a head when, as part of a new corporate program, Gyre had been requested to submit their five-year sales and profits forecast (see Exhibit 1, page 15). After reviewing it briefly, Mr. Meter, the vice president of finance, was not happy. He called John Pens into his office and said, "John, this forecast from Gyre is impossible. I can't believe they're going to sell that much product or make that much money. Get out there and check it out." John had just enough time to make appointments with Gyre's accountant, marketing manager, production personnel manager, and purchasing manager before he caught his plane.

His meeting with Mr. Wittenberg, accountant for the Gyre Division, had revealed the basis used for the original income forecast. Wittenberg had proven himself unfamiliar with forecasting techniques. He had estimated sales volumes by asking each of Gyre's salesmen for an estimate of "the amount he could sell" for the next five years in dollars. Wittenberg had totaled these estimates to arrive at the sales forecast. He had calculated the cost of goods sold and the gross margin on sales by assuming that the cost of goods sold was 70 percent of net sales; this had been the average for the last three years. This figure was to include direct labor. overhead, and cost of raw materials, under Bemish's system of reporting. Selling and administrative expense estimates were based on the 1975 payroll expenses for this class of employees.

The Bemish Corporation had a policy of charging each division a carrying cost for the book value of accounts receivable and fixed assets. This was the interest-expense entry shown on the forecast; in reality, no division borrowed money independently. The rate of charges was currently 10 percent. Wittenberg has applied this rate to the book value of fixed assets ($45,000,000 net in 1975, being depreciated, for corporate-reporting purposes, on a straight-line basis over 20 years starting in 1976) and to accounts receivable, which were currently $5,000,000. Wittenberg had used this figure for accounts receivable in future years, also. The remainder of the calculations were straight forward.

John Pens' other interviews had provided much additional information. The marketing manager, Mr Weslager, had been very helpful and interested. "Well, John," he had said, "you know salesmen. They're given to overestimating their selling capacity in the long run, and they don't have much feel for prices. I'm sure Art Wittenberg felt he was getting information straight from the source when he went to them for estimates, but they don't see the market as a whole, and they don't see our constraints. We sold 60,000,000 pounds of our product last year; we'll sell 80,000,000 pounds in 1976, and sell at capacity in 1977 and thereafter. Prices, as you know, are unstable, but I'd guess they'll increase about 3 percent per year over 1975 levels in our marketplace. We'll be selling to the same customer base, but in bigger volumes. Once we reach capacity, we believe that the market growth in this area will have peaked. We don't plan to put in requests for plant expansion in the foreseeable future." From his interview with the production manager, John found out that practical production capacity was about 90,000,000 pounds per year.

The personnel manager, Mr. Aaker, and the purchasing manager, Mr. Winter, had also been cooperative. From Aaker, John Pens had found out that the plant was now fully staffed with production workers, and that a new union contract had just been signed which would keep the production payroll at its 1975 level of $6,300,000 per year through 1978. After that, Aaker expected that the new three-year contract would result in a 20 percent wage increase. The payroll expense for selling and administrative employees is expected to increase 10 percent per year above 1975 levels.

Mr. Winter had grumbled about inflation and the cost of raw materials. "We're paying 20 cents for raw materials per pound of product sold in 1976. We paid the same in 1975. I can remember when it was 10 cents. I guess that will go up about 5 percent per year after this year. Fortunately, I've hog-tied all suppliers we classify as overhead with contracts; we're safe from their increases beyond 1975 levels for five years at least."

Questions

1. Compute a new income forecast based on the information John Pens got from the Gyre personnel. (*Hint:* to get overhead from cost of sales, compute the other two components, and subtract.)

2. Assuming that the information gleaned by John Pens from the department managers was valid, what incorrect assumptions did

Mr. Wittenberg make in deriving his original forecast of sales and income? Why did he make them?

3. Make a chart showing Wittenberg's profit forecast, your profit forecast, and the differences. Given Bemish's 10 percent return policy on fixed assets and accounts receivable, is this Gyre Division making a reasonable contribution to corporate profitability?

4. The Bemish Corporation's method of evaluating corporate profitability based on allocation of a percent of assets (see question 3) is called the ROI (return on investment) method. The accept-reject decisions for projects yielded by this method are not necessarily consistent with the more modern net present-value method. However, the ROI method is still used by many firms and is used by the Bemish Corporation; the student should be familiar with it, and therefore, we have illustrated it here. Assume that Bemish will sell the Gyre Division for $50,000,000 on December 31, 1980, and that the appropriate rate of discount is 20 percent for firms in Gyre's risk class. If Bemish was offered $75,000,000 for Gyre on January 1, 1976, should they sell? Use the NPV method of calculation.

EXHIBIT 1

Gyre Manufacturing Division

Five-Year Income Forecast

(rounded thousands of dollars)

	1975 (actual)	1976	1977	1978	1979	1980
Net sales	$31,200	$35,000	$41,000	$50,000	$63,000	$75,000
Cost of goods sold	21,840	24,500	28,700	35,000	44,100	52,500
Gross margin on sales	9,360	10,500	12,300	15,000	18,900	22,500
Selling and administrative expenses	2,000	2,000	2,000	2,000	2,000	2,000
Interest expense	5,000	4,775	4,550	4,325	4,100	3,875
Depreciation on new plant	0	2,250	2,250	2,250	2,250	2,250
Net profit before taxes	2,360	1,475	3,500	6,425	10,550	14,375
Taxes (50 percent)	1,180	737	1,750	3,212	5,275	7,187
Net profit after taxes	$ 1,180	$ 738	$ 1,750	$ 3,213	$ 5,275	$ 7,188

Case 4

CENTRAL DATA SYSTEMS, INC.*

FINANCIAL FORECASTING AND RATIO ANALYSIS

In mid-1975, it was announced that Itel Corporation had proposed the acquisition of Central Data Systems, Inc. (CDSI). An investor in CDSI decided to analyze the merger. As a first step, he decided to look at CDSI's past performance, and thereby, to forecast key financial items for CDSI.

Central Data Systems, Inc. was incorporated in Ohio in June, 1965, and maintained its corporate offices in Cleveland. CDSI was principally engaged in providing computing and software services. Its growth had been rapid and had been partially accounted for by acquisitions. CDSI acquired the Electronic Tabulating Company in June, 1969, the Pittsburgh Computer Company in June, 1971, Computer-Analysts, Inc. in March, 1972, Accounting and Business Forms, Inc. in July, 1972, and Computab, Inc. in September, 1972. CDSI's income statements for 1968 through 1974 are shown in Exhibit 1. Revenues increased from $420,000 in 1968 to $8,985,000 in 1974. During this same time span, net income increased from $60,000 to $337,000. CDSI's balance sheets for 1968–1974 are shown in Exhibit 2. From 1968 to 1974, total assets increased from $142,000 to $4,791,000. Other related, per-share statistics for CDSI are shown in Exhibit 3, page 18.

The software and data-processing industries have been characterized by rapid growth in the last few years. The software industry provides programming services to businesses. The data-processing industry provides companies with access to computer centers on a leased-time basis. As companies' data-processing needs have grown and become complex, more and more of them have found it easier and cheaper to be on-line with a computer center, rather than try to maintain in-house facilities. Just like any other emerging industries, the software and data-processing industries have been undergoing rapid change. They include small, one-city companies as well as companies that are truly international in scope. This flux in these industries had cautioned the investor against too much emphasis

---

*This case was prepared from public information. It is designed for educational purposes, and not for purposes of research or to illustrate the correct or incorrect handling of administrative practices.

on "industry averages." Rather, it was felt that a more appropriate procedure might be to look at trends in CDSI's performance in absolute terms.

EXHIBIT 1

Central Data Systems, Inc.

Income Statements, Year Ending May 31, 1968 to May 31, 1974[*]

(in thousands of dollars)

	1968	1969	1970	1971	1972	1973	1974
Revenues	$ 420	$1,212	$2,005	$1,780	$2,396	$7,292	$8,985
Expenses	317	1,018	1,720	1,705	1,960	6,653	8,198
Income before taxes	103	194	285	75	436	639	787
Taxes	43	88	133	43	207	332	410
Net income	$ 60	$ 106	$ 152	$ 32	$ 229	$ 307	$ 377
Dividends	. 2	2	4	17	18	32	37
To retained earnings	59. 8	104	148	15	211	275	340
Depreciation				153	131	253	268

EXHIBIT 2

Central Data Systems, Inc.

Balance Sheets, May 31, 1968 to May 31, 1974

(in thousands of dollars)

	1968	1969	1970	1971	1972	1973	1974
Cash	$ 43	$ 184	$ 325	$ 191	$ 433	$ 150	$ 71
Net receivables	71	207	345	329	385	1,593	1,452
Inventories	–	–	–	–	–	276	616
Other current assets	–	–	–	–	45	131	174
Total current assets	144	391	670	520	863	2,150	2,313
Net plant	9	221	432	414	699	1,317	1,428
Long term receivables	–	17	34	28	28	26	14
Other long term assets*	19	327	634	638	717	1,226	1,036
Total assets	142	956	1,770	1,600	2,307	4,719	4,791

[*]Firms acquired have been included from dates of acquisition. Average number of shares outstanding: 1968 – 300,000; 1969 – 400,000; 1970 – 431,150; 1971 – 431,150; 1972 – 450,733; 1973 – 459,313; 1974 – 460,883.

EXHIBIT 2 (Cont'd)

Notes payable	2	69	136	81	133	326	389
Accounts payable	14	56	96	133	372	1,223	1,150
Income taxes payable	35	60	86	6	128	27	37
Total current liabilities	51	185	318	220	633	1,576	1,576
Long-term debt	–	54	108	34	81	1,181	917
Deferred income taxes	8	17	26	12	30	42	47
Total liabilities	59	256	452	266	744	2,799	2,540
Common stock	5	6	7	7	7	7	7
Surplus	1	489	976	976	982	1,066	1,056
Returned earnings	77	205	335	351	577	850	1,191
Treasury stock	–	–	–	–	(3)	(3)	(3)
Net worth	83	700	1,318	1,334	1,563	1,920	2,251
Total liabilities & net worth	$ 142	$ 956	$1,770	$1,600	$2,307	$4,719	$4,791

*Mainly acquisition costs.

EXHIBIT 3

Central Data Systems, Inc.

Selected per Share Statistics

(in dollars)

Per Share Statistics	1968	1969	1970	1971	1972	1973	1974
Earnings	0.20	0.27	0.35	0.07	0.51	0.68	0.82
Dividends	0.00	0.00	0.01	0.04	0.04	0.07	0.08
Price – low	–	13.25	3.50	4.00	4.50	3.00	3.00
Price – high	–	22.50	9.00	6.75	10.25	9.00	4.50

Questions

1. Evaluate the performance of Central Data Systems. Answering this question involves calculating liquidity, efficiency, leverage, profitability and stockholder (P/E ratio, dividend payout, dividend yield and book value per share) ratios for CDSI. The answer should also encompass the trends in the ratios.

2. Using extrapolation, forecast 1975 and 1976 sales and earning per share for CDSI.

3. Assume that you are interested in buying a firm in the data-processing and software services fields. Taking into consideration your answers to Questions 1 and 2, what factors would you find attractive and unattractive about CDSI?

Case 5

WASHINGTON PAPER AND WOOD CORPORATION (A)

PRO-FORMA STATEMENTS AND CASH BUDGETING

As 1976 began, Robert Louis, treasurer of the Washington Paper and Wood Corporation, was somewhat apprehensive. (Detailed information on the Washington Paper and Wood Corporation is contained in Appendix A of this case. This information is material to the solution to the case.) He and the firm's president, Ed Richards, had renegotiated the company's short-term line of credit with their bank, the previous year, based on sales estimates available at the time. The firm's economists and sales personnel had developed a new, higher forecast of sales, based on economic and industry trends:

Month	Net sales (thousands)
1/76	12,105
2/76	17,293
3/76	19,022
4/76	17,293
5/76	15,563
6/76	15,563
7/76	15,563
8/76	15,563
9/76	12,105
10/76	12,105
11/76	12,105
12/76	8,646

Louis was concerned that three of the covenants in the line-of-credit agreement might be violated if the firm's sales actually reached these levels: (1) that the firm be out of debt on the credit line for 90 consecutive days during the calendar year; (2) that the maximum borrowings on the line be $15 million (no other short-term borrowings were allowed); and (3), that the firm's current ratio not fall below 1.7 at the end of each quarter.

Louis knew that several facts regarding the firm's cash flow, costs, and expectations were pertinent to resolving his apprehensions:

1. Interest on the line of credit for the month was payable during the following month.

2. Louis expected that the prime rate would be 7 percent for the first half of 1976, and rise to 7½ percent thereafter.

3. Gross margin on sales was expected to be 10 percent throughout the year.

4. Louis felt that the firm should continue to honor raw-materials suppliers' terms of sale of net 30 days.

5. Receivables also turned in 30 days.

6. Selling and administrative expenses were expected to be $12,684,000 for the year (approximately the 1975 level). These expenses were expected to occur evenly throughout the year, and were payable in the month in which they were incurred.

7. Taxes were to be 50 percent of quarterly net income, payable the month following the quarter's end. If the firm took a net loss during any quarter, 50 percent of this amount was to be immediately refundable. Net income, for tax and reporting purposes, was computed on an accrual basis. The fourth quarter of 1975 was break-even, so no tax accrual was shown on the end-of-year balance sheet.

8. Preferred dividends were to be $43,000 per quarter, payable at the end of the quarter. No common stock dividends were to be paid in 1976 to preserve capital.

9. Louis considered that $1 million was the minimum level of cash necessary to operate the firm, and intended to reduce cash balances to this level during January of 1976.

10. Depreciation was on a straight-line basis, both for reporting and tax purposes, and was to be $460,000 per month in 1976. This entry had been included in selling and administrative expenses on the income statements in past years.

11. Wages were 25 percent of cost of goods sold, and must have been paid in the month, incurred; raw-materials purchases, on a net 30 day basis, comprised the balance of cost of goods sold.

12. Interest on long term debt was to be $3,836,000 for 1976, payable in December, but accrued over the year. Principal payment was also due in December.

13. No capital spending was expected in 1976.

14. With the exception of any changes specified above, no differences in balance sheet items were expected between year-end 1975 and year-end 1976. The items that were to be constant over the period included inventories (turnover was expected to increase), pre-paid expenses, other current assets,

other assets, other accruals, preferred stock, and common
stock.

Questions

1. Generate a monthly cash forecast for Washington Paper and
   Washington Paper and Wood Corporation for 1976 (to get tax
   payments, you will also have to generate *pro forma* income
   statements). Use the net sales figures shown in the forecast.
   Assume all transactions occur on the first day of the month.

2. Will Washington Paper have to violate either the 90-day, out-of-
   debt constraint or the maximum-borrowing constraint in order
   to gain the higher sales level? If the 90-day, out-of-debt constraint is violated, how much short-term, credit-line debt must
   be converted to long-term debt to avoid this problem?

3. Generate *pro forma* balance sheets for the firm as of the end
   of each quarter in 1976. Does the firm have to violate the
   current ratio constraint?

4. If the bank lender for the short-term credit line is not also
   the long-term lender, and if the firm could renegotiate the short-
   term credit line with another bank at no increase in interest,
   would you suggest that they do so?

APPENDIX A

Washington Paper and Wood Corporation (A)
Background Information

Note: This appendix contains background information for Washington Paper and Wood Corporation (A). This background information
is also used in Washington Paper and Wood Corporation (B) and
Washington Paper and Wood Corporation (C). Each case is designed
to be solved independently of the other two cases.

The Washington Paper and Wood Corporation, founded in 1925,
was a major producer of paperboard and lumber. For the first
twenty years of its existence, the company concentrated its efforts
within these lines of business, building a series of production facilities on the West Coast and in the Pacific Northwest. In 1946,
the company began a series of acquisitions, the closings of some

operations, and the sale of other operations. This series of maneuvers lasted until the early 1970's. Acquisitions were made for cash or stock. Washington Paper stock held by other firms was also repurchased. The firms acquired by Washington Paper during this period were generally within Washington Paper's established lines of business and market area (examples: a lumber mill in California, a lumber distributor in Oregon). The operations that had been closed or sold were generally out of the firm's market area or business lines (examples: a Detroit carton manufacturer, a plastic molder). This series of maneuvers gave Washington Paper a large market position in its primary, geographical and product areas; however, no diversification was achieved, if any was intended. Neither did these moves provide new production facilities to replace the firm's aging plants, or give the firm access to additional timberland.

Washington Paper was organized into two divisions based on product line. The container products division, with about 66 percent of total sales, produced the two principal types of paperboard, containerboard and boxboard. Containerboard is a highly versatile and relatively inexpensive material, consisting of a corrugated layer glued between two liners. Boxboard is the material used in the manufacture of folding cartons, milk cartons, and food-service containers. Both products are used almost exclusively for packaging applications.

The container products division manufactured paperboard at two paperboard mills, one located in Washington and one in Oregon. The Washington mill used virgin fibers as raw material. There were two paperboard machines at this mill, one producing materials for containerboard and one producing materials for boxboard. The boxboard machine had undergone substantial modification in the years immediately prior to 1975, but outputs were still limited in product range as compared to the outputs of newer machines available.

The Oregon mill had three paperboard machines, all of which manufactured materials for boxboard from recycled fibers. The Oregon mill was older and less efficient than the recycling mills being constructed as of 1975. One of the paperboard machines in the Oregon mill was shut down for all of 1975, and the company had stated that this machine would remain shut down unless demand improved substantially.

About 70 percent of the output of these mills was used by Washington Paper as feedstock for the firm's two carton and four container plants. These plants, also located on the West Coast and in the Pacific Northwest, produced corrugated shipping containers, packaging for fresh produce, ice cream containers, cereal boxes, detergent containers, and many similar products. All the plants of the container products division were owned outright by the firm.

Sales in the paperboard industry are highly correlated with GNP, and closely follow general economic activity. Paperboard industry production fell, for the second straight year, in 1975. After advancing at an annual rate of 4 percent from 1964 to 1973, output declined 2.2 percent in 1974 and 14.5 percent in 1975. Sales began to recover in late 1975. Standard and Poors forecast that 1976 production would increase 16.9 percent. Benefiting from price increases, volume expansion, and operating efficiencies, industry profits were expected to increase substantially in 1976. However, pollution-abatement costs, conversion to the metric system, and economic uncertainties might have adverse effects in future years. Additionally, the entire paper-packaging industry was threatened by the intrusion of plastic into the container industry, although this threat had abated somewhat, due to the energy shortage's effect on plastic prices.

The firm's other division was the wood products division, with the remaining 34 percent of the company's sales volume. This division produced lumber and plywood from virgin timber. As of 1975, the firm owned six lumber mills and two plywood plants. The company was not one of the industry leaders in terms of volume of lumber produced; in 1974, the firm ranked below 25th in volume of sawtimber produced. The output of this division was sold to wholesale outlets.

The financial performance of this division had been adversely affected because the firm owned relatively little timberland. The raw-materials costs of the division were, therefore, dependent on the increasing cost of government lumber. As a consequence, the division had decided to shut down two of its mills in an area where timber costs were particularly high, where it had no captive supply, and where sales had been particularly low. At best, the lumber mills in other areas received 30 percent of their raw materials from captive sources.

The wood products division ran Washington Paper's only recently-constructed production facility. This plant, which started into operation in 1975 and which cost $7.2 million, used wood shavings, sawdust, and other wood wastes to produce building products. Start-up expenses had been higher than expected, resulting in an expense of $1.9 million in 1975 (See Exhibits 1 and 2, pp 26-27, for Washington Paper's balance sheets and statements of income and retained earnings).

Since the products made by the wood products division primarily went into construction (and, to a lesser extent, into furniture), sales for this group were primarily dependent on activity in the housing industry. Specifically, sales had been found by company economists to be highly correlated with housing starts.

The year ending December 31, 1975 was not a good one for Washington Paper. It was distinguished by plant start-up expenses, low demand for output, inventory liquidation by customers, increasing costs, and resistance by customers to price increases. The latter two factors were emphasized by the 1975 income statement. Though the firm's sales dropped by $17.7 million, cost of goods sold declined by only $4.2 million. The firm's gross margin on sales declined from 14.6 percent to 7.0 percent. Increased debt had been used by Washington Paper to finance operating losses and for capital expenditures due to the low price (by historical standards) of the firm's stock, which was publically traded. From 1974 to 1975, the firm's total debt to net worth ratio had increased from 1.55 to 1.81.

The company's long-term debt was composed of four issues; as of December 31, 1975, the current and long-term portions of these were:

1. Bank notes, totalling $20,352,000, interest at 7 percent; principal due, $2 million per year, 1977 to 1987, interest and principal payable on the last day of the year. A special payment of $352,000 against the principal was due on December 31, 1976. This amount is already included in "Current Principal Portion of LTD" in Exhibit 1.

2. Secured 6 percent Debentures, totaling $5.4 million, principal due $600,000 per year, 1976 to 1985, interest and principal payable on the last day of the year. The principal due 1976 is shown in Exhibit 1 in the "Current Principal Portion of LTD."

3. Convertible Subordinated 5¾ percent Debentures, totalling $36,308,000, principal due 1995, interest payable on the last day of the year. Under the sinking fund covenant of

these securities, 5 percent of this issue was to have been redeemed every October 15, starting in 1980.

4. A $952,000 note to an insurance firm, due on March 31, 1982.

The firm had also used leasing extensively, to acquire the use of some assets. These leasing agreements were not capitalized on the balance sheet. Minimum levels of these lease commitments are shown in Exhibit 3, p. 28. Under the firm's accounting system, these payments are included in selling and administrative expenses.

The bank line of credit shown on the balance sheet required no compensating balance. Interest was paid on this credit line at prime plus 2½ percent and the line must not have been utilized for 90 consecutive days during each calendar year. This provision is a standard one on bank credit lines, and is designed to show that the line represents short-term lending, only.

EXHIBIT 1

Washington Paper and Wood Corporation

Balance Sheets, December 31, 1974 and December 31, 1975

(rounded thousands of dollars)

	12/31/74	*12/31/75*
Cash	$ 1,858	$ 1,576
Accounts receivable	12,647	12,168
Inventories	32,525	28,494
Prepaid expenses	6,863	7,385
Other current assets	1,126	5,504
Total current assets	55,019	55,127
Other assets	5,722	7,180
Property, plant, land, and equipment	135,285	141,255
Less: depreciation	57,336	62,282
Net fixed assets	77,949	78,973
Total assets	138,690	141,280
Current principal portion of L.T.D.	1,251	952
Principal due on bank credit line	13,110	11,400
Accounts payable – raw materials	11,276	11,286
Accruals (see Note 1)	4,374	5,268
Preferred stock dividends payable	43	43
Total current liabilities	30,054	28,949
Long-term debt	54,209	62,060
Preferred stock	3,440	3,440

EXHIBIT 1 (Cont'd)

Common stock (less treasury stock)	14,851	14,851
Retained earnings	36,136	31,980
Total owners' equity	54,427	50,271
Total liabilities and owners' equity	$138,690	$141,280

Notes to December 31, 1975 Balance Sheet

Note 1: Breakdown of accruals as of 12/31/75

Accrued interest on bank credit line, due 1/76	$ 90
Accrued interest on long term debt, due 12/76*	0
Accrued taxes payable for previous quarter, due 1/76	0
Other accruals	5,178
Total accruals	$ 5,268

*Interest for 1975 has been paid. Interest for 1976 has not yet started to accrue.

EXHIBIT 2

Washington Paper and Wood Corporation

Statements of Income and Retained Earnings, for the Years Ending December 31, 1974 and December 31, 1975

(rounded thousands of dollars)

	12/31/74	*12/31/75*
Net sales	$167,481	$149,823
Cost of goods sold	143,471	139,311
Gross margin on sales	24,010	10,512
Selling and administrative expenses	12,012	12,683
Interest expense	3,492	3,996
Start-up costs of new plant	–	1,862
Income before extraordinary items	8,506	(8,029)
Other income	4,513	1,309
Other expenses	5,264*	0
Income before taxes	7,755	(6,720)
Taxes	3,609	(3,299)**
Income after taxes	4,146	(3,421)
Retained earnings, beginning of year	33,788	36,136
Common and preferred stock dividends	1,798	735
Retained earnings, end of year	$ 36,136	$ 31,980

*Loss from terminated operations.

**An increase in income due to tax loss carry-forward.

EXHIBIT 3

Washington Paper and Wood Corporation

Minimum Non capitalized Lease Commitment Expenditures, 1976–1980

Year	Expenditure (thousands)
1976	$1,208
1977	1,123
1978	684
1979	462
1980	314

Case 6

WASHINGTON PAPER AND WOOD CORPORATION (B)

SOURCES AND USES OF FUNDS

Robert Louis, the Treasurer of Washington Paper and Wood Corporation, felt that the meeting with John Evans, Investment Manager for Linear Life Insurance, on June 10, 1976 had gone rather well. (Detailed information on Washington Paper and Wood Corporation is contained in Appendix A of Case 5. This information is material to the solution to this case.) Despite Washington Paper's recent losses, Evans had been quite receptive to the firm's preliminary inquiries regarding long-term financing. Evans' remarks had been most encouraging.

"We realize your position, Bob, and we have confidence in you in the long run," Evans had said. "We realize that those losses are only temporary. Your new asset-management program should help your position greatly. Your long-term notes and debentures are beginning to become due, and the interest rate on that bank credit line is certainly high. We believe that Washington Paper still has debt capacity. Here's our preliminary proposal. We'll make your firm a four and one-half year loan, due January 1, 1981, at 7¾ percent, the interest payable at the end of each year, but we'd prefer that you take the entire sum now, since we have funds available for any reasonable amount. Just tell us how much you need. We can negotiate future lending in 1980."

Robert Louis felt that this was quite reasonable. He had his assistant draw up profit forecasts for 1976 through 1980, and a *pro forma* income statement for 1980. It was expected that the minimum level of cash necessary to support 1980 sales would be $2 million. He had decided that $7 million of the bank credit line would have to be converted into long-term debt, which would help the firm's current ratio. The approximate effect of the financing change on taxes, interest expense, and profits had been included in the profits' forecast. Preferred dividends were scheduled at $43,000 per quarter; no common dividends were to be paid through 1980. Depreciation was on a straight-line basis for both reporting and tax purposes, and was to be $460,000 per month through 1980. However, it was expected that fixed assets would be replaced, at the same rate, starting in 1977 and thereafter. No fixed-asset purchases were planned in 1976. Receivables generally turned over in 30 days; all sales were made on a credit basis. Wages and selling expenses were paid in the month in which they were incurred. Raw-material purchases were paid on a 30-day basis, and were 75 percent of monthly CGS. As of 1980, the firm expected that inventories would turn-over in about 45 days (based on CGS). Expected 1980 levels of some other balance sheet items, in thousands of dollars:

Prepaid expenses	$7,000
Other current assets	5,000
Other assets	7,000
Principal due on bank credit line	5,400
Accruals	5,000
Preferred stock dividends payable	43

No changes were expected on the Common and Preferred stock accounts before 1981.

EXHIBIT 1

Washington Paper and Wood Corporation (B)

Projected Statement of After-Tax Profit and Loss, 1976–1980[*]

(rounded thousands of dollars)

	1976	1977	1978	1979	1980
Profit after tax	$ (91)	$1,525	$2,500	$3,700	$4,300
Preferred stock dividends	172	172	172	172	172
Additions (reductions) of retained earnings	(263)	1,353	2,328	3,528	4,128

[*]The approximate effect of the financing change on taxes, interest expense, and profits has been taken into account in this forecast.

EXHIBIT 2

Washington Paper and Wood Corporation (B)

Projected Income Statement, 1980

(rounded thousands of dollars)

Net sales	$250,000
Cost of goods sold	222,400
Gross margin on sales	27,600

EXHIBIT 2 (Cont'd)

Selling and administrative expenses	15,000
Interest expense	4,000
Income before extraordinary items	8,600
Other Income	0
Other expenses	0
Income before tax	8,600
Taxes	4,300
Income after tax	4,300
Common and preferred stock dividends	172
Additions to retained earnings	$4,128

Questions

1. Using the balance sheet of December 31, 1975 from Exhibit 1, Washington Wood and Paper (A), as a starting point, generate a *pro forma* balance sheet as of December 31, 1980. It is best to start with a reconciliation of the long-term debt existing as of December 31, 1975 to the December 31, 1980 date.

2. Generate a detailed-sources and uses-of-funds statement for the period January 1, 1976 to December 31, 1980. How much will Washington Paper ask to borrow from the insurance company, given that December 31, 1980 is the high balance of the loan?

3. Generate a summary sources and uses of funds statement for the period, of the form:

Sources	Uses
Funds from operations	Dividends
(after-tax profits and	Increase in working capital
depreciation)	Increase in assets
	Decrease in long-term debt

This type of statement is used for management purposes, and is probably the one which would be presented to Mr. Evans.

4. What will the firm's ratio of total debt to net worth be as of December 31, 1980? How does this compare to December 31, 1975? What can we say about the firm's debt capacity as of December 31, 1980?

Case 7

SULLIVAN TOY COMPANY

OPERATING LEVERAGE

The Sullivan Toy Company was a small manufacturer of children's toys, located just outside a major metropolitan area. The firm operated primarily as a job shop, producing toys for larger firms to service their peak-demand seasons. The firm also did some manufacturing of proprietary items, which were sold by retailers in the area. The management of the Sullivan Toy Company liked to do the latter type of business when the firm's machines were not occupied with contractual production. It preferred to manufacture items with specialized local appeal, where there was an opportunity to make a significant contribution to company profits in a short period of time. Such an opportunity occurred in the winter of 1977.

The local, college football team had experienced an excellent year, and the demand for sports items affixed with its insignia was high. For example, baseball caps with the college insignia were selling for $7.00 on campus and $6.50 off campus. Similarly-styled caps with other non school insignias were commonly sold for $2.50. The management of Sullivan Toy decided to enter the market with another college-specialty item.

The marketing and sales manager, Mr. Riley, seemed to have come up with a good plan for marketing the item: a set of four drinking glasses with the school emblem, which fit into holders in the corners of plastic snack trays. The tray was molded in the school colors. Mr. Rilery had estimated that the demand for an item of this type would be high, initially, but would taper off as more units were sold. Consequently, he intended to use a staggered pricing strategy, pricing the first 25,000 units at $4.00 and any remaining sales at $3.00 (prices are received by Sullivan Toy from retailers, after allowances and discounts).

Mr. Tipe, the production manager, agreed that the item could be produced on Sullivan Toy's primary assembly line. Fixed costs were $50,000, and he estimated that the item would cost $1.75 to produce in variable costs (materials, direct labor, as so on), if manufactured on that line. However, if volumes of over 35,000 units were to be produced, the firm would have to use an outmoded line, which was presently idle. This would increase fixed costs by

32

$28,750 (for additional indirect overhead, maintenance, etc.), and items produced on this line would cost $1.80 per unit in variable costs. Alternately, Mr.Tipe suggested that new equipment be purchased to do the whole job, which would increase fixed costs to $75,000, but would have variable costs of only $1.70 per unit for any output level.

Mr. Sullivan, president of the firm, considered Mr. Riley's plan and Mr. Tipe's cost estimates. The decision to use present equipment or buy new machinery seemed to hinge on the expected sales volume. Mr. Sullivan asked Mr. Riley if he had any idea of how many units might be sold. Mr. Riley replied that it depended on whether the item caught on, but that sales in the 40 to 50,000 units range seemed most reasonable.

Questions

1. Construct break-even graphs for both the present, obsolete equipment system and the new equipment system. What are the break-even points from these graphs?

2. Calculate the break-even points for both prospective systems. (*Hint*: Some revenue and cost functions contain inflection points and discontinuities. Standard break-even formulas cannot be used over regions where these occur. Break-even points can be calculated, however, by calculating the loss at the last previous inflection point or discontinuity; then applying the break-even formulas, using this loss as fixed cost.)

3. From the break-even graphs, are there any output levels where one method or another is superior? Are there any levels where they seem to achieve nearly the same profit results?

4. From the break-even graphs and Mr. Riley's estimates, what should the firm do? (*Hint*: the firm does not necessarily have to produce and sell the entire 40 to 50,000 units, despite demand levels.)

5. If Mr. Riley is wrong and demand turns out to be 60,000 units, how much profit will the superior strategy provide?

PART II

Working
Capital
Management

Case 8

BUTLER MANUFACTURING COMPANY

CASH MANAGEMENT

The Butler Manufacturing Company was started in the mid-1950's, and was a subsidiary of a large French firm. By 1976, annual sales had reached the half-billion dollar level. The company was organized into five divisions of unequal size. The organizational system was partly the result of the piecemeal fashion in which the company had grown through acquisitions, and partly the result of attempts to parallel the parent organization in terms of product lines. Each division had, until recently, operated quite autonomously; in fact, they had been separately-incorporated, subsidiary organizations until 1970.

In 1972, the firm had decided to centralize certain operations. Operating autonomously, each division had developed (or inherited from a predecessor) different methods for handling various operations. The top management felt that these operations could be better handled on a centralized basis. The corporate offices in New York City were closed and the company's top management was moved to recently-constructed headquarters in Philadelphia. The site was adjacent to the headquarters of Butler's largest division in terms of sales volume.

An example of how differently the five divisions were managed is provided by their respective accounts-receivable and cash-applicaton systems. The largest division of the firm had annual sales of $325 million. Its cash-application system was a manual-computer hybrid, wherein the cash-application clerk identified the items being paid from alphabetical listings, and manually removed a computer card from a deck of such cards signifying the outstanding items. The computer was used to total cards and generate listings. The firm's second-largest division (headquartered in St. Louis, with yearly sales of $100 million) used an entirely different system. As checks came in, data from them were keypunched. The computer then scanned a tape of outstanding items and applied the cash. Lists of the items paid were presented to the clerk for auditing on a CRT output device. A slightly smaller division, headquartered in Charlottesville, Virginia ($80 million annual sales) used a totally manual system; copies of invoices generated by this division were filed alphabetically as generated. When paid, they were removed from the file and stored by day of payment. The firm's smallest division, headquartered in New York, (with $10 million in annual sales) used a similar system. The remaining division was headquartered in Los Angeles and had sales of $40 million per year. Its cash-application system was similar to that of the Philadelphia division, except that no manual card removal was necessary. After ascertaining what items were paid, this data was keypunched and compared to a computer tape. The two divisions with the closest sales volumes (St. Louis and Charlottesville) had the most- and least-advanced, cash-application systems. A chart of the divisions, with associated sales volumes, is presented in Exhibit 1, page 40.

It was the company's policy to keep the minimum number of bank accounts, and to pay banks for their services on a straight-fee, rather than a compensating-balances, basis. Each division kept a central receiving and disbursing bank account for cash receipts and trade payments. Each division also had a payroll account at a local bank for each plant and/or headquarters location. Money was wire-transferred into these payroll accounts on the day that paychecks were written, and drawn out by employees shortly thereafter. The permanent balance in these accounts was nominal. Sales offices were not allowed to have local bank accounts; emergency needs were met from petty cash. Other disbursements were made from the divisional receipts and disbursements accounts. Paychecks for field salesmen were mailed to their homes, and were drawn on payroll accounts at their divisional-headquarters locations. Corporate headquarters used the bank accounts of the Philadelphia division.

In addition to the receipt and disbursement and payroll accounts, the Philadelphia division had several small accounts with New York City international banks. The Philadelphia division did a sizable export business, and it was felt that having these accounts open was necessary to facilitate receipts of export collections. Balances in these accounts were nominal. A chart of divisional bank accounts is provided in Exhibit 2, page 41.

To facilitate the deposit of checks, most of the divisions kept lock boxes at the bank handling their receipts and disbursements account.[1] The exception was the Los Angeles division. The credit

---

[1] A lock box is a post office box where customers are instructed to send remittances. The firm's bank bicks up the checks directly from thw lock box and puts the checks into the processing system. Copies of the checks are then sent to the firm. This eliminates the delay inherent if checks are sent directly to the firm and must be forwarded to the bank for deposit.

manager for this division was opposed to using a lock box because he felt that too large a portion of the checks for his division were not routine items; they were restrictively endorsed, post dated, and so on. Lock box systems do not handle such items well. It had not been determined if this contention was valid, but the Los Angeles division did deal with a more "retail" class of customers than the other divisions.

One of the changes contemplated, in the process of centralization, by Butler's management was a study of the location of these lock boxes. Prior to the centralization program, each division had maintained only one central-receiving point (either lock box or deposit account). This had the advantages for the divisions of local accessibility, and additional bargaining power if the bank involved was also a lender. The result was in keeping with the corporate policy of minimum-number bank accounts. Also, there were some doubts by the managers of individual divisions that they could generate the volume of receipts necessary to make additonal lock boxes economical if receipts volume was split up.[2] A multiple lock box system would speed cash flow through the corporation by reducing mail float. Partial data on mail times and customer receipts is given in Exhibits 3, page 41, and 6, page 42. Data on the effects of such a change in *clearing float*[3] had not yet been investigated.

Centralization of Butler's finance function had already resulted in several changes in the cash management area. Individual divisions were required to submit weekly forecasts showing book (not cleared[4]) bank balances, receipts, and disbursements on their combined payroll and receipts and disbursements accounts (see Exhibit 5). By applying a standard lag or lead factor for clearing of received remittances and mail time, and clearing for disbursements, an "available funds" forecast could be made for each division on a daily basis. This forecast showed which division would need money and which would have surplus funds on a day-to-day basis. Excess moneys, even if available for only a few days, were used to temporarily reduce the firm's short-term, bank line of credit (Butler was extremely high-leveraged). If one division needed money, transfers were made from other divisions, or short-term borrowing

---

[2] A rule of thumb used is that if monthly receipts do not exceed $500,000, a lock box is probably not economical.

[3] *Clearing float* is the time it takes the bank to convert a check into usable funds, either through deposit with the Fed, through correspondent banks, or via local clearing houses.

[4] *Cleared:* available for use by the firm.

was arranged. The only division not included in this procedure was New York; the balances involved were considered too small to be of significance.

This cash forecast was updated on a daily basis. At the end of each banking day, a clerk in the Philadelphia cash-control office would call each division's receipts and disbursements banks and get an end-of-day balance of available funds (also known as "federal funds" or "good money"). A report would then be made to the relevant parties. (See Exhibit 6). If balances seemed inappropriately high or low, transfers were made between banks. If the receipts forecasts were slightly in error (as often occurred), a division's receipts and disbursements account might be overdrawn. The banks involved had been instructed to advise the corporate cash-control office immediately, and transfers would be made to cover the shortage. A total of between 30 to 50 transfers were made per week to cover shortages (both forecast and unexpected), and to repay or draw on short-term debt.

Under the new centralized system, the disbursement of large checks was closely controlled. Previously, the individual divisions had not reviewed this closely, or had specifically anticipated due dates to important suppliers. It was felt that the latter was necessary to maintain good supplier relations, since Butler did not give out financial statements to suppliers. Many of the divisions bought from common suppliers. Under the centralized system, division accounts-payable managers were instructed to write and mail checks over a certain value exactly on the due date. These large checks involved about 50 percent of Butler's disbursements by dollar volume.

EXHIBIT 1

Butler Manufacturing Company

Chart of Divisions, Locations, Sales Volumes, and Plant Locations

Division Headquarters Location	Plant Locations	Annual Sales Volume, Millions of Dollars per Year	Lock box Locations
Philadelphia	Virginia, Texas	325	Philadelphia
St. Louis	St. Louis	100	St. Louis
Charlottesville	Charlottesville, Newark	80	New York

EXHIBIT 1 (Cont'd)

| Los Angeles | Los Angeles | 40 | None–checks sent to division headquarters. |
| New York | None– Material imported. | 10 | New York |

EXHIBIT 2

Butler Manufacturing Company

Location and Number of Bank Accounts

Division Headquarters Location	Receipts- Disbursements Account Location	Payroll Account Location	International Bank Account Locations	Total Number of Bank Accounts
Philadelphia	Philadelphia	Philadelphia Virginia Texas	New York (5)	9
St. Louis	St. Louis	St. Louis	None	2
Charlottesville	New York	Charlottesville Newark	None	3
Los Angeles	Los Angeles	Los Angeles	None	2
New York	New York	New York	None	2
		Total Number of Bank Accounts		18

EXHIBIT 3

Butler Manufacturing Company

Average Mail Times between Parts of the Country in Days*

	Northeast	Southeast	N. Central	S. Central	Northwest	Southwest
North- east	2.3					
South- east	2.3	2.1				
North Central	2.8	3.2	2.5			
South Central	3.0	2.9	3.0	2.3		
North- west	3.5	4.2	2.9	3.1	2.5	
South- west	4.2	3.6	3.0	3.2	2.6	2.5

*Data shown here has been considerably simplified to aid calculation. Mail times vary considerably, depending on mail service to various cities; lock box studies normally use data from zip code areas to major cities.

EXHIBIT 4

Butler Manufacturing Company

Analysis of Customer Pay— from Location by Division

(percent of total receipts)

Division

	Philadelphia	St. Louis	Charlottesville	Los Angeles	New York
Northeast	31	12	30	0	76
Southeast	21	32	61	0	20
North Central	20	2	0	0	0
South Central	9	27	9	0	0
Northwest	2	10	0	26	0
Southwest	17	17	0	74	4
Location of Present Lock box or Receipt Point	Northeast	S. Central	Northeast	Southwest	Northeast

EXHIBIT 6

Butler Manufacturing Company

Daily Cash Report (Collected Balances)

	Starting Balance	Receipts	Disbursements	Ending Balance
Philadelphia Division	———	———	———	———
St. Louis Division	———	———	———	———
Charlottesville Division	———	———	———	———
Los Angeles Division	———	———	———	———
New York Division	———	———	———	———
Totals	———	———	———	———

To: Treasurer
Asst. treasurer, cash control
Controller
Manager, general accounting
Accounts payable supervisor

EXHIBIT 5

Butler Manufacturing Company

Divisional Weekly Cash Forecast (Book Balances)

Day, Date *Starting balance*	*Monday, / /*	*Tuesday, / /*	*Wednesday, / /*	*Thursday, / /*	*Friday, / /*	*Weekly Totals* */ / to / /*
Receipts 　　Trade 　　Other						
Total receipts						
Total funds						
Disbursements 　　Notes 　　Trade 　　payables 　　Payroll 　　Other 　　disbursements						
Total disbursements						
Balance, end-of-day						

43

Questions

1. Give your general impression of Butler Manufacturing Company's cash management system. Has it been well thought out? Is it complete?

2. Can you give some reasons why a firm might want to minimize its number of bank accounts?

3. Do the objections of the Los Angeles division's credit manager make sense? Should a lock box be arranged in Los Angeles?

4. Using the data from Exhibits 1, 3, and 4, and a 13 percent yearly cost of capital, calculate how much the firm could save per year, on a gross basis, by arranging for a lock box for each division in each area, in terms of mail-float carrying costs. Are all these necessary? Which division will reduce its float the most (in terms of days)?

5. Should the lessening of clearing float be investigated?

6. Would there be any advanatage to combining receipts and disbursements bank accounts from the division into a central account?

7. Should the New York division be included in the forecast—transfer procedure?

8. Should a daily report also be made on book (as checks are received but not cleared; as checks are written) cash balances as well as cleared balances?

9. Assess Butler's policy on large checks. Do you think this is a common policy?

Case 9

FOXTROT INCORPORATED

RECEIVABLES MANAGEMENT

Foxtrot Incorporated, a medium-sized manufacturer of chemicals and machinery, had personnel policies which fostered long-term employment. Promotions were made when vacancies arose; there was little hiring from outside the firm. Employees, who seemed promising, were nurtured slowly and given an opportunity to learn the various areas of their chosen specialty, in anticipation of the eventual retirement or promotion of their boss.

The unexpected death of Foxtrot's treasurer due to an automobile accident, however, had distrubed the firm's plans. Lucy Krenn, the assistant treasurer, had been picked to fill the treasurer's job. Ms. Krenn had started with the firm about five years ago as a financial analyst, having had previous experience in capital planning and acquisitions. Since being promoted to assistant treasurer, three years ago, her assignments had been related to Foxtrot's cash-management system. Her exposure to the receivables-management area had been rather limited. In reviewing the firm's recent financial statements, she noticed that the receivables balances were rising rapidly. This had necessitated increased borrowing on the firm's bank line of credit, and additional interest expense had been incurred. Bad debt losses, however, seemed within normal limits for the firm's sales volume. Lucy had scheduled an appointment with Jay Natalli, the firm's credit manager, to discuss the increasing receivables balances.

"Receivables management is a method of evaluating credit policy and decisions," said Mr. Natalli, "and credit management is probably the most nebulous area of finance. There is little, hard, proven credit theory; we have to rely on rules of thumb, comparisons of customers' financial statistics with industry norms, and similar measures. The results of our credit decisions determine receivables balances and bad-debt levels. We try to coordinate our efforts with those of the marketing department, though the departments often disagree in regard to specific accounts.

We can present the receivables data to you in any form you want, but let me warn you that there is a good deal of controversy as to how this data should be presented and evaluated. By far, the most common statistic is days sales outstanding, known in the trade as DSO.   This statistic shows the turnover of accounts receivable in days, and is computed by this formula:

$$DSO = \frac{\text{Average Receivable Balance For Period}}{\text{Sales For Period}} \times \text{Days Per Period}$$

For example, if the firm had sales of $3000 for a quarter, and the average receivables balance was $1000, DSO would be:

$$DSO = \frac{\$1000}{\$3000} \times 90 \text{ days/quarter} = 30 \text{ days}$$

There are some problems with DSO in that it is sensitive to sales volume changes, since it is normally computed on a short-term (60- or 90-day) basis.   However, this statistic, along with the percent of receivables over 90 days past due and the percent of bad-debt losses, are the ones generated by the industry reporting agencies on a quarterly basis, and in this way, we have compared our receivables statistics with those of other firms in the industry.   For this reason, Mr. Newington, when he was treasurer, had the credit department prepare these   three statistics on a quarterly basis. Here is part of the latest report (see Exhibit 1) for our domestic and foreign receivables.   Keep in mind that our domestic sales are growing at a much faster rate than the industry as a whole; the work load in the credit department is very heavy.   In view of this, I think its remarkable that we are so close to the industry mean in terms of DSO, and that DSO for domestic sales has not increased over the year. Overall DSO, however, is increasing.

Another measure of receivables management is the percent of month's sales outstanding (PMSO).   This is computed by dividing the end-of-month, accounts-receivable balance due from a particular month by the sales for that month.   The result is a vector of percents from previous months.   Here is a hypothetical case.

	12/74	11/74	10/74	All Prior Months
Month's sales	$1,000.0	$900.0	$1,200.0	
12/31/74				
Accounts receivables balance (total = 1,750)	1,000.0	400.0	200.0	$150.0
PMSO (due from current month)	100.0			
PMSO (due from first prior month)	44.4			
PMSO (due from second prior month)	16.7			

All our sales are nonseasonable, so comparisons can be made with preceding quarters. Terms of sales, as you know, are net 30 days for domestic sales. Here are the raw accounts-receivable data (see Exhibit 2). We'll provide you with any calculations you need."

EXHIBIT 1

Foxtrot Incorporated

Sales and DSO for Domestic Sales, Foreign Sales, and Industry Averages

(DSO in days, sales in rounded thousands of dollars)

Quarter Ending	3/74	6/74	9/74	12/74
Foxtrot domestic DSO (Sales on 30-day terms)	42.1	43.4	42.9	42.9
Quarterly sales	$50,220	$54,240	$57,900	$60,800
Industry domestic DSO (Sales on 30-day terms)	42.2	42.4	42.1	42.2
Foxtrot foreign DSO (Sales on 120-day terms)	153.2	160.1	155.1	154.0
Quarterly sales	$ 9,180	$10,234	$11,353	$12,408
Foxtrot overall DSO	59.3	61.9	61.3	61.6
Foxtrot total Quarterly sales	$59,400	$64,474	$67,253	$73,208

EXHIBIT 2

Foxtrot Incorporated

Statement of Domestic Sales and Accounts Receivable, 1974

(rounded thousands of dollars)

Month	1/74	2/74	3/74	4/74	5/74	6/74	7/74	8/74	9/74	10/74	11/74	12/74
Sales	$16,000	$16,720	$17,500	$17,850	$17,990	$18,400	$19,000	$19,100	$19,800	$19,700	$20,300	$20,800
End-of-month accounts receivable	21,108	24,200	25,100	24,367	26,150	28,000	26,500	27,200	29,100	29,300	26,600	31,000
Due from current month			17,500			18,400			19,800			20,800
Due from 1st prior month			6,050			7,060			7,620			8,320
Due from 2nd prior month			1,000			1,500			1,300			1,500
Due from all other prior months			550			1,040			380			380

Questions

1. The previous treasurer of Foxtrot had focused on overall DSO to compare the firm's receivables-management performance between quarters. For 1974, what does this statistic seem to indicate? How does this compare to an evaluation made on the basis of the individual, foreign and domestic statistics? Explain any differences.

2. Mr. Newington had compared the quarterly, domestic DSO statistics to the industry statistic in order to assess Foxtrot's performance relative to the industry. Given the relative sales trends, what bias is inherent in this comparison?

3. Compute PMSO statistics for Foxtrot for 1974, on a quarterly basis. How would you evaluate the firm's receivables-management over this period? Does This evaluation differ from that made on the basis of foreign and domestic DSO figures? Why?

4. Why do you think DSO is more popular than PMSO for management evaluation of receivables management?

Case 10

ALLOYED COMPANIES, INC.

RECEIVABLES MANAGEMENT

Alloyed Companies, Inc., was one of the more successful mini-conglomerates, perhaps because of two policies: (1) no firm was acquired that Alloyed did not think it could manage properly, and (2) after acquisition, certain functions of the acquired firms were centralized to take advantage of the economies of scale. One of these centralized functions was receivables management. Mr. Juliett, assistant treasurer of Alloyed, acted as credit and receivables manager for all five of Alloyed's divisions.

Sales had been expanding over the past few years, as had Alloyed's customer base, in each of the five divisions. The average receivables balance for each of the credit department's three, accounts managers had reached $9 million, which Mr. Juliett thought was uncomfortably high. Though there had been no complaints from the accounts managers, who reported to Mr. Juliett directly, he felt that they could do a better job with a decreased work load and he decided to add another accounts manager to the force. Mr. Juliett also felt that the time was right to review the firm's credit- and receivables-management policies, in general.

Despite the fact that Alloyed's five divisions were similar, in terms of the processes used and the physical products sold, they each sold to different markets. There were no common customers. As each firm had been acquired, its receivables had been centralized and sorted into Alloyed's receivables system. This system was a fairly complex one, using much computer assistance and capable of producing the numerous management reports as requested, sorted in almost any fashion. All sales were within the continental United States. Credit and receivables management was one of the areas where Alloyed felt that future financial executives should have experience, and so the company rotated promising people into the accounts-manager positions on a regular basis. Average tenure within the position was about two and one-half years, after which the employee would go on to another position within the firm. The accounts of customers from all five divisions were sorted alphabetically and assigned to the accounts managers in this fashion;

each manager had about the same total dollar exposure and total number of accounts, as well as the same number of accounts and dollar exposure from each division. The strategy for handling accounts had been to treat each customer similiarly, and to try to keep the time spent on each account proportional to dollar exposure. Accounts managers were instructed to be courteous to all, but not to make concessions from stated terms of sale (net 30 days from date of invoice for each division), even when it was confirmed that this was meeting competition in good faith. To assure that none of the accounts managers grew bored with his or her group of customers, assignments within the department were rotated on a regular basis. Though policies of the type used by Alloyed were quite common in credit and receivables management, Mr. Juliett wondered if they were optimal, in view of the differences between the divisions on customer characteristics, competitive situation, correlation with other divisions, and profitability (see Exhibit 1, page 54, for divisional statements of income for 1977).

The imported products division brought products into the United States from other countries. Sales were by contract to large, very credit-worthy firms. Though the division sold a substantial portion of Alloyed's sales volume in terms of dollars, it handled relatively few orders, and consequently had relatively few employees in the sales and marketing areas. Because bargaining power was on the buyer's side, profit margins tended to be slim, as reflected in the divisional income statement. Sales were uncorrelated with those of other divisions. Despite the low risk of default, the effort of the credit and receivables department per dollar of sales tended to be higher for this division than for the other four divisions. This was because of paperwork problems. The large customers sold by this division did not respond significantly to the computer-generated form letters, which were effective in collecting from smaller firms sold by the other divisions. Also, the management of this division tended to make special "deals" with customers which were not reflected in paperwork, resulting in nonpayment of invoices. When this occurred, the division was slow to correct the matter. Consequently, the accounts managers spent a significant amount of time following up unpaid items on a personalized basis, and attempting to get the division to correct their own errors so that payments could be collected. The average time to pay an invoice for this division was 42 days. Extended time for payments was almost never requested by these customers.

Notes to Divisional Statements of Income

[1] This depreciation refers to that on the actual facilities producing the materials for sale. It is computed on an accelerated basis, and transferred to the divisional income statements from the corporate tax reports.

[2] Sales salaries are only for the salesmen who are actually selling the division's products. A salesman's time is highly utilized and each salesman has about as much volume as he can handle.

[3] Marketing department expenses include all salaries for this department for the related division. In general, this department's time is not fully utilized.

[4] For all costs with this footnote number, costs were allocated based on sales volume. Charges of this type continue, regardless of changes in the sales volume of the individual divisions.

[5] Nonplant depreciation includes tax-statement depreciation on administrative buildings, recreational facilities, and so on. It is allocated to the divisions based on sales volume.

[6] This interest-expense entry is an allocation based on the sales volume of interest expense on corporate debt to support assets. Accounts receivable are a minor part of these assets.

[7] Other income is basically royalties on the patents which divisions have licensed out to other firms.

The paint supplies division dealt with paint manufacturers of various sizes. Its sales were not correlated with those of other divisions. In general, the firm and its customers were of equal bargaining power. The risk of default was in the medium range, but payments were often received far beyond terms. Accounts could be collected in a routine fashion with computer assistance. There had been numerous requests in the past for lengthened terms of sale to meet competitive situations, but in keeping with department policy, these had been rejected. The average time taken to pay an invoice was 60 days.

The plastic resin division presented the highest degree of default risk of any of the divisions. The customers were small job shops with highly-variable cash flows, little management expertise, and almost no profitability. Though market power should have been on the seller's side, with few sellers of resins and many buyers, a "huckster" attitude prevailed among the industry sellers, and requests for extended terms to meet competition were constant. Sales in this division were highly correlated with those of the consumer products and chemical divisions. Because of poor financial situations, customers of the plastic resin division did not generally respond to computer-assisted collection methods, and required much personal-collection effort and financial counseling. The divisional statements of income showed profits to be higher for this division than for the imported products or paint supplies divisions. Average time to pay an invoice for the plastic resin division was 55 days.

The consumer products division sold items to wholesalers and jobbers. Though customers tended to be highly levered, and therefore, very risky from a default standpoint, their asset turnover was very high and their cash flows substantial; they tended to pay promptly. Routine follow-up was sufficient in order to collect any past-due items. Though analysis of the financial condition of these customers was necessary on a regular basis, in general, less than an average amount of time of the accounts managers was taken up with accounts from this division. Because demand for the consumer products division's products was high on the retail level, bargaining power was on Alloyed's side, and there were few requests for concessions in terms of sale. The average time taken to pay an invoice was 35 days. Sales were correlated with those of the plastic resin and chemical divisions.

The chemical division had the largest share of company sales, and also, the highest margins. The average time taken to pay an invoice was 36 days, and the customers were of the medium, default-risk category. The chemical division sold to a moderately large group of medium-sized, well-established firms, and held a major share of the market. However, because the number of buyers of the division's products was not large, bargaining power was about equally distributed between buyer and seller. On a frequent basis, requests had been made in the past for extended terms of sale, which had been refused. This had resulted in some lost sales. Most of this division's customer base had dealt with Alloyed for several years, and had developed working relationships with the accounts managers. When there was some payment problem (which occurred in the great minority of cases, as indicated by the 36-day payment average), some personal contact by the accounts manager was required.

In considering all the data, Mr. Juliett wondered if a change to a divisionalized, credit- and receivables-management system might be in order. This would enable him to formulate different policies for different divisions. He wondered how such an organization could be staffed equitably. He would liked to have put the greatest effort and expense where it would net the firm the most profit. His decision variables were dollars exposure per staff member (a measure of credit cost per dollar of sales and exposure), policy with regard to competition (meeting longer-terms requests), and collection aggressiveness. However, he could not estimate the sales response from the use of each of these tools.

EXHIBIT 1

Alloyed Companies, Inc.

Divisional Statements of Income for Fiscal 1977

(rounded thousands of dollars)

	Imported Products Division	Paint Supplies Division	Plastic Resin Division	Consumer Products Division	Chemical Division
Gross sales	$41,800	$24,200	$61,600	$26,400	$66,000
Returns and allowances	209	242	616	792	660
Net sales	41,591	23,958	60,984	25,608	65,340
Cost of goods sold:					
Direct labor	0	1,978	3,297	1,512	5,213
Direct materials	36,421	14,916	32,450	15,026	29,657
Direct overhead	1,011	1,412	1,932	1,020	1,764
Depreciation [1]	0	1,100	4,400	880	4,620
Gross margin on sales	4,159	4,552	18,905	7,710	24,806
Selling and administrative exp.:					
Sales salaries [2]	1,501	1,121	8,703	3,121	13,101
Marketing Department [3]	539	1,962	5,232	1,127	3,020
Headquarters Staff [4]	190	110	280	120	300
Computer department [4]	152	88	224	96	240
Nonplant depreciation [5]	836	484	1,232	528	1,320
Other indirect overhead [4]	105	61	154	66	165
Operating margin	836	726	3,080	2,112	5,940
Interest expense [6]	167	97	246	106	264
Other income [7]	50	0	0	0	111
Profit before tax	$ 719	$ 629	$ 2,834	$ 2,006	$ 5,787
Gross margin on sales (%)	10%	19%	31%	28%	37%
Operating margin (% of sales)	2.0%	3.0%	5.1%	8.2%	9.1%
Profit before tax (% of sales)	1.7%	2.6%	4.6%	7.8%	8.9%

Questions

1. Restate the divisional statements of income to give the profit on a dollar of marginal sales. It is this type of data which is critical to assessing the returns from changes in credit policy, just as marginal figures are used in capital-budgeting decisions.

2. Make a chart, with a column for each division, showing the relative levels of the following measures of profit or cost:

   1. Profit per dollar of marginal sales
   2. Possible changes in sales volume via the granting of requests for extended terms (low–medium–high)
   3. Default risk (low–medium–high)
   4. Payment characteristics (average days to pay)
   5. Effort required to collect (low–medium–high)
   6. Correlation of the receivables asset with that of other divisions (low–high)
   7. 1977 Average exposure (thousands of dollars)

3. In your opinion, which division (or divisions) is a candidate for the acceptance of extended terms? Keep in mind that this will proportionately increase the necessary management effort with regard to increased receivables balances. Is there any division (or divisions) which is definitely not a candidate for this acceptance?

4. In which division, should staff time be the highest per dollar of sales? Where should it be lowest? Why?

5. Using four staff members, how would you assign these employees?

Case 11

KOSS REFINING COMPANY

INVENTORY-MANAGEMENT SYSTEM

In April, 1975, Mr. Dan Olson, manager of retail sales for the Koss Refining Company, had asked the operations research staff to develop an inventory-management system that could be used by the company's service station managers to control their inventories of tires, batteries and accessories (known in the trade as TBA items). Mr. Olson knew that reducing inventory levels by more-frequent reordering would put an increased load on the distribution system and, perhaps, be disruptive for operations. Larger inventories were generally frowned on by the firm's controller, who considered excessive inventories to be unproductive assets. Mr. Olson was interested in a rapid completion, test, and implementation of the system, since quite a few of the service station managers were relatively new on the job and had not really developed a "feel" for managing TBA inventory under the existing system.

The Koss Refining Company traces its history back to the days of John D. Rockefeller. In 1859, an ex-railroad conductor, "Colonel" Drake, struck oil in Titusville, Pennsylvania and ushered in a new industry. In 1860, John D. Rockefeller, a Cleveland merchant, became interested in the oil business and started to apply his resources to production financing, mergers, shipping, and so on. By 1911, the Standard Oil Trust controlled 70 percent of the refining capacity in the United States. Koss was created from the breakup of the Standard Oil Trust in 1911. By 1975, Koss had become a refiner and distributor of gasoline. It had to depend on other oil companies for its supply of crude oil.

The existing TBA inventory system was not considered to be very effective by Mr. Olson. Experienced station managers would order TBA items, periodically, based upon their "feel" for demand. If shortages occurred, they purchased TBA items from local auto-supply stores. New managers were given a standard, recommended inventory list. Often, this list was not very appropriate for a particular store, due to competition.

Overstocked items had to be returned to the central warehouse. However, if the item was received at the warehouse in a damaged condition, it was charged against the station's sales. Groups of stations constituted a sales division, which was supervised by a division supervisor.   Damaged goods were also charged against division sales.   Thus, the usual procedure for a division supervisor was to try to arrange for the clandestine transfer of overstocked and damaged goods between the stations in his division. This was beneficial for both the station managers and the division supervisor.   However, this procedure was highly inefficient from Mr. Olson's viewpoint.

Mr. Jeff Levenberg from the operations research staff, who was assigned to develop the TBA inventory-management system, decided to evaluate the use of the order-quantity/order-point (OQ/OP) system. The OQ/OP system is designed to indicate how many items should be ordered and when.   This system would require each station manager to forecast demand, and then utilize tables to determine order quantities and when the orders should be placed. The concept of the OQ/OP system is illustrated in Exhbitit 1, page 59.

Order Quantity (OQ) Mr. Levenberg used the following formula for determining order quantity:

$$OQ = \sqrt{\frac{2DC}{MP}}$$

> where D = annual demand in units
>   C = cost of reordering in dollars per reorder
>   M = maintenance cost, fraction per year
>   P = purchase price

Reorder Costs Mr. Levenberg wanted to make sure that reorder and maintenance costs were properly estimated. He interviewed the station managers and accounting supervisors, and found that reorder costs were fairly difficult to determine. He learned that certain variable costs were difficult to identify. The placement of an order by the service manager fell in this category. Mr. Levenberg felt that this cost would be approximately 1 cent per line item. That is, each size of tire was considered to be a separate line item. The number of items in a line ordered at the same time did not affect order costs. At the regional office, the clerical labor cost was estimated to be 20 cents per line item. The computer time to process orders was determined by regression analysis to be

1.5 cents per line item.   Other direct labor costs were determined to be 37.5 cents per line item.   No costs were associated with truck delivery, since the company-owned truck followed a fixed route, regardless of the items ordered or stations ordering.   A summary of these costs is shown in Exhibit 2.

Maintenance Costs   Property taxes were 4 percent of 70 percent of the purchase price.   The cost of capital was 10 percent.   The inventory of stations was insured by Koss Refining through a master policy.   Thus, no direct costs were available.   However, the accounting office stated that insurance would be 1 percent of the purchase price.   Obsolescence was determined to be 5 percent of the purchase price, based on the national average.   Finally, based on inventory turnover, average annual rent per square foot, TBA item volume and stacking properties, the storage costs were estimated to be 1 percent.   These costs are summarized in Exhibit 3.

Based upon these reorder and maintenance costs, Mr. Levenberg was able to develop order-quantity table, which could be utilized by the station managers to determine the order quantity.   This table is shown in Exhibit 4, page 60.

Order Point (OP)   Mr. Levengerg assumed that, 95 percent of the time, the service station would be able to provide a customer with an item from its inventory.   The station with the longest lead time was used to establish the lead-time distribution.   Based upon prices, and the probability distributions of demand and lead times for various TBA items, Mr. Levenberg was able to develop a table for order points.   This table is very similar in concept to the table in Exhibit 4; however, it is not presented in this case.

Mr. Levenberg decided to test the system by using data from a service station.   He obtained the following data:

Items	Price	Annual Demand
Tires (GR–78)	$20	240
Batteries (F22)	20	84
Filters (323)	3	240
Wiper blades (16")	1	120
Lamps (5")	1	36
Tune-ups (6 C)	10	240

The above items, of course, do not refer to all types and sizes of TBA items. For example, the first two items refer to just one particular size and type of tire, and one type and size of battery. For the items listed above, Mr. Levenberg estimated the present average inventory to be $530. The total average inventory for all items in the station was estimated to be $11,897. Mr. Levenberg was interested in calculating average inventory under the new system to see if he would recommend its implementation to Mr. Olson.

EXHIBIT 1

Koss Refining Company

Graphic Illustration of OQ/OP System

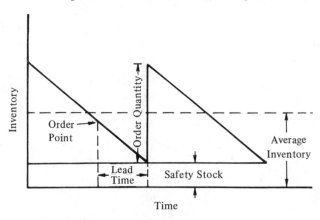

EXHIBIT 2

Koss Refining Company

Summary of Reorder Costs

Source	Cost
Station	$ .01
Regional office	.20
Computer time	.015
Warehouse labor	.375
Total	$ .60

EXHIBIT 3

Koss Refining Company

Summary of Maintenance Costs

Source	Cost
Taxes (4% of 70%)	3 percent
Insurance	1
Cost of capital	10
Obsolescence	5
Storage	1
	20 percent

EXHIBIT 4

Koss Refining Company

Order Quantity Table

Reorder costs = $0.60; Maintenance costs = 20%

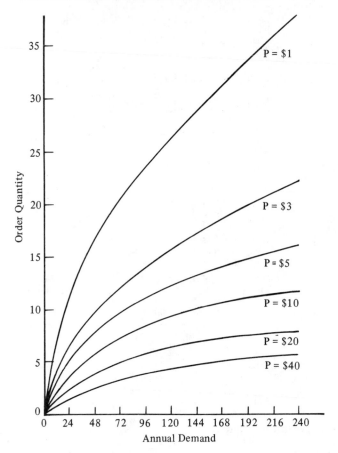

Questions

1. For the first item on which Mr. Levenberg obtained price and demand information–tires–determine the order quantity and the number of orders the service manager will place for tires every year.

2. Mr. Levenberg determined that for the GR-78 tires, based upon the distribution for lead-time and stockout requirements, six days of inventory should be carried as safety stock. How many

tires would be in the safety stock, and what will be the average inventory for the size and type of tires mentioned in the case?

3. For the six items that Mr. Levenberg used to test the OQ/OP systems, calculate the total average inventory in dollars. How does this compare with the same cost, without using the inventory system? Is use of the system justified?

PART III

Capital Budgeting and Risk Analysis

Case 12

GENERAL LIGHTING CORPORATION

CAPITAL BUDGETING: CERTAINTY

In January 1977, the commercial lighting division of the General Lighting Corporation was considering entrance into the reflector market for high-intensity discharge lamps. The corporation had discovered a new process for making the reflectors out of anodized aluminum. The division's marketing department felt that the company's reflector had more desirable properties than competing reflectors.

The marketing department had conducted a survey, which indicated that with a selling price of $5 per unit, 400,000 units could be sold the first year. The market for reflectors had maintained a steady growth of 4 percent over the past few years. The marketing department felt that the company could easily maintain this growth rate for its own reflector over the foreseeable future. The accounting department provided the following estimate for the unit cost of a reflector:

Materials	$0.95
Labor	1.70
Overhead	0.85
Total	$3.50

Overhead had been estimated at 50 percent of labor. It was assumed that overtime manufacturing efficiencies would offset increases in labor costs, and that over the next ten years, the manufacturing costs would remain constant.

If the company decided to proceed with the production of the reflectors, it would have to buy new equipment at a cost of $2 million. Although the equipment was expected to last longer than 10 years, the research and development personnel felt that, after ten years, the equipment would be technologically obsolete. As a result, the new equipment would be depreciated over ten years. Its expected salvage value after 10 years was $100,000.

The accounting department generated *pro forma* income statements for the next ten years, based on its own cost estimates and the marketing department's projections. These projected income statements are shown in Exhibit 1, page 66.

One final issue that the commercial lighting division had to clarify

EXHIBIT 1

General Lighting Corporation

Pro Forma Income Statements for Reflector Project
(rounded thousands of dollars)

	1977	1978	1979	1980	1981	1982	1983	1984	1985	1986
Sales	$2,000	$2,080	$2,163	$2,250	$2,340	$2,433	$2,531	$2,632	$2,737	$2,847
CGS	1,400	1,456	1,514	1,575	1,638	1,703	1,772	1,842	1,916	1,993
EBDT*	600	624	649	675	702	730	759	790	821	854
Depreciation	190	190	190	190	190	190	190	190	190	190
EBT	410	434	459	485	512	540	569	600	631	664
Taxes	197	208	220	232	246	259	273	288	303	319
Net income	$ 213	$ 226	$ 239	$ 253	$ 266	$ 281	$ 296	$ 312	$ 328	$ 345

*Earnings before depreciation and taxes

was the appropriate discount rate to be used in this analysis. The company had a policy of recommending 12 percent as a basic discount rate, which could be adjusted upward or downward to reflect the riskiness of the project being evaluated. Certain assumptions made by the division regarding market share, growth in the market, price, salvage value of the equipment to be purchased, materials and labor led it to believe that the project was relatively risky. Thus, it was decided to use a discount rate of 18 percent in the analysis.

Questions

1. Calculate the net present value and internal rate of return for the reflector project. What decision should the division make with respect to manufacturing the reflector?

2. Restate Exhibit 1, assuming that the firm uses the sum-of-the-years digit method of depreciation. Recalculate the net present value, using data from the restated Exhibit 1. What effect does using accelerated depreciation have on the net cash flows and net present value? Why? How would the internal rate of return and the payback period be affected? (Do not calculate the IRR and the payback period. A descriptive answer on the effects of SYD on IRR and payback period will suffice.)

Case 13

CUSTARD, INC. RESTAURANTS*

CAPITAL BUDGETING: CERTAINTY

On January 7, 1976, Mr. Ronald Johnson, managing partner in an insurance agency, recieved the following letter from Mr. Robert Davis, who specialized in the sales and mergers of restaurants, retail stores and franchised restaurants.

Dear Ron:

It was good to see you and Joan at the Andersons' New Year's Eve party. I was delighted to hear that your insurance agency has done tremendously well. I can appreciate your concern for utilizing your savings in a manner more consistent with the financial needs of your family.

As I indicated to you, recently, I am frequently asked to facilitate the transfer of ownership of retail stores and restaurants. Yesterday, I was asked to identify a qualified buyer for Custard, Inc. Custard, Inc. owns and operates three retail franchises of a nationally-known, ice cream and food business operation. The owners of Custard, Inc. are willing to sell the non-cash assets of the company for $500,000. In addition, the purchase is expected to assume the accounts payable. Custard, Inc. currently owns equipment and buildings whose book value is $108,100. As you will notice from the attached Exhibit 1, the market value of these depreciable assets is $137,300. You know, of course, that the Internal Revenue Service allows you to establish your own depreciation schedule. So you are not bound to maintain the cost and life figures given in Exhibit 1.

In addition to the assets described above, the selling price of $500,000 also includes three parcels of land, on which the buildings are located. All three sites have paved parking lots. The market value of the land is $150,000. Also included in the selling price is inventory, valued at $12,700. A rough estimate of the breakdown for the selling price is as follows:

Equipment and building	$137,300
Land	150,000
Inventory	12,700
Goodwill	200,000
	$500,000

As the above figures indicate, you would be paying $200,000 for the goodwill associated with using the franchisor's name. From my viewpoint, this purchase price for using the franchisor's name is a "steal" at $200,000, since the same franchisor has a current franchise fee of around $100,000 per unit.

*This case is an abbreviated version of Custard, Inc., Copyright © 1976 by Iqbal Mathur.

While the purchase price is $500,000, I do not feel that you will need $500,000 in cash to purchase this company. With your solid reputation and by pledging the assets of Custard, Inc., you should not be required to make a down payment of more than 30 percent, with a local bank financing the remaining 70 percent. Your cash requirements for acquiring Custard, Inc., would be as follows:

Down payment	$170,000
Transfer & lawyer's fees	20,000
Organization expense	1,000
	$191,000

I also feel that to properly manage the three franchises, you will need to increase working capital by approximately $10,000.

Ron, I am sure that by this time you are beginning to wonder about the return on investment for this venture. I am enclosing a copy of the 1975 income statement for Custard, Inc.–Exhibit 2. As you can see, the firm's earnings equaled $26,349 for 1975. However, these figures would not be directly relevant for your case. In calculating the return on investment, it would not be appropriate to treat interest as expenses. This, the firm's true "net income" is closer to $30,000. Furthermore, since depreciation is a noncash charge, the firm's real cash flow is around $48,000–$49,000. Based on the selling price of $500,000, this constitutes a return of around 10 percent—much better than you would obtain by leaving your funds in a savings account. Actually, the correct way to calculate ROI is to do it only for the invested capital. Since you will be investing only $201,000 in acquiring Custard, Inc., your ROI is approximately 24 percent per annum. And you tell me, Ron, where else can you get ROI like this?

Ron, I shall be in touch by phone with you to seek your reaction to Custard, Inc., and also to answer any questions you may have.

Best regards.

Sincerely yours,

Bob Davis

Mr. Johnson, on reading this letter, was considerably intrigued by the prospects of owning this franchised operation. Mr. Johnson was forty-one years old and the father of two sons and two daughters, all in their teens. The eldest was a freshman in college. Another child was getting ready to enter college in Fall, 1976. Mr. Johnson was very familiar with the Custard, Inc. stores, since he used to take his family to an outlet near his home, quite frequently, for after-dinner snacks. He knew that all three franchises were located on main roads near highways and could be easily patronized, not only by residents in the trading areas, but also by travelers passing through the areas.

While Mr. Johnson knew some details about the company and found the information contained in Mr. Davis' letter to be of value, he had a number of questions considering Custard, Inc. Thus, when Mr. Davis called him to provide any further information desired, he posed a number of questions. In response to his questions, Mr. Davis sent him the 1975 balance sheet for Custard, Inc. (Exhibit 3). Mr. Davis also told him that a conservative approach would be to assume that future sales would be at the 1975 dollar volume; that no "other income" would be generated in his case; that *purchases,* which include the four percent of the sales royalty payment to the franchisor, would be 50 percent of sales; that wages and salaries would increase to $90,000 and $102,000, respectively; that contributions could be lowered to $600 per year; and that other income-statement items would remain constant.

As Mr. Johnson considered the additional details provided by Mr. Davis, he started to think very seriously about the idea of purchasing Custard, Inc. and operating it on an absentee-ownership basis. He felt that by retaining the present managers, he could avoid the day-to-day details of running the business, while earning a safe return on his investment. However, before Mr. Johnson could commit himself to purchasing this company, he needed to get a more precise estimate on what he would earn on his investment. His current net worth was approximately $600,000. A major portion of this amount represented certificates of deposit, which were yielding eight percent before taxes. He know that he could borrow money from a local bank at nine percent interest to finance this purchase. However, the loan would have to be repaid in ten equal, annual payments of principal and interest. Mr. Johnson's marginal tax rate was 32 percent.

EXHIBIT 1

Custard, Inc. Restaurants

Depreciable Assets, December 31, 1975

Item	Quantity	Year of Acquisition	Original Cost	Life	Annual Depreci- ation Charged	Present Book Value	Appraised Market Value
Dispensers	6	1971	$ 18,000	10 years	$ 1,800	$ 10,800	$ 15,000
Cookers	6	1971	30,000	6	5,000	10,000	8,000
Friers	6	1972	12,000	8	1,500	7,500	9,000
Freezers	12	1971	60,000	10	6,000	36,000	43,700
Fixtures	3	1971	21,000	10	2,100	12,600	17,800
Buildings	3	1971	36,000	30	1,200	31,200	43,800
Total			$177,000		$17,600	$108,100	$137,300

EXHIBIT 2

Custard, Inc. Restaurants

Income Statement

(For Year Ending December 31, 1975)

Net sales	$655,667
Other income	1,500
Total revenues	$657,167

Expenses

Purchases	$343,000
Wages	85,800
Salaries	99,600
Local taxes	17,500
Utilities	15,534
Advertising	3,700
Maintenance	7,000
Insurance	6,276
Depreciation	17,600
Contributions	1,800
Interest	9,700
Miscellaneous	8,960
	$616,470
Gross profits	40,697
Income tax	14,348
Net income	26,349
Dividends	6,000
Retained earnings	$ 20,349

EXHIBIT 3

Custard, Inc. Restaurants

Balance Sheet, December 31, 1975

Cash		$ 10,100	Accounts payable	$ 7,500
Inventory		12,700	Bank loan	114,100
Plant	177,000		Total liabilities	$121,600
Less: Accumulated Depreciation	68,900			
Net plant		108,100	Common stock	132,400
Land		85,300	Retained earnings	82,200
Intangibles		120,000	Total liabilities and	
Total assets		$336,200	net worth	$336,200

Questions

1. Assuming that Mr. Johnson acquires the noncash assets of the Custard, Inc. stores on January 1, 1976, construct a *pro forma* balance sheet as of January 1, 1976 for the Custard Restaurants to be used by Mr. Johnson. You may assume that the purchase is 100 percent equity financed.

2. Construct a *pro forma* income statement for the year ending December 31, 1976. You may assume that Mr. Johnson acquires the stores on January 1, 1976. What assumptions did you make in generating this financial statement?

3. Compute the net present value, internal rate of return, and payback period for the purchase of the stores by Mr. Johnson.

4. What additional factors need to be taken into consideration in the purchase decision? What would you recommend to Mr. Johnson?

Case 14

CARNEGIE HOSPITAL

CAPITAL BUDGETING: UNCERTAINTY

In October 1976, Mr. Jerome Rosenberg, assistant hospital administrator at Carnegie Hospital in Pittsburgh, Pa., was thinking about the presentation that he would have to make before the hospital's capital expenditure review committee within the next few days. Another hospital committee, concerned with evaluating the quality of health-care delivery at the hospital, had suggested equipping one or two of the hospital's operating rooms with radiographic diagnostic equipment. The deployment of this equipment would not only expedite the availability of diagnostic test results, but would also permit surgeons to constantly monitor the patient's physical condition in highly complicated surgical procedures. The evaluation procedure had established, beyond doubt, that installation of the equipment would greatly improve the quality of health care for certain patients. Thus, it was certain that the equipment would be installed in at least one operating room. A more pertinent question was whether it would be desirable to simultaneously equip two operating rooms with the equipment. If there was not sufficient demand for the second operating room, it would be under-utilized, and the hospital would prefer not to follow this course, since it could use the additional moneys elsewhere.

Carnegie Hospital, located a few miles from downtown Pittsburgh, was opened more than thirty years ago. It has been committed to the delivery of the best health care possible. In keeping with this goal, it has kept pace with the incorporation of technological innovations in its equipment, and has been closely associated with the medical school of a nearby university. A number of doctors on the hospital's staff have pioneered new diagnostic and operational procedures. The capital expenditure review committee was formed in 1969, when the hospital began to feel the impace of sharply-rising medical costs. The primary purpose of the committee is to carefully review expenditures for new equipment and facilities. Currently, a lawyer, a university finance professor, an insurance-company executive, two doctors, the hospital administrator and the director of Carnegie Hospital Foundation—the fund-raising arm of the hospital—serve on this committee. This committee had emphasized that capital-expenditure analysis for a "not-for-profit" institution, such as Carnegie Hospital, was not much different than analysis in the "for-profit" sector of the economy. In fact, the committee felt that typical concepts of opportunity costs of funds, allocation of scarce resources among competing projects, tight managerial controls, and rigorous economic analysis and planning would result in the ultimate delivery of better health care. Mr. Rosenberg had received his MPH five years ago with a major in hospital administration. He had felt certain weaknesses in his academic background and had, in the last two years, taken three courses in managerial accounting and financial management.

As Mr. Rosenberg started to develop his presentation, he knew that he would have to analyze two alternatives initially. One alternative was to equip only one operating room now, at a cost of $200,000 and, depending upon the demand for its use, decide whether to equip a second room two years from now. If the hospital chose to follow this alternative, it would need to decide two years from now whether to spend an additional $200,000 to equip the second operating room. The second alternative was to equip two operating rooms now, at a cost of $304,000. Strictly from a cost basis, it made sense to equip the two rooms now, rather than one, now, and one, two years from now. However, if the demand was not sufficient for adequate usage of both operating rooms, this alternative would not be very desirable, since the additional $104,000 could easily be utilized elsewhere.

As Mr. Rosenberg considered these costs, he realized that he would need more information on the demand for the newly equipped room or rooms, and on the probability of that demand occurring. He decided, somewhat arbitrarily, to classify the demand into three categories: High, medium and low. Secondly, to obtain a subjective estimate of the probabilities associated with each state of demand, he enlisted the help of a couple of influential department heads. They were instrumental in getting a group of surgeons and other specialists to provide their input regarding the probability of various states of demand occurring. From these responses, Mr. Rosenberg was able to derive the following estimates: If one operating room (OR) was equipped, the probability of demand being high, medium or low would be .5, .3 or .2, respectively. If it turned out that in two years the demand was high and a second OR was added, the probabilities associated with high, medium and low demand for the second OR would be .6, .3 and .1, respectively. If after two years, the demand was medium and a second OR was added, the probabilities associated with high, medium and low demand for the second OR would be .3, .4 and .3, respectively. If after two years, the demand was low and a second OR was added, the probabilities for high, medium and low demand for the second OR would be .1, .3 and .6, respectively. Finally, if Carnegie decided to equip both OR's at once, the probabilities associated with high, medium and low demand for both OR's would be .4, .4 and .2, respectively. One additional question that Mr. Rosenberg had with respect to the assessment of probabilities was why the probability of high demand for one OR equipped now would be .5, but the probability of high demand for two OR's equipped now would be .4 and *not* lower than .4, as he had expected. He was informed that hospital equipment, to a certain extent, tend to generate their own demand. Thus, the second OR equipped now would tend to generate some demand on its own. Also, in certain emergency cases when one equipped OR was being utilized, the patient would not have to be transferred to another university-affiliated hospital, as would be the case with only one equipped OR.

It had been estimated that the equipment would have a useful life of ten years, with no salvage value at the end of this period. Working with the accounting department and chief surgeon, Mr. Rosenberg was able to derive net cash flows for each alternative. The cash flows for each alternative are shown in Exhibit 1. For example, cash flows for one OR throughout the ten years and high demand are −$200,000 initially, $60,000 in year 1, and so on. If one OR is equipped now, demand is high, a second OR is added in two years and demand for OR 2 is high also, then cash flows are −$200,000 initially, $60,000 in year 1, $80,000 minus $200,000 = −$120,000 in year 2, $200,000 in year 3, and so forth. If two OR's are equipped now and demand is high, cash flows are −$304,000 initially, $120,000 in year 1, $160,000 in year 2, and so on.

Mr. Rosenberg felt that 10 percent was an appropriate discount rate to use, and proceeded to calculate net present values for each alternative. His calculations are shown in the last column in Exhibit 1. For example, the NPV for one OR, throughout, with high demand is $456,750.

EXHIBIT 1

Carnegie Hospital

Expected Net Cash Flows for Various Alternatives

(in thousands of dollars)

	0	1	2	3	4	5	6	7	8	9	10	NPV
One O.R. Throughout												
High demand	-200	60	80	100	120	140	140	140	120	110	100	$ 456.75
Medium demand	-200	45	68	85	102	120	120	120	100	80	70	342.09
Low demand	-200	30	45	56	67	78	78	78	67	56	45	157.14
One or Two O.R.'s												
High demand for 1 & high 2	-200	60	-120	200	240	280	280	280	240	220	200	827.52
High demand for 1 & med. 2	-200	45	-132	185	222	260	260	260	220	190	170	712.81
High demand for 1 & low 2	-200	30	-155	156	197	218	218	218	197	166	145	539.40
Med. demand for 1 & high 2	-200	60	-120	185	222	260	260	260	220	190	170	736.38
Med. demand for 1 & med. 2	-200	45	-132	170	204	240	240	240	200	160	140	621.66
Med. demand for 1 & low 2	-200	30	-155	141	169	198	198	198	167	136	115	436.78
Low demand for 1 & high 2	-200	60	-120	156	197	218	218	218	197	166	145	595.61
Low demand for 1 & med. 2	-200	45	-132	141	169	198	198	198	167	136	115	469.43
Low demand for 1 & low 2	-200	30	-155	112	134	156	156	156	134	112	90	284.53
Two O.R.'s Throughout												
High demand	-304	120	160	200	240	280	280	280	240	220	200	1,009.46
Medium demand	-304	105	148	185	222	260	260	260	220	190	170	894.75
Low demand	-304	90	125	156	197	218	218	218	197	166	145	721.36

Questions

1. What is an appropriate method of analysis that Mr. Rosenberg could use in his presentation?

2. What conclusion could Mr. Rosenberg draw upon completion of his analysis?

3. Are there any other factors that you may want to take into consideration for analyzing similar types of situations?

4. What can be said about the method by which Mr. Rosenberg obtained his probability assessments?

Case 15

PENN PLASTICS, INC.

CAPITAL BUDGETING: UNCERTAINTY

Mr. Jamal Ahmed, owner and president of Penn Plastics, Inc., was pondering over the economics of introducing a new line of products. As Mr. Ahmed looked over the financial projections, he realized that the new product line had the potential of either firmly establishing Penn Plastics as a viable minority enterprise, or leading the company into insolvency.

Penn Plastics, Inc. was founded by Mr. Ahmed four years ago. Prior to founding Penn Plastics, Mr. Ahmed had received his Bachelor of Science degree in Chemical Engineering from a "Big Ten" University and an MBA from the same school. Upon graduation, Mr. Ahmed had accepted employment with a New York bank. After an 18-month stay with the bank, Mr. Ahmed had moved to a major chemical firm as a senior credit analyst. Over a period of time, Mr. Ahmed had assumed positions of increasing responsibility. Four years ago, the company had proposed that it would provide the "seed money" to set Mr. Ahmed up in business. Mr. Ahmed viewed this as an opportunity to further his own personal goals. Penn Plastics was formed by equity contributions by Mr. Ahmed and additional funds, in the form of equipment and supplies, provided by the chemical firm. At its inception, Penn Plastics was purchasing its raw materials from the chemical firm, and also, selling 100 percent of its output to it. Gradually, Mr. Ahmed had been successful in generating additional sources of relatively cheap raw materials and in developing other markets for the company's products.

As Mr. Ahmed looked at the new product line's revenue and cost figures, he realized that Penn Plastics had the potential of substantially increasing its sales. Investment in the new project would amount to $250,000. Mr. Ahmed did not anticipate any problems in raising the funds. He did realize that the cost of incremental funds would be 10 percent. Virtually all of the $250,000 amount would be utilized to buy new equipment. For purposes of analysis, he assumed that Penn Plastics would be able to utilize the new equipment for five years. The investment tax credit at 3.33 percent would be available in the current year, and earnings from the existing operations were substantial enough to fully utilize the investment tax credit. The equipment would be depreciated by using a straight-line method towards a salvage value, after *five* years, of $130,000.

Mr. Ahmed had also derived the expected sales-and-net-income figures.   For purposes of analysis, he used a five-year planning horizon.   His belief was that any financial forecasting or planning beyond five years might prove to be injurious to Penn Plastics. He felt that estimates in the low, medium and high categories, with probabilities of occurrence of .15, .65 and .2, respectively, were appropriate.   His estimates for sales and net income for the low, medium and high categories are shown in Exhibit 1(a)–1(c), respectively.

As Mr. Ahmed started to analyze these figures, he realized that the salvage value was not deterministic.   In fact, it was not farfetched to assume that the $130,000 salvage value was an expected value, which had a dispersion not unlike that for the net-income figure. Mr. Ahmed felt that from Penn's perspective, the after-tax, risk-free rate was 5 percent.   Mr. Ahmed wanted to use this rate in assessing the probability of the project's net present value being negative.

EXHIBIT 1

Penn Plastics, Inc.

Low, Medium, and High Estimates, New Product Line

Item	Year 1	Year 2	Year 3	Year 4	Year 5
(a) Low Estimate, Probability = .15					
Sales	$120,000	$130,000	$140,000	$150,000	$170,000
Income	7,300	9,200	11,300	13,000	16,100
(b) Medium Estimate, Probability = .65					
Sales	160,000	170,000	190,000	200,000	220,000
Income	14,000	19,000	24,000	30,000	33,000
(c) High Estimate, Probability = .2					
Sales	200,000	220,000	240,000	260,000	290,000
Income	28,000	35,000	42,000	49,000	53,000

Questions

1. Calculate the expected net present value for the project under consideration by Penn Plastics. The 10 percent discount rate is

appropriate for use. Based upon the net present value criterion, is the project acceptable?

2. Calculate the standard deviation of the net present value of the project. Use the following formula:

$$SD(NPV) = \left[\sum_{t=1}^{5} \frac{SD(t)^2}{(1+k)^{2t}} \right]^{1/2}$$

Here k = appropriate discount rate and $SD(t)$ is the standard deviation for annual net cash flows. It is assumed that cash flows are independent from one time period to the next. Ignore the salvage value dispersion effects in your calculations.

3. What is the probability that net present value would be negative? (Hint: Expected net present value will have to be recomputed at the after-tax, risk-free rate.)

4. Why were two different discount rates used in answering questions 1–3?

5. What qualitative factors need to be taken into consideration by Mr. Ahmed?

6. What should Mr. Ahmed do with respect to the proposed, new product line?

Case 16

ROSS CONTROLS, INC.

REPLACEMENT OF FIXED ASSETS

In December, 1976, Joanne Ross, president and principal owner of Ross Controls, Inc., was evaluating two new systems to replace the existing, sanitary, waste-water-disposal system. Two events had prompted the need to consider replacing or upgrading the old system. First, hydraulic and organic overloading of the existing system had necessitated frequent cleaning of the storage tanks. In conjunction with the overload, soapy water was causing clogging of the leaching wells. Secondly, a governmental agency, concerned with environmental pollution, had concluded that the frequent overloading and clogging of the existing system would ultimately result in the bacteriological contamination of the underground water table. Thus, it was possible that by early 1980, the governmental agency would determine that community health was being endangered, and would issue an order to Ross Controls, Inc. to bring its waste-disposal system within compliance. Ross was told by the company lawyers that appealing the compliance order and related litigation would permit the company not to install a new system until early 1982. Ross was also told that it was almost certain that the company's appeal would be found lacking in merit, and would result in assessments and court costs of $4,000 for both 1980 and 1981.

Ross Controls, Inc. was founded in 1946 by John Ross, father of Joanne Ross, to manufacture fluid controls for the oil industry. The company had prospered through the mid-fifties, when sales leveled off at the $3 million level. John Ross had been satisfied by the financial performance of the firm, and had not sought to seek applications of the firm's products in areas other than the oil and related-refining industries, nor had he sought to expand the firm's product line. By 1969, when Joanne Ross assumed active management of the firm, the firm's unit sales had started to decline, and other small manufacturers of competitive products had begun to make inroads into the firm's markets. Ross, utilizing her mechanical-engineering background, designed and patented a number of fluid-control devices; notably, a butterfly valve that was made of polymerized plastic, which in addition to having excellent shear resistance, was also anticorrosive. The valve found application in the production and distribution of reactive chemicals; especially sulphuric acid, which was being utilized in large quantities in markets close to Ross Controls' manufacturing plant. Ross also hired two fulltime salesmen to supplement the manufacturer's representatives who were handling the company product time. The net result was that the company's sales started to increase very rapidly and, by 1976, had reached the $7.5 million level.

Ross Controls, Inc. is located in a township north of Pittsburgh, Pennsylvania. In 1946, when the company was founded, the township consisted principally of farms. Even until 1968, when the present waste-disposal system was installed, the area was rural in nature. The existing system had been designed for 300 people, working 1.5 shifts per day, six days a week. However, by early 1976, the number of people contributing sanitary waste to the system had more than doubled to 610. Sales and manpower projections indicated that, by 1980, more than 800 people would be employed by Ross Controls.

The two main problems associated with the existing system were the frequency of the storage-tank cleaning and the clogging of the leaching-well drainage material. The storage tank required cleaning once every four months. This frequency of cleaning was necessary because the retention time and sludge-storage capacity was insufficient to permit solid decomposition and digestion. The cleaning service was provided by an outside contractor at a cost of $4,000 per cleaning. The cleaning action consisted of removing the top 8 to 12 feet of gravel in the storage tank. While the gravel-removal operation is being performed over a period of three to four days, it is necessary to continuously pump out all sanitary waste-water discharged for off-site disposal. The gravel is then replenished, after the cleaning operation is completed. The gravel replenishment and off-site disposal costs an additional $800 per cleaning.

As the work force and waste flows increase, and the system ages, it is logical to assume that operating costs will increase. The potential of higher operating costs, coupled with the pollution caused by seepage of the raw, waste waters, appeared to indicate that, both on economic and environmental factors, alternative systems might be desirable.

Three alternatives were available for consideration. The first one was to upgrade the existing storage-tank system; the second one was an "Extended Aeration" system; the third alternative was a "Bio-disc" system. The second and third alternatives would require the use of the storage tank from the existing system.

Upgrading the Present System

The present system has a processing capacity of 13,500 gallons per day (gpd) of waste water. The system can be upgraded to a 22,000 gpd capacity. With the increased capacity, the system would be able to assimilate hydraulic surges better; thus, substantially reducing the likelihood of upsets to the sedimentation and anaerobic processes, which are necessary for the decomposition and digestion of solids. As a result, the interval between cleanings would be longer.

The engineering firm doing the system-replacement study also suggested that eliminating the soapy water bypass, and combining the soapy-water and waste-water flows prior to entrance to the storage tank, would eliminate the leaching-well clogging problem. This would be accomplished with piping changes, instituted following the completion of the excavation work.

Concrete for the system would cost $16,000. Excavation would cost $10,500 and installing manholes would cost $2,000. Additional piping required would cost $500. The upgraded system would need to be cleaned only once a year, at an annual cost of $6,000. Pennsylvania Department of Environmental Resources regulations prohibit the modification of subsurface absorption systems for waste-flow rates in excess 10,000 gpd. The firm's lawyer had indicated that there was a 100 percent chance of obtaining a waiver to upgrade the present system. Lawyers' fees would be approximately $10,000 and would be expensed immediately. Capitalized expenditures would be expensed over five years, by using the straight-line depreciation procedure. None of the equipment would have any salvage value.

Extended Aeration

Extended aeration is an aerobic, biological and activated-sludge process which provides secondary treatment for the sanitary waste water. Both the waste-water and soapy-water flows would be discharged into a pump station, prior to entering the existing septic tank. The waste water would be pumped to the aeration tank for biological treatment. The aeration tank would overflow to the clarifier for removal of suspended solids, prior to effluent chlorination and discharge. Activated sludge from the clarifier would be returned to the aeration tank, with excess sludge being discharged to the existing storage tank.

The extended-aeration process is generally considered to be as effective as other secondary treatments, and does not require a primary sedimentation step. Among the disadvantages of the system are relatively large, surface-area requirements, high power consumption, and susceptibility to hydraulic surges and thermal conditions. Consequently, this system requires a greater amount of operator attention to assure efficiency. A surge tank is also necessary to handle hydraulic surges.

The extended-aeration system consisted of a package treatment plant costing $24,500. Erection costs would be $6,800. Concrete would cost $5,700 and excavation $3,700. Pumps required for the system would be $3,800, the surge tank would cost $2,000, piping would be $1,000 and electrical equipment would cost $2,700. The system would have a useful life of five years, and would be depreciated on straight-line basis. The treatment plant can be salvaged and resold for approximately $9,200 after five years.

Use of the extended aeration system would result in the existing storage tank being cleaned only once a year, at a cost of $6,000 per cleaning. Other annual, system-operating costs include power consumption, $5,400; maintenance, $1,400; and operator attendance, $3,000.

Bio-disc System

The bio-disc system is a four-stage, secondary, biological-treatment process. After primary sedimentation in the existing septic tank, the sanitary waste water is pumped to a four-compartment tank, where the biological step takes place. After the biological treatment, the effluent from the last compartment overflows to the clarifier. The clarifier-effluent flow is chlorinated and discharged while the underflow sludge is recycled to the storage tank.

Slow-moving parts and an absence of internal piping and diffusers result in lower power consumption and lower maintenance costs for the bio-disc system. Since the system is essentially self-controlled, it is not affected by hydraulic surges, thus obviating the need for either high operator attention or a surge tank.

The package treatment plant for the bio-disc system costs $45,000.

Erection and excavation costs are $2,500 and $3,700, respectively. $4,800 of concrete is required, as well as pumps costing $3,800. Piping costs are $700, while electrical equipment will cost $3,100. This system would also have a useful life of five years. Capitalized expenditures would be depreciated over five years. The treatment plant would have a salvage value of $11,600 after five years.

Annual operating costs for the bio-disc system include storage-tank cleaning, at a cost of $6,000; power consumption, $1,800; maintenance $300; and operation attendance, $500.

As of January 1977, the existing system would have a book value of $15,000. Annual depreciation charges, on a straight-line basis, are $3,000. If either the extended-aeration or the bio-disc system is used, existing equipment, with a book value of $5,000, would be scrapped. A scrap dealer has agreed to remove the equipment from the premises at no cost. The remaining $10,000 book-value cost is associated with the existing storage tank, which would continue to be utilized in the two new systems. Ross Controls, Inc., which has been profitable since 1948, has a marginal tax rate of 48 percent, and its marginal cost of capital is 12 percent.

Question

1. What alternatives are available for consideration by Ross?

2. Evaluate the economic desirability of each of the alternatives by using the net present value method.

3. What noneconomic factors have an influence on the final decision?

4. What should Ross do?

Case 17

NATIONAL CHEMICAL PRODUCTS

ABANDONMENT

In anticipation of an expected increase in market size, National Chemical Products and its competitors had, over the last several years, invested significant amounts of capital in the expansion of their production facilities for a plastic called Tensoplast. However, the expected increase in market size, which was based on anticipated use of Tensoplast in certain aircraft parts, had not come about. The aircraft producers had redesigned the parts, and the new specifications could not be met with Tensoplast, as produced by National Chemical Products or its competitors. Forced to operate at less than half of nameplate capacity, and with substantial overheads from newly expanded facilities, price cutting in the industry had become rampant. For the last two years, the profit and loss statement for National Chemical's Tensoplast product line had shown consistent losses, and conditions were not expected to get any better (see Exhibit 1 for this 1976 profit and loss statement).

Sam Springer, product manager for Tensoplast, not feeling comfortable with the cost-allocation methods used by National Chemical Products, had done some investigation regarding the basis for several of the cost numbers. The cost-of-goods-sold figure included $690,000 per year, straight-line depreciation on the plant book value of $3,000,000, as of December 31, 1975. Also included was $600,000 in direct labor, representing the salaries of 22 plant workers employed to produce Tensoplast. If the Tensoplast product line were discontinued, these plant workers could be reassigned very rapidly to other production areas within the firm's growing labor force.

As in the production of many chemical products, two of the raw materials used in producing Tensoplast were produced elsewhere within National Chemical Products. Cost of goods sold included 1.2 million pounds of one of these raw materials, at an interdivisionally-negotiated transfer price of 68 cents per pound. Out-of-pocket costs for this material were 44 cents per pound, but the market price was 90 cents per pound. There were also sales-volume difficulties with this product, and it was not expected that the 1.2 million pounds would be sold if production of Tensoplast was discontinued, unless the production facilities could be sold to another firm. The intermediate chemicals used by National Chemical Products to make Tensoplast were produced on spare, fully depreciated machinery in a corner of the plant. The other product produced by National Chemical Products and used in Tensoplast was shown at a price of 62 cents on the Tensoplast cost statements; out-of-pocket costs to make this product were 60 cents per pound; the market price was 70 cents per pound. For Tensoplast production, 2 million pounds per year were used. Like the first intermediate, it was not expected that this sales volume would continue if Tensoplast was abandoned. The remainder of the Tensoplast cost-of-goods-sold figure were materials purchased from other firms.

The selling, administrative expenses and allocated-costs number had also come under Mr. Springer's scrutiny. Of the $1,350,000 shown on the profit and loss statement, $600,000 was due to salaries associated with Tensoplast. If Tensoplast was discontinued, the 14 people associated with this expenditure could be reassigned to other areas, avoiding new hiring to fill these positions, but the process of reassignment would take about two years. The remainder of this entry on the statement was composed of costs allocated from other departments; computer costs, depreciation on headquarters facilities, and so on, which would continue, despite the abandonment of the Tensoplast product line.

In the beginning of 1977, a competitor of National Chemical Products made a surprise offer: to purchase the assets of the Tensoplast product line for book value, either in January of 1977 or 1978. To Sam Springer, it appeared that there were three options for National Chemical Products: first, the firm could continue to produce Tensoplast, which would produce the losses shown in Exhibit 1 for the next 10 years (adjusted for changes in depreciation), at which time the plant would be worn out and scrapped at no salvage value. Second, the firm could sell the assets of the Tensoplast product line to the competitor, either in January 1977 or January 1978, in which case the sales of the two chemical intermediates would continue for the 10-year period. Finally, the firm could discontinue the product line at any time during the 10-year period, which would stop sales of the intermediate chemicals for Tensoplast production. Since the plant and equipment were specially built for Tensoplast production, scrap value would be zero.

A meeting had been held between Mr. Springer, Mr. Fletcher, the firm's controller, and Mr. Sullivan, the division manager for the part of National Chemical Products which included Tensoplast.

Mr. Fletcher was of the opinion that the product should be sold immediately.

"I don't know why they would want to buy Tensoplast, but by all means let's sell immediately," Mr. Fletcher had said. "I've done some calculations, and the net present value of future profits and losses for Tensoplast is negative, using our 13 percent discount rate, even though small profits are shown after depreciation on the plant runs out. If we hit a snag in negotiations, we should terminate the operation immediately."

Mr. Sullivan was not so sure. "I don't know about the comparison of sale or continuance, but I disagree about termination. When operating profit is positive, as we have defined it for this product line, the product can make a contribution to fixed costs. That's called the 'shut down point' in economics. Whatever we do, I think termination should be ruled out."

EXHIBIT 1

National Chemical Products

Profit and Loss Statement for Tensoplast Product Line, for Year Ending December 31, 1976

(rounded thousands of dollars)

Net sales	$7,088
Cost of goods sold	6,248
Operating profit	840
Selling, administrative expenses and allocated costs	1,350
Net loss	$ 510

Questions

1. Is Exhibit 1 an adequate representation of cash flows for present value analysis? If not, show the proper cash flows for the life of the Tensoplast product line, assuming continued operation. Assume a 50-percent tax rate.

2. Compare the three alternatives, using the net present value method. Consider abandonment only for 1977. Assume all cash flows take place on the last day of the year. What should the firm do?

3. What is wrong with Mr. Fletcher's logic? Mr. Sullivan's?

Case 18

T.N.B. EXPORTERS CORPORATION

RISK MANAGEMENT

John Tabor, Bob Neese, and Ed Baker had started T.N.B. Exporters two years ago. All three had extensive experience in export sales; Baker and Neese as salesmen, Tabor as an accountant. The idea of T.N.B. Exporters was to serve as an intermediary between small and medium-sized United States firms with little export expertise and few foreign buyers. T.N.B. bought goods from the United States firms and resold them overseas. Baker and Neese did the purchasing and selling; Tabor handled the extensive paperwork involved with foreign selling and kept the books.

The firm's sales quickly grew, and for the last eighteen months, the volumes were just about all that the firm could handle without additional employees. Since the three owners were men with modest standards of living, they had no wish to expand or to take on further business.

One area that had worried John Tabor was credit risk. T.N.B. Exporters had had no bad debts over the short history of the firm, and was not reserving any money against this possibility. Tabor had some exposure to insurance, in general, and export credit insurance, in particular, and he felt that he had a grasp of some of the basics. He was aware that any insurance is not usually viable from a returns standpoint; that is, unless the insured knows something adverse that the insurer does not know in setting the rates, the expected value of losses is less than the premiums. Insurance is intended to cover the catastrophic, very-low-probability loss. In a business context, the firm wants to be protected against the unusual, extensive, and possibly business-ending loss, such as a fire, theft, or bankruptcy of a major customer.

The three owners had put most of their savings into T.N.B. Exporters and were making an adequate living out of the business. To protect their livelihood, Tabor was evaluating the possibility of obtaining export credit insurance. A large portion of this type of insurance, he knew, was issued by the Foreign Credit Insurance Association, in affiliation with the Export-Import Bank of the United States. However, for several reasons, Tabor preferred to deal with another insurer, who offered a similar, but not identical, program. He had obtained quotes and conditions on several, alternate policies.

Tabor knew that there were five aspects of foreign credit insurance that can vary among policies. These were:

1. Types of risk covered—there are two types of credit risk in export sales; commercial risk (the risk of nonpayment due to firm conditions, such as insolvency) and political risk (the risk of nonpayment due to war, confiscation, decree preventing import, and so forth).

2. Length of terms of sale covered—there are considered to be two types of terms; short terms (up to 180 days) and medium terms (up to 3 years for contracts of less than $25,000; longer for larger contracts).

3. Number of buyers covered—policies can either be taken out on one buyer at a time (single-buyer policies), or over several buyers (multiple-buyer policies). In the case of multiple-buyer policies, the insurer usually requires that these include all of the insured's export sales, not specific groups of countries or buyers.

4. Pre- or post-shipment risk covered—policies usually do not cover preshipment risks, such as cancellation of order. Preshipment endorsements covering other risks (political or commercial) are added to the base policy on a case-by-case basis, with premiums depending on the exposure during the preshipment period.

5. Deductability—policies that cover political risk insure 95 percent of the loss for short-term sales, 90 percent for medium-term sales, no deductability provision. Policies covering commercial risk insure 90 percent of the loss, less some yearly-deductable amount.

The insurer had presented five plans, with associated premiums based on current customer and country sales volumes (see Exhibit 1). Tabor was concerned not so much with preserving the firm's net worth, but with avoiding default on the bank loans, which might force the firm into liquidation and stop the principals' source of income. Tabor had reason to believe that, in the event of cash-flow problems, he could work out an extended payout arrangement with suppliers for balances. He also had no fear of lost sales volumes. Should one or several buyers default, there were plenty of other buyers in need of the firm's services.

It had been Tabor's policy to pay the firm's suppliers in accordance with their terms of sale of net 30 days, taking out short-term notes from the bank, as needed, to keep the firm's cash balances at $20,000, which he considered an optimal level. Note: repayments were scheduled on the basis of expected receipts. Exhibit 2 shows the balance sheet for T.N.B. Exporters as of the previous month; Exhibit 3 gives details in the accounts-receivable figure shown. Exhibit 4 is a typical statement of income for one month. In view of the paperwork that Tabor already had to prepare, he did not believe that export credit insurance would change the paperwork costs. Claims for either political or commercial defaults, under the policy proposals, were proven to the insurer by nonpayment by the customer for a specific period beyond the due date. Tabor felt that if the claim was covered by insurance, the bank would not exercise its foreclosure rights in the event that the monthly credit-line-note payment was not made in full.

EXHIBIT 2

T.N.B. Exporters Corporation

Balance Sheet as of December 31, 1975

(rounded thousands of dollars)

Cash	$ 20
Accounts receivable	1,850
Total current assets	1,870
Office furniture	20
Total assets	$1,890
Accounts payable	$ 456
Notes due bank (secured by accounts receivable)	1,269
Interest due bank	13
Accrued salaries	6
Other current liabilities	5
Total current liabilities	1,749
Capital stock	99
Retained earnings	42
Total owners' equity	141
Total liabilities and owners' equity	$1,890

EXHIBIT 1

T.N.B. Exporters Corporation

Export Credit Insurance Proposals

Policy Number	Type of Risk Covered	Length of Terms of Sale Covered	Number of Buyers Covered	Pre- or Post-Shipment Risk Covered	Commercial Deductability	Premium ($ per $100 in Sales)
1	Commercial	Short	all	both	$10,000	$.15
2	Political	Short	all	both	Does not apply	$.19
3	both	Short	all	both	10,000	$.23
4	both	both	all	both	10,000	$.25
5	both	both	one	both	10,000 per policy	*

*Depends on country risk class and firm composite credit appraisal—see table below.

Country Risk Class	Firm Composite Credit Appraisal			
	1	2	3	4
A	$ .02	$ .10	$ 1.00	$ 5.00
B	.15	.75	2.00	7.25
C	1.00	4.25	8.25	10.25
D	6.25	8.25	10.25	11.75

EXHIBIT 3

T.N.B. Exporters Corporation

Schedule of Accounts Receivable as of December 31, 1975

Firm Number Country #1.	Country Risk Class: A. Firm Composite Credit Apprasal	Terms of Sale: 120 days.; Monthly Sales (thousands)	12/31/75 Receivable
1	2	20	80
2	3	10	40
3	1	30	120
4	1	5	20
Country #2.	Country Risk Class: C.	Terms of Sale: 180 days.	
5	1	80	480
6	1	10	60
7	3	20	120
Country #3.	Country Risk Class: A.	Terms of Sale: 90 days.	
8	2	50	150
9	1	40	120
10	2	40	120
11	3	20	60
Country #4.	Country Risk Class: B.	Terms of Sales: 90 days.	
12	2	100	300
13	1	40	120
14	2	20	60

EXHIBIT 4

T.N.B. Exporters Corporation

Monthly Income Statement—for the Month of December 1975
(in thousands of dollars)

Sales	$485
Cost of goods sold	456
Gross margin on sales	29
Interest expense	13
Office rental	1
Depreciation on office furniture	1
Officer's salaries	6
Cable charges, travel expense, other expenses	4
Profit before tax	4
Tax (50% of above line)	2
Dividends	0
Increase (decrease) in retained earnings	$ 2

Questions

1. If the officers' salaries could be cut by 25 percent for a period of time, and accounts payable deferred into future months, what is the approximate, minimum, monthly cash flow necessary to avoid bank default?

2. Tabor believed that commercial and political probabilities of default for the next year could be estimated as follows:

Political Risk

Country Risk Class	Yearly Probability of Default
A	.0002
B	.0025
C	.0050
D	.2000

Commercial Risk

Firm Composite Credit Appraisal	Yearly Probability of Default
1	.0005
2	.0050
3	.0100
4	.1000

   If each political and each commercial risk is independent of each similar risk, what is the expected, bad-debt loss from each source for the next year? Can these be added to get the total, expected, bad-debt loss? Why or why not?

3. Is there a probability that T.N.B. Exporters cash flow will fall below the critical level of Question 1?

4. If the firm's aim in taking out the insurance is to prevent default on the bank notes at the lowest cost, which policy should be used? Does a comparison of the costs of this policy and the expected, bad-debt losses show export credit insurance to be a financially viable expenditure? If the insurance is taken out, what does this say about the firm's principals utility functions? Can you give a reason for the shape of these functions?

PART IV

Capital
Structure
and
Valuation

Case 19

GENERAL INDUSTRIAL CORPORATION

FINANCIAL LEVERAGE

General Industrial Corporation had been founded in the late 1950's as a partnership to manufacture a new type of building product. Jack Harrison and John May, the founders, had developed the product, which had several safety advantages over materials which were then in use, but was slightly more expensive. Sales grew slowly and profits were small. In 1965, Harrison and May had sold control of the firm to a group of local investors, and stock in the firm was listed on a regional exchange in 1971. No new stock had been issued since 1970, and borrowings had been made through the private placement of bonds.

In 1974, a federal agency made a ruling which was to result in significant earnings increases for General Industrial Corporation. The agency, which set federal standards for the use of certain types of materials, had raised the safety standards for materials that were similar to those produced by the firm. This negated the cost disadvantage which General Industrial had suffered, and considerably raised the demand for the firm's products. General Industrial's management responded by increasing the production capacity, raising prices, tightening the payment terms and credit policy, and decreasing inventories. All these responses are reflected in the financial statements of the firm, which are shown as Exhibits 1 and 2, pages 100-101.

Although the firm's production process was not patentable, it was difficult to copy. Mr. Larsen, treasurer of General Industrial, noted that, by late 1977, there were other firms within the industry that were producing comparable products; this had slowed General Industrial's sales growth in 1977 and had reduced its gross profit margins. Profits during the last quarter were considerably below previous levels. However, he expected that profit margins would remain considerably above industry averages, and that there would be considerable opportunities for profitable asset investment in the firm's line of business. Due to the decreased margins, however, this asset growth could not be financed by retained earnings to the extent that it had been in the past. During 1978, Mr. Larsen wished to finance $4 million in asset investment beyond that which he expected could be paid for out of internally-generated funds. He saw two possible financing methods:

New stock issue. Stock could be sold at $175 per share via a rights' offering to current stockholders. Given the profitability of the past few years, Mr. Larsen felt that there would be no problem in getting the stockholders to exercise these rights, and the flotation costs would be negligible.

New bond issue. Several institutional investors had approached the firm, recently, with offerings in response to Mr. Larsen's inquiries. Again, the flotation costs would be negligible and the interest rate would be 7.5 percent.

Mr. Larsen's estimate of the amount of needed funds was based on the 1976 financial statements. He had assumed:

a. a 10 percent increase in sales.

b. Cost of goods sold to be the same percent as in 1976.

c. Selling and administrative expenses to increase by 5 percent.

d. no other income or expenses.

e. interest rate on prior debt at 7.3 percent when applied to the long-term portion; the amount of this debt to be constant.

f. taxes at 48 percent of earnings before taxes.

g. dividends of $200,000.

Mr. Larsen's main concern was that the entry of other firms into the industry would draw sales volume away from General Industrial. He consulted with the sales manager of the firm and obtained the sales estimates that are shown in Exhibit 3, page 102. Armed with the above information, Mr. Larsen felt that he was prepared to arrive at a decision for selecting the most appropriate financing method.

EXHIBIT 1

General Industrial Corporation

Balance Sheets, 1974–1976

(in thousands of dollars)

	12/31/74	*12/31/75*	*12/31/76*
Cash	$ 501	$ 1,011	$ 704
Accounts receivable	2,573	2,768	2,755
Inventories	3,859	4,497	4,182
Prepaid expenses	213	373	175
Total current assets	7,146	8,649	7,816

EXHIBIT 1 (Cont'd)

Property, plant, & equipment	3,867	7,283	10,678
Total assets	11,013	15,932	18,494
Accounts payable	1,645	2,420	2,487
Accruals	1,456	627	370
Federal income tax	112	612	299
Current portion L.T.D.	338	567	771
Total current liabilities	3,551	4,226	3,927
Long-term debt	2,663	4,497	6,160
Common stock	2,031	1,995	2,017
Retained earnings	2,768	5,214	6,390
Total owners' equity	4,799	7,209	8,407
Total liability and owners' equity	$11,013	$15,932	$18,494
Current ratio	2.01	2.05	1.99
TD/NW	1.29	1.21	1.20

EXHIBIT 2

General Industrial Corporation

Statements of Income and Retained Earnings, for years Ending December 31, 1974 to December 31, 1976

(in thousands of dollars)

	12/31/74	*12/31/75*	*12/31/76*
Sales	$20,562	$30,260	$36,920
Cost of goods sold	15,669	21,445	29,606
Gross margin on sales	4,893	8,815	7,314
Selling and administrative expenses	3,549	3,691	4,211
Operating profit	1,344	5,124	3,103
Other income	13	1	2
Other expenses	6	9	13
Earnings before interest & taxes	1,351	5,116	3,092
Interest	240	391	450
Earnings before taxes	1,111	4,725	2,642
Taxes	497	2,079	1,242
Earnings after taxes	614	2,646	1,400
Dividends	203	200	202
Change in retained earnings	$ 411	$ 2,446	$ 1,198
EPS (200,000 shares)	$ 3.07	$13.23	$ 7.00
Gross margin (percent)	24	29	20

EXHIBIT 3

General Industrial Corporation

Estimates of 1978 Sales Volume

(in thousands of dollars)

Volume	Probability
$35,000–$37,000	.05
37,001– 39,000	.20
39,001– 41,000	.50
41,001– 43,000	.20
43,001– 45,000	.05

Questions

1. Compute the net profit after taxes, degree of financial leverage, and EPS for the alternative of new bonds and new stock for each sales level for 1978. Assume that 200,000 shares of stock are currently outstanding. Use the midpoint of each sales level as your sales estimate. What are the expected earnings per share?

2. Graph earnings per share versus sales. What is the break-even point between the financing methods?

3. In your opinion, which financing method should be undertaken? Why?

4. The use of debt financing increases both the expected earnings per share and the standard deviation of the earnings per share. Under the bond-financing alternative, where the bonds will be traded at par value, how much will the value of the firm increase under each of the following assumptions?

   a. The Modigliani and Miller propositions hold, no taxes.

   b. The Modigliani and Miller propositions hold, with taxes.

Case 20

KEOKUK PRECISION PRODUCTS

VALUATION

Keokuk Precision Products, located in Iowa, was a small manufacturer of metal and plastic products. It had been started in 1960 by Fred Mifflin, a professional manager with a degree in business administration from a major midwestern university. The initial capital had been provided by Mr. Mifflin and his wife's relatives, but the founder had allocated himself the majority of the common stock. As of 1976, the profitable operations of the firm had provided the equity capital necessary for expansion, and (except for deaths and inheritances) the stock remained in the hands of the original capital contributors (see Exhibit 1, page 105).

Over the years of its existence, the firm had never suffered a loss, although in some years, profits had been small (see Exhibit 2 for the firm's consolidated statements of income for the years ending December 31, 1971 to December 31, 1975). Profits had been reinvested, originally, in additional plant and equipment at the firm's main location; then in similar, wholly owned subsidiary operations in neighboring states. During the years 1972 through 1975, sufficient opportunities to use profits had not presented themselves to the firm, and substantial funds were held over these years in certificates of deposit. The firm had never paid a dividend.

Exhibit 1 presents the firm's consolidated balance sheets for December 31, 1971 to December 31, 1975. All data for Exhibits 1 and 2 were taken from the firm's annual reports, which are audited by a major auditing firm. In all cases, the accountant's opinion showed no disclaimer. All significant intercompany accounts have been eliminated. Investment tax credits have been applied as a reduction of the Federal income tax provision. Sales were recognized on the date that shipments were made to customers. Long-term debt consisted of a 9.5 percent note, payable to an insurance company in quarterly installments. This note, which was undertaken in 1972, contained provisions which limited the amount of other debts which the company might acquire, and also set minimum levels on working capital and quick assets.

Early 1976 was not an easy time for Mr. Mifflin. Because of the high tax brackets of himself and the other family investors, he had always preferred to have the generated profits retained in the business, rather than distributed as dividends and taxed as ordinary income. The other investors agreed—as long as the income on sales seemed to be rising at a relatively rapid rate. However, the costs of raw materials had risen in 1975, and profits were essentially the same, although sales had increased. Now the relatives, after years of waiting, were asking for some return on their investment. They had made it clear to Mr. Mifflin that they wanted him to either start paying dividends, or arrange for the sale of his and the family's stock in the firm. Considering that the latter alternative would result in a less heavily taxed, long-term capital gain, and that he was nearing retirement, Mr. Mifflin found the sale approach more attractive. He contacted several parties, who had in the past expressed an interest in buying into Keokuk Precision. One of the people he notified was Mr. John Hall, business manager for a Miami-based group of aggressive investors.

Mr. Hall was certainly interested in the purchase of the firm for his group. The profits for Keokuk Precision's main lines of business, though quite unstable, had been good in the 1971 to 1974 period, and the firm had a very good reputation. However, there were several problems in arriving at a fair market value for the firm. Mr. Hall did not know whether the trend in earnings after taxes, shown in the 1971 through 1974 period, would continue, or whether the "flat" profits picture of 1975 was the correct one. Also, since most of the firms in Keokuk Precision's industry were privately held, it was going to be difficult to get data to value the firm on a price/earnings basis. After an extensive search, Mr. Hall was only able to find one, publicly traded firm in the same industry with a similar profits history—an over-the-counter firm, selling at 13 times the earnings as of December 31, 1975. However, this firm pursued a different dividend policy than Keokuk Precision's, paying out 60 percent of its earnings in dividends. In addition, this company was about three times the size of Keokuk Precision.

As Mr. Hall tried to establish an appropriate price for the firm, he realized that his task was complicated by the difficulty of establishing an appropriate growth rate for Keokuk. He also knew that valuations could be based on book values, as well as on a "comparable firm" basis.

EXHIBIT 1

Keokuk Precision Products

Consolidated Balance Sheets,
December 31, 1971 to December 31, 1975
(rounded thousands of dollars)

	12/31/71	12/31/72	12/31/73	12/31/74	12/31/75
Cash and certificates of deposit[*]	$ 50	$ 159	$ 113	$ 224	$ 225
Notes and accounts receivable	259	311	588	498	520
Inventories[†]	253	286	321	546	461
Prepaid expenses and other current assets	8	11	12	16	15
Total current assets	570	767	1,033	1,284	1,220
Fixed assets less depreciation	628	658	670	738	709
Other assets	17	24	30	37	59
Total assets	$1,216	$1,448	$1,734	$2,060	$1,989
Notes payable	$ 96	$ 0	$ 58	$ 0	$ 43
Accounts payable and accruals	185	203	437	568	357
Federal income taxes	46	54	12	109	57
Current portion of long-term debt	14	34	31	31	31
Total current liabilities	342	292	538	708	488
Long-term debt	146	357	323	293	262
Deferrals	38	32	12	13	16
Common stock[‡]	330	330	330	330	330
Retained earnings	361	438	531	717	894
Total owners' equity	691	768	861	1,046	1,224
Total liabilities and owners' equity	$1,216	$1,448	$1,734	$2,060	$1,989

[*]Certificates of deposit   12/31/71 - $ 0
                                  12/31/72 - 77,000
                                  12/31/73 - 96,000
                                  12/31/74 - 96,000
                                  12/31/75 - 96,000

[†]Valued at lower of FIFO or market.

[‡]330,000 shares outstanding.

EXHIBIT 2

Keokuk Precision Products

Consolidated Statements of Income, for Years Ending December 31, 1971 to December 31, 1975

(rounded thousands of dollars)

	12/31/71	12/31/72	12/31/73	12/31/74	12/31/75
Net sales	$2,282	$2,446	$3,051	$4,223	$4,749
Cost of goods sold	2,045	2,034	2,631	3,557	4,071
Gross margin	237	412	420	666	678
Expenses	270	239	246	280	296
Net income on sales	(32)	172	173	387	382
Other income (expenses)	119	(28)	(35)	(32)	(28)
Earnings before taxes	87	144	138	355	353
Federal income taxes	(18)	67	45	169	176
Earnings after taxes	$ 105	$ 77	$ 92	$ 186	$ 177

Questions

1. Calculate book value per share for Keokuk Precision Products.

2. Estimate an appropriate growth rate for Keokuk. (Hint: Take into consideration its dividends, sales, earnings, and assets.) Justify your answer.

3. Estimate a value for one share of Keokuk Precision by using the dividend capitalization model. Assume that Keokuk will pay a 1976 year-end dividend of 30 cents per share, that paying this dividend and not retaining earnings will reduce Keokuk Precision's growth by half, and that the appropriate capitalization rate is 12 percent.

4. Can Keokuk Precision be valued by using the price/earnings ratio for the firm mentioned in the case? Why or why not? What adjustments, if any, need to be made before using the P/E ratio? What value do you get for Keokuk by following this procedure?

5. What value should Mr. Hall place on Keokuk Precision Products?

Case 21

MEMOREX CORPORATION[1]

VALUATION AND CHANGES IN FIRM RISK

The Memorex Corpoation was founded in 1961. As of 1970, the companys' product lines could be broken down into two areas: computer peripheral equipment and magnetic tape products. The peripheral equipment product line included data storage file products, terminals, control units, and a computer-output-to-microfilm system. Magnetic tape products encompassed computer tape, video tape, audio cassettes, and recording tape. Also, the company was in the process of developing its own computer systems, the MRX40 and MRX50. Headquartered in Santa Clara, California, the firm was a major manufacturer in its two main product areas, with plants and sales offices throughout the United States and around the world. The company had 23 subsidiaries, both domestic and foreign, including ILC Peripherals Leasing Corporation, which was formed in 1970 to purchase computer equipment from Memorex for lease to firms in the United States and Canada. As originally formed, Memorex Corporation held only 20% of the ILC stock; the remainder was owned by institutional investors.

The creation of ILC to support the leasing of Memorex products, as well as the increasing investment in the MRX40 and MRX50 computer systems, represented a substantial shift in emphasis by the firm. This shift was reflected in the firm's accounting methods. Lease revenue was recorded as earned. Initial lease acquisition costs were deferred and amortized on a straight-line basis over four years (the estimated life of the equipment being between four and five years). Research and development costs, including those on the computer systems, were expensed for tax purposes, and deferred and capitalized for book purposes. Amortization of research and development costs was to begin when the commercial production of the products involved commenced. If it was determined that any of these deferred costs could not be recovered from future revenues, they were to be written off at that time. As of December 31, 1971, the firm had deferred unamortized research and development costs

---

[1] This case was prepared from public information. It is designed for educational purposes, and not for purposes of research or to illustrate the correct or incorrect handling of administrative practices.

totaling $17,648,000; up from $12,149,000 as of December 31, 1970. See Exhibit 1, page 112, for Memorex's balance sheets from 1970 to 1975.

Total sales volumes grew in 1971, although not to the extent that was anticipated by the firm. This variance was attributed to: 1) retail income reductions due to competition, 2) video tape production problems, and 3) computer tape placing problems. To support the additional assets necessary for the leasing of equipment, deferred research and development costs, and deferred lease acquisition costs, Memorex and ILC borrowed increasing sums. On a consolidated basis, their debt grew to over $228 million as of December 31, 1971. This was well in excess of their net worth of approximately $26 million. Their interest expense totaled $9,967,000; up from $5,233,766 in 1970. This contributed to the consolidated net loss of $13,390,000 during 1971. See Exhibit 2 for Memorex's profit-and-loss statements from 1970 to 1975.

The year ending December 31, 1972 included some very significant events for Memorex. Sales were again up, from $107,006,000 in 1971 to $145,422,000 in 1972, and the company returned to profitability, with a final net income of $1,193,000. For the first time, the sales resulting from leases exceeded those resulting from other sales. Long-term debt grew from $140,146,000 as of December 31, 1971 to $206,439,000 as of December 31, 1972. Current debt increased, also, from $53,426,000 to $76,428,000. During 1972, the firm arranged for the sale and leaseback of the Santa Clara administration and equipment manufacturing facilities.

In November of 1972, Memorex acquired 100 percent voting control of ILC, in return for 300,000 shares of Memorex common stock. ILC had been paying 12 percent interest on its loans, and lenders agreed to reduce this to the prime rate plus 1½ percent, subject to certain minimum and maximum rates. $10 million additional borrowing power was made available to ILC if, 1) current loans were repaid in the same amount, and 2) Memorex increased its subordinated capital (either by the issue of common stock or subordinated debentures) by $10 million, which Memorex agreed to do. The year-end total investment in intangibles (which included deferred research and development costs) reached $32,410,000, up from $21,772,000 in 1971. The auditors, Arthur Anderson and Company, issued a qualified opinion in auditing the firm's 1972 financials, indicating that the statement was subject to the realization of revenues associated with the computer systems. Interest expense for the year was $19,951,000. Equipment for lease was shown as $116,929,000 on the balance sheet dated December 31, 1972; this entry had been $45,394,000 as of December 31, 1971.

During 1973, there were substantial changes in the Memorex balance sheet and in the firm's loan agreements. Effective June 31, 1973, the firm changed certain of its accounting policies and revalued some of its assets. In Note 2 of its annual report, the firm gave two reasons for these changes: reduced scale of the company's peripheral equipment operations, resulting in less future revenue then anticipated, and the effect upon Memorex of alleged anticompetitive acts by the firm's dominant competitor, International Business Machines. Adopting a new policy of charging research and development expenses and lease acquisition costs against income, rather than deferring these costs, the firm wrote off $37,373,000 against income. The firm announced the termination of its computer systems program. This resulted in a charge of $38,716,000 against income. Finally, the firm revalued certain assets and accelerated the depreciation on others, resulting in a $20,858,000 charge against income. A portion of these charges was included in current costs, and a portion was treated as extraordinary profit and loss. During 1973, the firm was delisted from the New York Stock Exchange. See Exhibit 3 for stock prices during the span of this case.

On December 14, 1973, Memorex, in a suit filed against I.B.M., alleged that I.B.M. was using its alleged monopoly power to control prices and eliminate competition. Another allegation was that I.B.M. had monopolized, or attempted to monopolize, the development, production, distribution, sale, lease, and servicing of electronic, data-processing equipment. The action was brought under the Clayton Act, and Memorex sought treble damages, totaling $3.1 billion, costs and attorney's fees, and permanent injunctive relief, including divestiture, as necessary to restore competition in the industry.

On September 28, 1973 and December 28, 1973, Memorex entered into revised credit agreements with lenders, changing the terms of certain loan agreements. These amendments and covenants were extremely complex, even in abbreviated form. It is unnecessary to review them here, since they were again revised shortly thereafter.

Nineteen-seventy-four was the first year in its corporate history that Memorex had a positive cash flow from operations, even though a net loss was recorded. On August 30, 1974, Memorex and the

Bank of America entered into a revised loan agreement. This agreement had been reached in principle between the parties in March, subject to the election of Robert C. Wilson as chairman of the board, president, and chief executive officer of Memorex. Mr. Wilson, who had been president of the Collins Radio Division of Rockwell International, assumed these positions with Memorex in May of 1974. During 1974 and 1975, several other new officers also joined the firm, including Henry C. Montgomery, vice president, finance, and treasurer, who came to the firm in October of 1974 from Fairchild Camera and Instrument.

The revised loan agreement contained a number of provisions, the major parts of which can be summarized as follows:

1. Certain additional credit facilities were provided.
2. Notes payable, due from both ILC and Memorex, were reduced by a total of $46,501,000. In consideration, the bank received preferred stock and warrants for the purchase of common stock. This preferred stock was to be redeemed from 1983 through 1992.
3. Principal payments on the remaining balance that was due the bank were altered.
4. Interest was reduced to 4 percent per year through December 31, 1977. This interest was made payable in cash or preferred stock, at Memorex's option.
5. The bank had taken security interest in all of Memorex's assets.
6. Cash dividends could not be paid, except on the new issues of preferred stock.
7. Certain mandatory repayments were to have been made if assets were sold, or if monies were realized from the suit against I.B.M.
8. The Bank agreed to exchange up to $20 million in debt for shares of preferred stock, if Memorex was able to force conversion, or redeem prior to December 31, 1977, any of its 5¼ percent convertible subordinated debentures due in 1990. The bank would exchange $500 of its debt for preferred stock for every $1,000 of convertible debentures converted or redeemed.

On April 22, 1975, the firm announced its intention to purchase the 5¼ percent, convertible subordinated debentures at a rate of $350 per $1000 principal amount, with the intent to require lenders to make the debt-for-equity exchange specified in the aforementioned point 8. In 1975, the company purchased $6,955,000 (principal amount) worth of debentures, and senior lenders exchanged $3,373,000 worth of debt for preferred stock. As well as increasing equity via the debt-for-equity exchange, this transaction also resulted in an extraordinary credit of $2,031,000 to income, net of income tax effect.

The year ending December 31, 1975, the first full year with Robert Wilson as chief executive officer, was significant in a number of other respects. Total debt was reduced by $52.5 million, to $225,046,000. Operating income after taxes was $8,245,000; extraordinary credits increased this to $18,022,000. Equity of all stockholders increased, from a deficit of $23,667,000 as of December 31, 1974 to a $3,091,000 positive amount as of December 31, 1975. Revenues increased from $217,627,000 to $263,994,000, despite recession conditions. A few quotes from the annual report are appropriate:

> 1975 was a very good year for Memorex. . . In many respects it was a time of restoration: restoration of positive attitudes, restoration of profitability, and restoration of positive net worth . . . We are proud of the progress made but we recognize that the restoration will not be complete until common shareholder's equity is strongly positive and the balance sheet significantly strengthened . . . The principle factor in this growth (of total revenues) was the sale of equipment products to both end-users and original equipment manufacturers. Yet, despite the high level of equipment sales, lease revenue was maintained at 1974 levels. [2]

> During 1975, Memorex continued its emphasis on financial integrity, credibility, and professionalism . . . Conservatism and propriety in all financial representations were stressed throughout the Company. Conservative accounting practices were consistently applied. Problems identified during the year were immediately recognized in the financial results . . . the propriety of the financial statements resulted in an unqualified opinion from Haskins and Sells, the Company's independent public accountants. [3]

[2] "Memorex Corporation 1975 Annual Report", page 2, Report to Shareholders, by Robert C. Wilson, President, Chairman, and Chief Executive Officer.

[3] ibid., page 22, Financial section, by Henry C. Montgomery, Vice-President, Finance, and Treasurer.

EXHIBIT 1

Memorex Corporation

Consolidated Financial Statements—1970 to 1975

(in thousands of dollars)

	12/31/70	12/31/71	12/31/72	12/31/73	12/31/74	12/31/75
Cash and Temporary investments	$ 4,705	$ 7,034	$ 5,340	$ 4,099	$ 11,783	$ 40,182
Marketable securities	541	0	3,488	0	0	0
Accounts receivable	32,598	32,135	30,428	41,365	42,285	40,413
Inventories	47,745	46,964	44,710	58,779	50,747	44,797
Prepaid expenses	2,746	3,461	0	0	0	0
Other current assets	0	5,573	0	0	0	0
Total current assets	88,334	95,167	83,966	104,243	104,815	125,392
Fixed assets	62,432	75,667	51,962	43,112	39,715	37,185
Investments	10,096	10,298	22,604	0	0	0
Intangibles	13,523	21,772	32,410	0	0	0
Equipment for lease	21,798	45,394	116,929	92,654	84,878	61,067
Other assets	4,842	7,107	8,608	6,195	6,987	4,493
Total assets	$201,021	$255,405	$316,479	$246,204	$236,395	$228,137
Due bank	$ 14,517	$ 18,296	$ 0	$ 0	$ 0	$ 0
Accounts payable and accruals	24,918	24,589	22,791	25,347	28,025	36,709
Taxes due except federal taxes	2,064	503	2,450	1,094	0*	4,503*
Federal income taxes due	0	0	0	0	0	0
Current portion of L.T.D.	528	10,038	51,187	47,549	27,000*	35,500*
Total current liabilities	42,027	53,426	76,428	73,990	55,025	76,262
Long-term debt	101,913	140,146	206,439	253,473	199,288*	143,444*
Deferred income taxes	8,908	1,685	1,393	5,598	5,759*	5,340*
Other liabilities	9,061	34,192	0	0	0	0

EXHIBIT 1 (Cont'd)

Common stock	3,870	3,922	4,305	4,322	4,340	4,484
Capital surplus	11,864	12,042	16,729	16,726	38,740	38,405
Preferred stock	0	0	0	0	50,390	59,057
Retained earnings	23,381	9,992	11,185	(107,905)	(116,877)	(98,855)
Total owners' equity	39,115	25,956	32,219	(86,857)	(23,677)	3,091
Total liabilities & owners' equity	$201,021	$255,405	$316,479	$246,204	$236,395	$228,137

*Indicates that the current and long term portions were estimated based on the total amounts and the notes to the financial statements.

EXHIBIT 2

Memorex Corporation

Consolidated Statements of Income — For the Years Ending December 31, 1970 to December 31, 1975

(in thousands of dollars)

	12/31/70	12/31/71	12/31/72	12/31/73	12/31/74	12/31/75
Gross sales, retail, and service income	$ 79,259	$107,006	$145,422	$176,923	$217,627	$263,994
Costs of gross sales, rentals, and service	46,487	64,836	87,434	139,451	147,743	163,651
Gross margin	32,772	42,170	57,988	37,472	69,884	100,343
Selling, general, administrative, and uncapitalized research and development expenses	21,100	58,062	36,542	52,200	59,077	67,225
Operating income	11,672	(15,892)	21,446	(14,728)	10,807	33,118
Interest expense	5,234	9,967	19,951	20,487	18,675	15,268
Extraordinary profit and loss	0	0	450	(78,950)	(1,104)	9,757
Provision for taxes	3,255	(12,469)	752	4,925	0	9,585
Net income	$ 3,183	$(13,390)	$ 1,193	$(119,090)	$ (8,972)	$ 18,022

EXHIBIT 3

Memorex Corporation

Price Range of Common Stock—January 1, 1970 to March 9, 1976

Year	High	Low
1970	$166 3/4	$44 1/2
1971	79 1/2	19 1/4
1972	38 1/2	14 7/8
1973	18 1/2	1 3/8
1974	4 3/4	1 3/8
1975	10 3/4	3 7/8
1976 (through 3/9/76)	26 1/2	7 3/8

From 1970 through 1972, the stock was traded on the New York Stock Exchange. In 1973 the stock was delisted and traded over-the-counter. The low price shown for that year is the OTC low-bid price. High and low prices for 1974 are bid prices. On July 28, 1975, the stock was listed on the Pacific Stock Exchange. Both the high and low prices for 1975 are OTC bid prices. 1976 prices are Pacific Stock Exchange trading prices.

Questions

1. In your opinion, what three business decisions led to Memorex's financial difficulties?

2. Did the capitalization and deferral of research and development and lease acquisition costs affect net cash flow?

3. Discuss the effects of Memorex's three decisions on a) the firm's business risk level and b) the firm's financial risk level. What was the combined effect on the riskiness of the firm as an investment? In your opinion, did the possible returns justify the risks that were taken? (Use traditional, financial-risk considerations.)

4. Based on the market price of the firm's stock, what did investors think of Memorex's increasing commitment to leasing and to the MRX computer systems development? What does this say about efficient capital markets?

5. Were Memorex's decisions in line with the theoretical objectives of the firm, if such objectives are taken to be maximizing the value of common stock held by present shareholders?

Case 22

UNITED PAPER CORPORATION (A)

COST OF CAPITAL

In early January, 1977, Mr. Murphy, controller of United Paper Corporation, was reviewing the various investment proposals that he had received from the vice presidents of United's four divisions. Under the direction of Mr. John Craven, president of United, the company had started an ambitious expansion program. All four divisions had been encouraged to generate proposals for review and possible funding, and had responded enthusiastically. As Mr. Murphy started to read through the details of the proposals, it became apparent to him that some proposals looked very good, some were obviously weak, and a significant number appeared to call for extensive evaluation. It also became apparent to him that United would not be able to finance even a small number of the proposals without raising funds from sources outside the company. As a preliminary to evaluating the proposals, Mr. Murphy wanted to estimate United's cost of capital for use in the evaluation process.

The United Paper Corporation is a diversified firm, involved in the manufacture of wood-based and other industrial products, and the mining and selling of coal. In the year ended December 31, 1976, United earned $33.7 million on sales of $917.6 million. A consolidated statement of earnings is shown in Exhibit 1, page 117. At year-end 1976, United had total assets of $667 million (see Exhibit 2, page 117).

The company is organized in four divisions. The fiber paper division makes writing paper, commercial/newsprint paper and specialty paper. Near-term prospects for the industry look good. It is anticipated that price boosts of about 5 percent will be instituted. The industry performance is being influenced by a number of factors, including a shortage of suitable mill sites, pollution-control requirements for existing mills, and environmental impact statements for proposed new mills. The division is the largest in terms of sales volume, contributing 35.4 percent of 1976 net sales. However, its contribution to pretax earnings was 18.1 percent (Exhibit 3, page 118).

The paperboard division produces a wide variety of paperboards with different chemical and physical performance characteristics. Within the division, the products fall into two broad categories: containerboard and boxboard. Containerboard products include corrugated containers, corrugating material and chipboards. Demand has been somewhat sluggish, although long-term prospects look good. Boxboards products are used for packaging consumer goods and, therefore, need to be lightweight and strong. The division has an excellent reputation in the trade for manufacturing boxboard suitable for high-fidelity graphic reproduction. However, the industry has been demonstrating a slow growth rate. The paperboard division has had to make pollution-control expenditures on some of its mills in recent years. In 1976 the division contributed 24.9 percent of sales and 11.5 percent of pretax earnings.

The industrial products division makes castings, cement and metal pipes, gaskets and valves, and small tools for use in the coal-mining industry. Intermediate and long-term growth prospects are good. The division contributed 27.7 percent of 1976 sales and 25.6 percent of pretax earnings. The smallest division, in terms of sales, is the mineral resources division, whose primary business is to mine and sell metallurgical coal. The division owns coal mines in Kentucky, Pennsylvania, and West Virginia. In recent years, the division has become extremely profitable, contributing 30.1 percent of pretax profits and 12 percent of sales. By coal industry standards the division is very small, mining just over 2 million tons of coal. The division is interested in acquiring additional mines to operate.

As Mr. Murphy started to estimate United's cost of capital, he decided on a number of assumptions for his calculations. First, he felt that the firm was overleveraged. However, he knew that his opinion on leverage was not overwhelmingly supported by the executive committee of United. Therefore, he decided to work under the assumption that the firm's existing ratio of total debt to total assets was optimal. Secondly, he was in favor of increasing the firm's common stock dividend per share from $1.00 to $1.10 in 1977. However, he knew that the majority of sentiment in the executive committee would be against a dividend increase and, therefore, he decided to use $1.00 for the expected 1977 dividend rate. Finally, based upon his calculations, he felt that a conflict existed between compound growth rates over the last ten years for total assets, sales, net income and dividends per share. He felt that the 8 percent growth rate for total assets was a good measure of the growth performance for United.

The recent price of United Paper Corporation common stock was $23 a share. Based upon conversations with an investment banking firm, Mr. Murphy felt that a reasonably sized issue of common stock could be floated with a cost of 3 percent of the selling price. United's preferred stock was currently selling for $55 a share. Any new $100 par, preferred stock issued would entail underwriting commissions of 2 percent of the selling price. Interest rates on recently issued, callable bonds of the same quality as United carried a coupon rate of 8.7 percent.

EXHIBIT 1

United Paper Corporation (A)

Consolidated Earnings Statement, Year Ending December 31, 1976

(in millions of dollars)

Net sales	$917.6
Cost of goods sold	751.8
Selling and administrative expenses	98.1
Interest expense	13.3
Operating income	54.4
Income equity in jointly-owned corporations	9.4
Income before taxes	63.8
Income taxes	29.1
Net income before preferred dividends	34.7
Preferred dividends	1.0
Net income	33.7
Common dividends	14.5
Retained earnings	$ 19.2

EXHIBIT 2

United Paper Corporation (A)

Consolidated Balance Sheet, December 31, 1976

(in millions of dollars)

Cash	$ 21.2
Net receivables	105.7
Inventory	107.1
Total current assets	234.0
Land and Mineral	52.5
Buildings, plant, net	254.1
Equity in jointly-owned corporations	126.4
	667.0

EXHIBIT 2 (Cont'd)

Accounts payable	60.2
Accrued liabilities	39.1
Other liabilities	4.9
Total current liabilities	104.2
Deferred taxes	30.1
Long-term debt	192.5
Total liabilities	326.8
Preferred stock, $5	20.0
Common, $1 par	14.5
Paid-in capital	90.5
Retained earnings	215.2
	$667.0

EXHIBIT 3

United Paper Corporation (A)

Sales and Earnings by Divisions

	% of sales	% of earnings
Fiber paper division	35.4	18.1
Paperboard division	24.9	11.5
Industrial products division	27.7	25.6
Mineral resources division	12.0	30.1
Jointly-owned corporations	-	14.7
	100.0	100.0

Questions

1. Assuming that United Paper Corporation's capital structure, before inclusion of 1976, marginal retained earnings, is optimal, calculate the proportion of capital-structure financing provided, respectively, by long-term debt, preferred stock and stockholders' equity. "Free" sources of funds, such as deferred taxes and accrued liabilities, should be ignored.

2. Calculate the cost of debt, preferred stock, and equity—both internal and external.

3. Develop a graph showing the relationship between the marginal cost of capital and the dollar amount of the capital budget. The graph and supporting calculations should clearly show all relevant percentages and dollar amounts. (Hint: Exhibit 1

indicates that 1976 retained earnings, which would be available for investment in 1977, equal $19.2 million. Depreciation-shielded funds, while available for investment, have no material impact on the calculation of the marginal cost of capital and should be ignored.)

4. Calculate the average costs of capital for United for capital budgets of $20 million and 60 million. Show your result on the previously drawn graph.

5. What is going to happen to the marginal and average costs of capital as United's capital budget for 1977 keeps getting bigger and bigger?

6. What additional factors need to be considered in estimating United's cost of capital?

Case 23

GBP INDUSTRIES

COST OF CAPITAL FOR AN INDUSTRIAL FIRM

In December 1976, Mr. Robert Singleton, vice president of finance for GBP Industries, was concerned that the firm would not be able to generate sufficient cash flows from retained earnings and depreciation to meet the anticipated capital-expenditure requirements for 1977. His feelings were that either GBP Industries (GBPI) would have to raise funds externally, or impose capital rationing. Raising funds externally would mean that GBPI would be able to fund all projects with expected internal rates of return in excess of GBPI's required 10 percent rate of return. Imposing capital rationing would mean that a number of projects with rates of return in excess of 10 percent would not be funded due to a shortage of capital. Mr. Singleton decided that, as a preliminary to deciding whether to raise funds externally, he would have his assistant, Miss Suzie Raymond, do an analysis on the long-range impact of capital rationing. Miss Raymond had been working for GBPI since last June, upon graduation from a graduate school of business. Mr. Singleton had been very pleased with the manner in which Miss Raymond had been able to handle assignments.

GBP Industries was founded in 1953 as the General Building Products Company. In the early years, GBPI was a manufacturer of products for the building and construction industry. However, by 1969 it had sufficiently diversified so that its investment bankers felt that a change in name was justified. Following the trend established in the late sixties by widely diversified firms, GBPI adopted its present name.

The company is organized into five divisions. The building products division is the largest of all, accounting for 30 percent of the total sales volume. The division manufacturers products for the building and home construction industry. Sales of the division are strongly influenced by fluctuations in new housing starts. The second-largest division is the pipe products division, which accounts for almost 20 percent of sales. This division provides various types of metal and ceramic pipes to the construction industry, oil industry and public utilities. In addition, the division also performs trench work on a contractual basis. Typical clients are electric utilities and rural electric cooperatives. However, in recent years, the division has also received many phone calls from farmers, who wanted trench work done to install milkers and feeders. The division is not advertising its trench work capabilities. Apparently, the farmers are finding out about its trenching capabilities through electric company representatives, who are promoting the increased use of electrical equipment on farms. This division has been one of the fastest growing. It had been acquired via a merger a few years ago. The thermal insulation division manufactures asbestos and fiberglass insulation and maintains its own sales force to service the construction industry. Sales of the division tend to fluctuate somewhat, but not as severely as those of the building products division. In fact, since 1973, with the advent of a shortage of energy resources, the division's sales appear to give all indications of being recession-proof. The market for selling insulation to older homes is growing very dramatically and the division is participating in this market growth. This division had been acquired by merger also. The electronics division is a manufacturer of wires, switches, fixtures, and so forth, used in wiring a building. Sales are to wholesalers selling to retail hardware stores and contractors. Sales in the division have been relatively flat over the past few years. Since 1974, the division has been acting as a distributor for a very small manufacturer that produces burglar alarms and fire alarms for residential and commercial buildings. Mr. Singleton knew that this manufacturer could not increase sales as rapidly as its potential without an infusion of additional working capital, and probably was an excellent merger candidate. The smallest division, euphemistically called the industrial products division, produces a mishmash of products and operates a half dozen retail electronics outlets, which sell hi-fi equipment, CB's, car stereos, and so on. The division has been a consistent money loser, and top management is considering selling off part of the division, and absorbing the remaining part in the other divisions. GBPI's most recent financial statements are shown in Exhibits 1 and 2, pages 122-123.

When Miss Raymond received her assignment, she asked why GBPI used a 10 percent hurdle rate for capital expenditures. Mr. Singleton responded that it had been his practice to use the 10 percent figure because that is what had been used in the past, and because he did not want potential new projects to be treated any differently than those projects that had met the 10 percent, required-rate-of-return criterion in the past. By continuing to maintain the rate at 10 percent, Mr. Singleton felt that new projects would be subject to the same risk and return criteria as the firm's existing business. Miss Raymond carefully pointed out the problems in using the existing approach. At Mr. Singleton's suggestion, she sent him a memorandum summarizing her viewpoints on, and justification for, a required rate of return. Portions of this memo are presented in Exhibit 3. She also sent him an illustrative example, which is not presented here.

GBPI's sales, earnings and dividends record for the past 10 years are shown in Exhibit 4, page 124. The recent market price of the company's common stock was $38 a share. GBPI's investment banker had informed Mr. Singleton that a medium-sized issue of new common stock could be underwritten with net proceeds to GBPI equalling 93 percent of the recent market price. The preferred stock that GBPI had issued a few years back was currently selling for $60.25. A similar type of issue could be sold, to net GBPI 93 percent of the selling price. GBPI's bond rating would be Aa, and a bond of this type could be sold with a coupon rate of 8.5 percent, to net GBPI par value.

EXHIBIT 1

GBP Industries

Balance Sheet June 30, 1976

(unaudited; in thousands of dollars)

Assets		*Liabilities*	
Cash	$ 2,400	Accounts payable	$ 6,320
Marketable securities	400	Accruals	5,541
Accounts receivable	23,710	Current LTD	1,200
Inventories	17,932	Taxes due	2,750
		Other CL	1,900
Total current assets	$ 44,442		
		Total CL	$ 17,711
Net plant	62,340	Long-term debt	24,600
Investment in subsidiaries	4,200	Preferred $5.75	
Deferred charges	3,965	($100 par)	2,000
		Common ($4 par)	5,200
Total assets	$114,947	Paid in capital	17,610
		Retained earnings	47,826
		Total liabilities	$114,947

EXHIBIT 2

GBP Industries

Income Statement for Year Ending March 31, 1976

(audited; in thousands of dollars)

Net sales	$122,500
Cost of goods sold	108,796
Operating income	$ 13,704
Depreciation	4,316
Income before tax	$ 9,388
Income tax	4,788
Net income	$ 4,600
Preferred dividends	115
Available to common	$ 4,485
Common dividends	2,340
Retained earnings	$ 2,145

EXHIBIT 3

GBP Industries

Excerpts of the Hurdle Rate Memorandum

TO:	Mr. Robert Singleton, Vice President of Finance
FROM:	Suzie Raymond
DATE:	December 14, 1976
SUBJECT:	Required Rate of Return for Capital Expenditures

Bob, as a follow-up to our discussion, last Friday, I am summarizing my understanding of determining a required rate of return for capital expenditures . . . The concept that we are using, currently, is quite sound; namely, that the projects selected should have an expected rate of return in excess of an opportunity cost, or hurdle rate . . . It is not immediately apparent that using the 10 percent rate would be quite appropriate, for a variety of reasons. . .

Because of some of the reasons that I have identified above, it may be more appropriate for us to consider a marginal cost of capital approach to capital budgeting. Since our capital structure is composed of debt, preferred stock and common stock, we should take into consideration the costs of all of these capital components in our determination of a hurdle rate . . .

Our current leverage ratio—ratio of total debt to total assets—is around 38 percent based on book value, while the median industry ratio is over 50

EXHIBIT 3 (Cont'd)

percent. Therefore, another question that we need to consider is whether to use our existing weights or to assume industry weights. I feel that . . .

Finally, for illustrative purposes, I have assumed four different levels of total financing requirements: $4 million, $8 million, $12 million and $20 million.

EXHIBIT 4

GBP Industries

Historical Record of Sales, Earnings and Dividends*

Year	Sales	Earnings	Dividends
1968	$ 69.8	$3.15	$1.40
1969	73.5	3.27	1.40
1970	72.3	2.85	1.40
1971	83.0	3.11	1.60
1972	90.7	3.25	1.60
1973	100.3	3.92	1.60
1974	107.1	3.30	1.60
1975	121.9	3.05	1.80
1976	122.5	3.45	1.80
1977 †	128.6	3.80	1.80

*Sales are in millions of dollars; earnings and dividends are on a per-share basis. All figures are *pro forma* adjusted for mergers.

† Fiscal year ending March 31, 1977 figures are estimated.

Questions

1. What are the problems in viewing the hurdle rate as Mr. Singleton does? What' approach might Miss Raymond suggest as an alternative to Mr. Singleton's approach?

2. What capital structure would you utilize in establishing your component weights; GBPI's or the industry median? Why? (For calculating the leverage ratios, preferred stock may be added to total debt; that is, use (total debt + preferred stock)/total assets.)

3. Assume that market prices, rates and costs, as given in the case, are applicable at fiscal year end, that net income available to common for fiscal 1977 will equal $4.94 million, that the present dollar-dividend payout policy will be maintained, and that cash flows attributable to the depreciation tax shield will equal $5.0 million for 1977. Calculate the marginal and average costs

of capital for the four total financing requirements mentioned in Miss Raymond's memo to Mr. Singleton. Show the results in a diagram.

4. What are the managerial implications in identifying marginal and average costs of capital?

5. Assuming that total financing requirements, net of internally and spontaneously generated funds, are $4.7 million, how should GBPI raise these funds? Why?

Case 24

F. W. WOOLWORTH COMPANY[1]

DIVIDEND POLICY

At its January, 1977 meeting, the board of directors of the F. W. Woolworth Company declared a regular dividend on common stock of 35 cents per share, payable March 1, 1977 to shareholders of record on February 1, 1977. This represented a 5 cent increase from the former quarterly rate of 30 cents per share, which had been paid since 1970. The yearly rate increased from $1.20 to $1.40. The May 18, 1977 issue of the *Wall Street Journal* quoted Ellis Smith, Woolworth's financial officer, as saying, "We wanted to be competitive with those we were related to." Common stock dividends had been paid, without interruption, for 65 years, since the company became a public corporation in 1912.

F. W. Woolworth Company was one of the world's largest retail chain stores, with 5,508 leased departments and retail stores in the United States and abroad as of early 1977. The firm was engaged primarily in the distribution of general merchandise. The firm had many units and subsidiaries, both consolidated and unconsolidated, including those doing business in Great Britain, Germany, Spain, and Mexico and, in the United States as Richman Brothers Company (a men's apparel store). However, about 88 percent of the 1976 consolidated sales (see Exhibit 1, page 130) of F. W. Woolworth was contributed by three units: Woolworth and Woolco U.S., Kinney Shoe Corporation, and F. W. Woolworth, Limited, Canada.

As of early 1977, 1,762 Woolworth and Woolco stores were in operation in the United States, Puerto Rico, and the Virgin Islands. In fiscal 1976, the U. S. Woolworth and Woolco Division had sales of $2,761 million (54 percent of the corporate consolidated total), up 8 percent over 1975. Income for this unit, before corporate expense, interest, and taxes, was $72 million, up 25 percent from 1975. Since 1972, sales for this unit had increased 49 percent and operating earnings, 213 percent; this included the 1974 fiscal year, which was a very difficult one for retailers, in general. The January 31, 1977 Woolworth Annual Report (firms in this line of business

---

[1] This case was prepared from public information. It is designed for educational purposes, and not for purposes of research or to illustrate the correct or incorrect handling of administrative practices.

often end the fiscal year on January 31) for fiscal 1976 cited several innovations which had contributed to this unit's improvements in sales and profits:

1. Reorganization of executive and regional staffs for greater efficiency.
2. A refined and improved merchandise mix in Woolco stores.
3. Sharp reduction of independent licenses operating in high-profit departments in Woolco stores.
4. Recycling retail operations formerly occupied by other firms.
5. Extensive analysis of future store locations.
6. More effective use of computerized management-information systems.
7. Centralization of purchasirg and planning of advertising functions.
8. Expansion and modernization of distribution facilities.

Kinney Shoes was one of the largest family-shoe retailers in the United States, Canada, and Australia, with 1,881 retail outlets. Kinney Shoe Corporation was a subsidiary operation, having been acquired some 13 years previously by Woolworth. With about 11 percent of Woolworth's 1976 consolidated sales, the unit's stores operated under several names, including Kinney, Lewis, Williams, Fredelle, and Foot Locker. The latter operation was a relatively new, 16-store retail chain, handling top-brand athletic shoes and apparel, such as Adidas, Pumas, and Converse. Sales of Kinney's operations for fiscal 1976 were $588 million, up 19 percent from fiscal 1975; earnings before corporate expense, interest, and taxes were up 28 percent over that period. In the 1972 to 1976 period, sales had increased 88 percent and operating earnings, 161 percent.

F. W. Woolworth, Limited, Canada was one of Canada's leading retailers; the subsidiary unit had contributed 23 percent of Woolworth's fiscal 1976 consolidated sales. The 1976 Woolworth Annual Reported cited, ". . . severe operating problems engendered by the Anti-Inflation Board."[2]   This may have been the reason that, although this unit's sales were up 17 percent over 1975, income before corporate expense, interest, and taxes was up only 8 percent. Over the period from 1972 to 1976, this unit's sales increased 104 percent, while operating earnings increased 56 percent.

The message to the stockholders in Woolworth's fiscal 1976 Annual Report seemed to paint a bright picture of that year, and expressed confidence in the future:

Earnings in the past year were again the highest of all time, exceeding $100 million . . . Income of consolidated companies of $101,500,000 was up 20% from 1975 . . . Gains in Woolco Stores were greater than those of Woolworth Stores. Both types of stores operate profitably and continued growth in sales and earnings is anticipated . . . A major objective was reached in the latter part of the year when customer receivables of Woolworth and Woolco stores in the U. S. and Canada were sold to separate financial institutions. The transactions strengthened the financial position of the Company greatly and enabled us to reduce foreign and eliminate all domestic short-term debt at year end and reduced long-term debt as well. The sale of consumer receivables improved debt ratios and places the Company in a much better position to plan its growth . . . Further financial strength was added during 1976 by realignment of banking relationships and securing of substantial increases in lines of credit to support seasonal borrowing requirements . . .

There is a general prediction that the economy of the U. S. will continue to improve in 1977. We expect that U. S. retailing will benefit from the improvement and that each of our domestic operations will increase its sales and earnings . . . In total, we are optimistic about the year and view the future with confidence. [3]

Consolidated Summary of Operations for F. W. Woolworth for the fiscal years 1972 to 1976 are presented in Exhibit 2; Balance Sheets, as of January 31, 1976 and January 31, 1977 in Exhibit 3, page 131.

Sales and profits of retail stores, in general, depend to a great extent on discretionary consumer spending. Consumer spending depends, in turn, on consumer income (the bulk of which consists of wages and salaries) and inflation. In early 1977, there was a feeling that consumer income would probably continue to rise, a positive factor for retailers. However, there was a great deal of uncertainty regarding inflation, which could partially or wholly offset gains in consumer income. At least part of this concern about inflaton may have been due to concern about energy problems.

In early 1977, some analysis of the industry seemed to indicate that, despite good prospects for the 3— to 5—year upcoming period, price-earnings ratios for retailing stocks were quite modest. Despite growth in earnings per share, F. W. Woolworth's annual, average price-earnings ratio had fallen in the 1972—1976 period. Exhibits 4, 5, and 6, pages 132-133, present average price-earnings ratios, earnings per share, and yearly dividends per share for F. W. Woolworth

---

[2] F. W. Woolworth Company 1976 Annual Report, page 14.

[3] *Ibid.*, pages 4—5.

and three other firms in the retail store industry.[4] Exhibit 7 gives a "thumbnail sketch" of the other three firms, with some dividend developments.

At any time, a firm has three alternatives which it might consider regarding cash dividend policy: 1) it may increase dividends per share, 2) it may keep dividends per share at previous levels, or 3) it may reduce dividends per share. There are many factors which may influence a firm's decision in this area. At any time, there are some stockholders who may wish the firm to raise dividends and others who believe that the firm should retain these monies, which might raise the rate of growth of the firm and result in capital gains. Financial management must also consider the effect of the disbursal of cash on the firm's liquidity and debt to worth positions. Cash for firm needs must come from somewhere; disbursal of increased dividends may raise share price, making future equity financing possible with less dilution, but the higher current debt to worth position necessitated by this disbursal may also increase the cost of debt financing.

A combination of these factors may have been affecting firms' decisions regarding dividends in mid-1977. The previously mentioned, *Wall Street Journal* article of May 18, 1977 ("More and More Firms Boost Dividends, Partly Due to Pressure from Stockholders") cited some factors in force at the time:

> The continuing trend toward higher payouts apparently is being pushed by a variety of forces, including a buildup of corporate cash and a change in investment fashions . . .
>
> Many . . . companies are declaring their first cash dividends, and they, like those disbursing increases, usually cite bright prospects for profits . . . many companies have been holding down capital expenditures and thus have less internal need for funds . . . boards of directors have been under heavy pressure from both institutional and individual shareholders to think about more dividends . . .
>
> As more and more companies have raised dividends, the corporations that haven't sweetened the pot for shareholders have come under increasing pressure to do so . . .
>
> An indication of that momentum is the current acute awareness of many corporate managements of how they stack up in comparison of the "payout ratio"—the ratio of dividends as a percent of earnings.

---

[4] It is up to the student to determine the extent of comparability of these firms with F.W. Woolworth.

EXHIBIT 1

F. W. Woolworth Company

Report of Sales and Income, by Operating Unit, for Fiscal Years 1972–1976

(rounded millions of dollars)

	1976	1975	1974	1973	1972
Sales					
Woolworth and Woolco					
United States	$2,761	$2,548	$2,347	$2,149	$1,853
Canada	1,163	992	858	706	570
Germany	492	469	428	376	271
Spain and Mexico	61	63	57	49	34
Kinney	588	495	410	359	312
Richman	160	145	128	123	126
Intercompany eliminations	(73)	(62)	(51)	(40)	(47)
Total sales	5,152	4,650	4,177	3,722	3,119
Income before corporate expense, interest, and taxes					
Woolworth and Woolco					
United States	72	59	39	45	23
Canada	56	52	45	37	36
Germany	53	55	45	47	34
Spain and Mexico	7	9	7	5	4
Kinney	60	47	35	28	23
Richman	8	6	1	8	7
Income before corporate expense, interest and taxes	256	228	172	170	127
Unallocated corporate expense	(4)	(2)	(4)	(1)	(3)
Interest	(64)	(63)	(70)	(48)	(30)
Income taxes	(87)	(78)	(48)	(54)	(40)
Income of consolidated companies	101	85	50	67	54
Equity in net income of F. W. Woolworth and Co., Limited	7	14	10	26	27
Net income	$ 108	$ 99	$ 60	$ 93	$ 81

Source: 1976 F. W. Woolworth Company Annual Report

EXHIBIT 2

F. W. Woolworth Company

Consolidated Summary of Operations, 1972–1976
(rounded millions of dollars)

	1976	1975	1974	1973	1972
Sales	$5,152	$4,650	$4,177	$3,722	$3,119
Costs of sales	3,638	3,286	2,941	2,619	2,190
Depreciation and amortization	69	67	63	61	53
Interest	64	63	70	48	30
Foreign exchange (gains) losses	(6)	(10)	12	3	(2)
Income taxes	87	78	48	54	40
Income of consolidated companies	101	85	51	67	54
Equity net income of F. W. Woolworth and Co., Limited	7	15	10	26	27
Net income	108	99	60	93	81
Dividend requirement of preferred stock	(4)	(4)	(4)	(4)	(4)
Net income available to common stock	$ 104	$ 95	$ 56	$ 90	$ 77

Source: 1976 F. W. Woolworth Company Annual Report

EXHIBIT 3

F. W. Woolworth Company

Consolidated Balance Sheets for
January 31, 1977 and January 31, 1976
(in thousands of dollars)

Fiscal year	1976	1975
Current assets		
Cash	$ 39,100	$ 46,500
Time deposits	10,200	27,700
Trade receivables less allowance	18,200	229,700
Other receivables	74,200	53,500
Merchandise inventories	1,026,300	914,100
Operating supplies and prepaids	21,900	22,600
Total current assets	1,189,900	1,294,100
Investment in F. W. Woolworth and Co., Limited	180,100	187,400

EXHIBIT 3 (Cont'd)

Properties

Land, buildings, fixtures, and equipment less accumulated depreciation	499,200	480,700
Buildings on leased ground, less amortization	41,300	41,100
Alterations to leased and owned buildings, less amortization	151,900	140,100
Total properties	692,400	661,900
Intangible assets	14,700	14,700
Deferred charges and other assets	15,700	15,000
Total assets	$2,092,800	$2,173,100

Current liabilities

Short-term debt—domestic	$ 0	$ 92,000
— foreign	3,900	56,300
Long-term debt due in one year	17,800	7,000
Accounts payable	262,100	235,200
Accrued compensation and other liabilities	162,700	141,500
Dividends payable	11,100	9,600
Income taxes	45,000	62,000
Total current liabilities	502,600	603,600
Long-term debt	428,900	485,800
Other liabilities	24,900	24,100
Deferred income taxes	59,600	54,400
Shareholders' equity	1,076,800	1,005,200
Total liabilities and owners' equity	$2,092,800	$2,173,100

Source: 1976 F. W. Woolworth Company Annual Report

EXHIBIT 4

F. W. Woolworth Company

Average Annual Price-Earnings Ratios—Woolworth and Other Firms, 1970–1976

Year	F. W. Woolworth	K Mart	G. C. Murphy	Zayre
1970	13.1	26.0	11.0	18.4
1971	19.5	34.2	14.4	20.0
1972	14.4	42.5	11.4	15.3
1973	6.8	32.0	7.8	6.2
1974	6.3	32.8	5.9	31.7
1975	5.1	18.3	5.9	5.6
1976	6.5	17.6	6.9	3.6

Source: Compiled from *Moodys* and *Standard and Poors* industrial manuals.

EXHIBIT 5

F. W. Woolworth Company

Earnings Per Share (Undiluted)—Woolworth and Other Firms, 1970–1976

Year	F. W. Woolworth	K Mart	G. C. Murphy	Zayre
1970	$ 2.52	$ .61	$ 2.10	$ 1.54
1971	2.50	.85	2.10	1.95
1972	2.60	1.00	2.00	2.05
1973	3.15	1.15	2.27	1.77
1974	2.14	.87	2.36	.14
1975	3.34	1.64	2.50	.98
1976	3.62	2.15	2.82	2.11

Source: Compiled from *Moodys* and *Standard and Poors* industrial manuals.

EXHIBIT 6

F. W. Woolworth Company

Dividends Paid Per Common Share—Woolworth and Other Firms, 1970–1976

Year	F. W. Woolworth	K Mart	G. C. Murphy	Zayre
1970	$ 1.20	$ .15	$ 1.20	$ 0
1971	1.20	.17	1.20	0
1972	1.20	.17	1.20	0
1973	1.20	.20	1.20	0
1974	1.20	.22	1.20	0
1975	1.20	.24	1.20	0
1976	1.20	.32	1.20	0

Source: Compiled from *Moodys* and *Standard and Poors* industrial manuals.

EXHIBIT 7

F. W. Woolworth Company

Business Synopses of K Mart, G. C. Murphy and Zayre as of June 1977

K Mart Corporation (formerly S. S. Kresge Company)—Second largest retail chain store in the United States. Operates approximately 1,200 discount department stores under the name of K

Mart, 91 Jupiter stores, and approximately 350 Kresge stores. The firm derives the majority of its sales and profits from the K Mart discount chain. At the board of directors' April, 1977 meeting, directors raised quarterly dividends to 14 cents per share from the 1976 quarterly level of 8 cents per share.

G. C. Murphy Company—Based in Mckeesport, Pennsylvania, operates 545 variety, department, and discount stores, mostly in Pennsylvania and neighboring states. In addition to Murphy's Mart and Murphy, the company also operates stores under a variety of other names. The company plans to open a number of new Murphy's Marts in 1977. Dividends from 1963 to 1976 were at an annual rate of $1.20 per share. Starting with the second quarter in 1977, dividends were raised to an annual rate of $1.28 per share. This change was made after Woolworth had announced its new dividend rate.

Zayre Corporation—Fifth largest discount merchandiser, operating about 250 self-service stores under the trade name of Zayre, Warwick, and Shopper's City. Zayre also owns approximately 200 stores, which sell women's fabrics and apparel. Management owns 34 percent of common shares. A dividend has not been paid on common shares since before 1960.

Source: Company annual reports, *Moodys* and *Standard and Poors* industrial manuals.

APPENDIX

F. W. Woolworth Company

Dividend Payout Model [1]

Let:

b = retention rate as a percent of earnings; $1-b$ is the dividend payout ratio

Y_0 = dollars of net income per share

r = expected annual return on reinvestment in future periods

k = capitalization rate of future dividends

Then, if r, k, and Y_0 are positive, $0 < b < 1$, and $r(b) > k$ at $b=0$, a possible model of the optimal retention rate, b^*, is:

[1] See James C. T. Mao, *Quantitative Analysis of Financial Decisions* (New York: Macmillan Publishing, 1969) pages 347–351.

$$r(b^*) = k - b^* \frac{\partial r}{\partial b} + b^{*2} \frac{\partial r}{\partial b} \quad (1)$$

And the wealth of the stockholders is

$$W = \frac{Y_0(1-b)(1+k)}{k - br(b)} \quad (2)$$

A firm using a dividend policy including b^* as calculated in formula (1) will maximize stockholders wealth W in formula (2). The problem, of course, is calculating $r(b)$, the relationship between retention rate and return on reinvestment.

Assume a simple, one-period accelerator model describes the linear relationship between r and b for F. W. Woolworth. Under this simple model, the return, r, is equal to the change in earnings per share (EPS) between periods divided by the earnings retained in the previous period:

$$r = \frac{EPS_{t+1} - EPS_t}{EPS_t - Div_t}$$

Where Div equals dividends per share. Then:

$$b = \frac{EPS_t - Div_t}{EPS_t}$$

Many other factors, of course, affect earnings per share besides the retention rate, and the accelerator model may not be a good approximation of $r(b)$. In the Woolworth case, the effects of changing economic conditions on earnings per share can partially be accounted for by eliminating 1974 from the data base (a recession year and an outlier), and using 1975 data for EPS_{t+1} in the 1973 calculations.

Questions

1. List and discuss the possible reasons why the F. W. Woolworth Company might have elected to increase its dividend.

2. Compare F. W. Woolworth's dividend policy with that of similar firms. Justify the firms you chose as being comparable.

3. Did similar firms react to Woolworth's decision? How? Why do you think these reactions occurred? Do these reactions (or lack of reaction as of June 1977) justify your selection of similar firms?

4. (Optional if not assigned) (a) Based on the Appendix, calculate b and r for Woolworth for 1970, 1971, 1972, 1973, and 1975. (b) Using linear regression, estimate $r(b)$. (c) If $k = 12\%$; can b^* be calculated? If so, do so. (d) Calculate W for this b^*. Use 1976 data for Y_0. (e) If b^* is the optimal retention percent, $1-b^*$ is the optimal dividend payout ratio. How does the $1-b^*$ term compare with Woolworth's dividend payout ratio prior to the dividend increase (1976)? If 1977 earnings were $3.90 per share, is the new, dividend payout ratio closer to the calculated optimal?

Case 25

INTERNATIONAL BUSINESS MACHINES[1]

STOCK REPURCHASE AND DIVIDEND POLICY

IBM is one of the most successful ventures in the history of United States business, but as of late 1976, the firm was embroiled in a series of legal disputes. The 1976 IBM annual report documented the status of this litigation as of year-end:

> Seven suits instituted against IBM since 1973, alleging Federal antitrust law violations, remain in progress. The plaintiffs, California Computer Products, Inc., Transamerica Computer Company, Hudson General Corporation, Memorex Corporation, Forro Precision, Inc., DPF Incorporated, and Sanders Associates, Inc., seek damages which, after trebling, aggregate $4,458 million (of which $3,150 million is sought by Memorex Corporation and subsidiaries alone) . . .
>
> IBM has denied the charges of all of these cases and is vigorously defending each action.[2]

IBM was a very conservatively managed company from a financial standpoint, especially considering the firm's profits record (see Exhibit 1 for IBM's balance sheets for 1975 and 1976). As of December 31, 1976, the total debt-to-net-worth ratio of the firm was 0.39, counting deferrals and reserves as debt. There was, essentially, no long-term debt in the firm's capital structure. In reviewing the December 31, 1976 balance sheet, it might be assumed that the very large investment in highly liquid, marketable securities was being held in reserve against possible, adverse court judgments. Events in February, 1977 seem to corroborate this assumption.

1976 had been a very good year for the firm from a profits' standpoint. On January 17, 1977, the *Wall Street Journal* reported that IBM had concluded 1976's fourth quarter with record profits of $674 million, a 15 percent increase from a year earlier. The result was a record for any quarter in the firm's history. Later that month the IBM directors increased quarterly dividends by 25 cents a share to $2.50. In early February, the firm received favorable news regarding some outstanding litigation:

[1] This case was prepared from public information. It is designed for educational purposes, and not for purposes of research or to illustrate correct or incorrect handling of administrative practices.

[2] "IBM Annual Report 1976", page 23. For more details on the Memorex suit, see Memorex Corporation, Case 21.

The antitrust suit brought abainst IBM by California Computer Products, Inc., was dismissed in Los Angeles Court February 11, 1977. Judge Roy McNicholas rendered a directed verdict for IBM, stating "There is not substantial evidence in the record to support a finding of unlawful monopolization or attempt to monopolize in any of the relevant markets suggested."

IBM Board Chairman Frank T. Cary said the decision 'once again proves that IBM competes fairly and has not violated the law.'[3]

With this type of favorable decision concerning a portion of the pending legislation, and with profits at high levels, the firm may have felt that the reserves of marketable securities were somewhat large. On February 22, the firm offered to buy 4 million shares of its outstanding capital stock at $280 per share. This offer represented a 2.7 percent interest in the firm at a cost of $1.12 billion. The market price at the time of the offer was about $270 per share. IBM allowed itself the latitude of purchasing an additional 1.5 million shares for a total cost of $1.54 billion. When the offer terminated on March 9 (after being extended), IBM had purchased 2,567,516 shares at a total cost of about $721 million, including fees and expenses.[4] "IBM board chairman, Frank T. Cary, termed the purchase 'an attractive investment' for a portion of the company's funds"[5]. The shares purchased were canceled and returned to the status of authorized, but unissued, shares. The repurchase moved IBM's sales/working capital ratio nearer to the industry average.

Three other factors may have had an influence on IBM's decision to repurchase a portion of its stock. First may have been the absence of profitable, near-term, unexploited investment opportunities in IBM's line of business. IBM has not really diversified to the extent that some other firms had, and may have felt that it had already utilized all the potential in its primary fields, which it dominates. Second, there may have been rumors of a stock overhang, with many investors waiting for a small rise in price before liquidating; for the previous 18 months, institutional investors had been reducing their holdings in IBM. Finally, IBM had put into effect, on July 1, 1976, a new, five-year, Employees Stock Purchase Plan. Under the plan employees could buy IBM stock from the firm at 85 percent of the average market price on the date of purchase; 8.5 million shares

[3] "IBM Stockholders' Quarterly Report April 31, 1977" page 3.

[4] Figures from April 31, 1977 quarterly report and are subject to final adjustment.

[5] "IBM Stockholders' Quarterly Report April 31, 1977", page 3.

EXHIBIT 1

International Business Machines

Balance Sheets, December 31, 1975 and December 31, 1976*

(rounded millions of dollars)

		12/31/76		12/31/75
Cash		$ 209		$ 184
Marketable securities†				
U. S. treasuries	3,428		2,214	
Federal agency securities	494		762	
State and municipal securities	192		452	
Time deposits–non-U.S.	1,501		893	
Corporate bonds, notes, etc.	332		264	
Total marketable securities		5,948		4,584
Notes and accounts receivable		2,626		2,300
Inventories‡		770		741
Prepaid expenses		368		306
Total current assets		9,920		8,115
Other investments and sundry assets		462		374
Land, buildings, etc., less depreciation		3,091		2,848
Rental machines and parts, less depreciation		4,250		4,194
Total assets		$17,723		$15,530
U. S. federal and non-U.S. income taxes		$ 1,384		$ 1,085
Accounts payable and accruals		2,583		2,064
Loans payable		116		214
Total current liabilities		4,082		3,363
Deferred investment tax credit		63		45
Reserves for employees' indemnities and retirement plans		553		412
Long-term debt		275		295
Capital Stock, par value $5.00 per share. Shares authorized: 162,500,000. Issued: 1976–150,766,927 1975–149,844,582		4,032		3,853
Retained earnings		8,737		7,563
Less: treasury stock		(20)		0
Stockholders' equity		12,749		11,416
Total liabilities and stockholders' equity		$17,723		$15,530

*   Source: 1976 Annual Report
†   Valued at lower of cost or market.
‡   Valued at lower of average cost or market.

were authorized for this plan, but this amount was not fully reserved.

At December 31, 1976, 2,000,000 authorized and unissued shares were reserved for issuance under the Plan. The total number of authorized shares was not reserved because the company intends to purchase the shares in the market to the extent feasible.[6]

Questions

1. Contrast the effect on stockholders of the disbursal of IBM's "surplus" funds via (a) a "special" dividend or (b) stock repurchase. Discuss tax and other differences; assume a stockholders marginal tax rate of 45 percent on ordinary income, that a repurchase of 4 million shares was intended, and that administrative expenses were not significant.

2. Based on the response to the repurchase offer, was there a significant overhang in the market?

3. Assess IBM's capital structure in light of the Modigliani and Miller, and traditional, capital structure-valuation positions. Does it seem optimal from a total, firm-value view?

4. Compare IBM's capital structure as of December 31, 1975 with that of Memorex Corporation (Case 21), based on debt/equity relationships (comparisons can also be made on the basis of fixed-charge coverage and cash flows). If there is an optimal capital structure (minimum cost of capital) for the industry, with non zero bond debt, is either firm probably close to it? Does this say anything about the two firms' profitability in other areas?

---

[6] "IBM Annual Report 1976", page 23.

PART V

Short-and Intermediate-Term Financing

Case 26

WASHINGTON PAPER AND WOOD CORPORATION (C)

APPLYING FOR A LINE OF CREDIT

"Modifying the convenants of your line of credit is a serious business, Bob," Jack Dean had said. "I know you could probably get the money elsewhere on a long-term basis at lower interest rates. However, we are the primary bank for Washington Paper and Wood Corporation, and we would like to keep your business. When we made that new credit arrangement last year, both you and I thought that Washington Paper's needs were covered for sometime to come, but conditions certainly have changed. Your new sales and profits forecasts do show some extensive improvements. If they are anywhere near the mark, I would agree that the interest rate on the credit line is too high and the covenants too restrictive. I think we can work something out."

Robert Louis, treasurer of Washington Paper and Wood Corporation, was inclined to agree. (Detailed information on Washington Paper and Wood Corporation is contained in Appendix A of Case 5, Washington Paper and Wood (A). This information is material to the solution of this case.) Washington Paper had an offer of a long-term loan, from the Linear Life Insurance Company, to replace the current bank credit-line arrangement, which Washington Paper felt was too restrictive and carried too high an interest expense. However, there were other factors to be considered. Washington Paper had dealt with the Dynamic Bank and Trust for more than 20 years, and with Jack Dean, vice president of Commercial Lending, for at least 10 years. The bank served as Washington Paper's depository, transfer agent, and long- and short-term lender. Robert Louis felt that Washington Paper was better off keeping these relationships, if at all possible. Consequently, he had scheduled a meeting with Mr. Dean in the hope that something could be arranged.

"Bank lending isn't confined to the borrower's stating his needs, as he perceives them, and the banker saying yes or no," Mr. Dean had continued. "We like to get together with the customer, get to know his business, and make decisions on more of a mutual basis. We like to think of ourselves partly as a counseling service; a wall off of which the customer can 'bounce his ideas,' so to say; a partner, more than a creditor. But, Bob, we've discussed these concepts before; there is no need for me to rattle on. We would like to get some ideas of the effect of your new sales and profit projections and asset-management program on Washington Paper's financial position about three years down the road. Let's get together again next week and discuss it."

Robert Louis agreed to meet again with Jack Dean the next week. The new asset-management program, referred to by Dean, was an attempt by Washington Paper to reduce the levels of certain assets, which the firm felt were at abnormally high levels. Included in this program were inventories, cash, prepaid expenses, other current assets, and fixed assets. The company had also instituted a one-year (calendar year 1976) moratorium on capital spending, and had discontinued the payment of common dividends until the firm was in a stronger position.

In preparation for the first meeting with Mr. Dean, Louis had prepared a *pro forma* income statement and balance sheet for Washington Paper as of December 31, 1978, showing the expected effects of the new sales and profit forecasts and the asset-management plan (see Exhibits 1 and 2). He knew that additional preparation would be required for next week's meeting, in keeping with Mr. Dean's philosophy of the bank as a partner and counselor.

EXHIBIT 1

Washington Paper and Wood Corporation (C)

Pro Forma Statement of Income and Retained Earnings for Year Ending December 31, 1978

(rounded thousands of dollars)

Net sales	$210,434
Cost of goods sold	187,284
Gross margin on sales	23,150
Selling & administrative expenses	14,000
Interest expense [*]	3,500
Income before extraordinary items	5,650
Other income	0
Other expenses	650
Income before taxes	5,000
Taxes	2,500
Income after taxes	2,500
Common and preferred stock dividends	172
Additions to retained earnings	$ 2,328

[*]Expected effect of new financial arrangements has been taken into account.

EXHIBIT 2

Washington Paper and Wood Corporation (C)

Pro Forma Balance Sheet, dated December 31, 1978

(rounded thousands of dollars)

Cash	$ 1,500
Accounts receivable	17,536
Inventories	23,411
Prepaid expenses	6,500
Other current assets	4,750
Total current assets	53,697
Other assets	6,750
Property, plant, land & equipment	152,295
Less: depreciation	78,842
Net fixed assets	73,453
Total assets	$133,900
Current principal portion of	
12/31/75 long-term debt	$ 2,600
Due on bank credit line	4,503
Accounts payable–raw materials	11,705
Accruals	4,500
Preferred stock dividends payable	43
Total current liabilities	23,351
Due on 12/31/75 long-term debt	56,860
Preferred stock	3,440
Common stock	14,851
Retained earnings	35,398
Total owner's equity	53,689
Total liabilities & owners' equity	$133,900

Questions

1. Generate a sources and uses of funds statement for Washington Paper and Wood for the period of December 31, 1975 to December 31, 1978 (the December 31, 1975 balance sheet is provided in Exhibit 1 of Appendix A, Case 5; a statement of projected, after tax profits and losses is provided in Exhibit 1 of Case 6). What percents of total sources have been provided by the asset-management program? If industry statements studies show that assets (on the average) are distributed as follows, are Washington Paper's expectations reasonable? Make a chart showing comparable statistics for Washington Paper for December 31, 1975 and December 31, 1978.

Assets	Percent of Total Assets
Cash	4.0
Marketable securities	3.6
Receivables (net)	19.7
Inventories (net)	15.2
All other current	1.3
Total current	43.9
Net fixed assets	51.7
All other noncurrent	4.4
Total assets	100.0

2. Generate a summary source and uses of funds statement for the period. This statement will include funds from operations (net income plus depreciation), dividends, changes in net working capital, changes in fixed and other assets, and changes in long-term debt.

3. Compute the following ratios, shown with industry medians, for Washington Paper as of December 31, 1975 and December 31, 1978. What can we say about the firm's current position? Debt capacity? Inventory management? Working capital management?

Ratio	Industry Median
Current ratio	2.2
Quick ratio (current assets less inventories)	1.1
Net fixed assets/net worth	0.9
Total debt net worth	1.0
Sales/receivables	8.6
Cost of goods sold/inventory	6.9
Sales/net working capital	5.8

4. What should Robert Louis expect Jack Dean to say about re-negotiation of the firm's bank credit line, given the outlook presented by the aforementioned analysis?

Case 27

ARIZONA ANTENNAS

RESTRUCTURING CURRENT DEBT

A note from the desk of Bruce Senior, president, Arizona Antennas:

February 10, 1974

To: Richard Knight, treasurer

Dick:

We certainly are in serious trouble. These creditors are constantly trying to contact me. They're withholding shipments from us and slowing production. See what you can do. I give you a free hand; I'm a technical man, not a finance man. If necessary, I can get the family to contribute $100,000 in equity to keep us afloat, but we'd rather not. It will take about 60 days to raise the money. Work out the best deal you can.

Bruce

Dick Knight agreed that the firm was in difficult straits. When he had joined the firm, two years ago, things had been fine; the company's finances had seemed strong and sales were growing. Now the picture was not bright.

Arizona Antennas was organized in 1946 by the Senior family, and had been run by them, personally, until very recently. The three Senior brothers, all of whom were radio operators, upon discharge from the service, used their accumulated pay to start Arizona Antennas. The firm had prospered in the 50's and 60's, manufacturing antennas on a long-term contract basis for commercial radio-equipment manufacturers and the military. The firm also made a line of amateur radio ("ham") antennas, which was sold on a mail-order basis. Each product line accounts for about one-third of sales volume.

A recent series of unfortunate circumstances had plunged Arizona Antennas into severe cash difficulty. First, a major commercial customer went bankrupt, leaving Arizona with an inventory of useless specialty antennas and work in process. A large receivable was also on the books at the time. These current assets had been charged off against profits, 18 months ago, but the loss had made the firm considerably less liquid. Next, there had been a sudden shift in demand for amateur radio antennas, from bulky, low-frequency equipment (Arizona's specialty) to compact, very-high-frequency apparatus. This had temporarily reduced sales for this product line, and decreased inventory turnover. Sales had since returned to traditional levels, but liquidity had been adversely affected.

When his brother retired, Bruce Senior, the last of the Senior brothers still active in the firm, had hired Dick Knight from a large corporation to handle the firm's finances. Knight was familiar with accounting and finance, but had not previously dealt with corporate distress. He knew that the firm needed to restructure its current debt, but had doubts as to how this should be done. Examination of the firm's recently-completed financial statements and long-term bank agreements had pointed out several facts.

First, it was probably not possible for Arizona Antennas to borrow further from the banks, and the banks were not receptive to changes in the structure of debt. All assets had been pledged as security for the long-term debt already outstanding. The property, plant, and equipment shown were of a specialized manufacturing nature; the banks were aware that their liquidation value would not be large. The personal assets of the Senior family had also been pledged to support the bank debt; it was, thus, imperative that the firm not default. If three creditors were to petition the courts, the firm would be forced into bankruptcy, possibly causing the bank to exercise its security and guarantees; so, creditors had to be satisfied. Knight believed that the top few creditors—who had been continuous suppliers for years, had good profit margins, to whom Arizona Antennas represented a significant customer—would go along with a payout agreement on past-due amounts. Such an agreement would also include a commitment to pay current and future obligations, promptly. The smaller creditors were generally specialty or service suppliers, with lower margins. The smaller creditors were demanding immediate payment of their entire balances. Several threatening telephone calls from these creditors had been received by Knight and Senior; at least one small claimant was in the process of suing the firm.

The banks knew the firm's situation with trade creditors, and had suggested that Knight call an informal meeting of creditors and propose some solution to the current problem. They had suggested that any creditor's arrangement result in a current ratio of not less than 1.5 to 1. Their research had shown that this was the critical survival parameter for firms in Arizona's industry.

Knight seriously doubted that a public sale, or private placement of equity, would produce much cash, given the firm's current problems. He also felt that the levels of cash, accounts receivable, accruals, and some inventories were in the range necessary for current and projected sales levels. He believed that $250,000 was an appropriate level for payables. This was approximately the level of Arizona's payables due for current purchases (see Exhibit 3). He had evaluated Arizona's sales contracts, and discussed profit levels at length with Arizona's production and sales managers. Depending upon certain external market conditions, he had projected the firm's profits before taxes for the next five years:

Probability	Profit per year before taxes
.2	$40,000
.6	60,000
.2	80,000

Arizona expected to make no purchases of capital assets during this time. No principal payments on long-term debts were due during this period.

EXHIBIT 1

Financial Statement of Arizona Antennas
as of December 31, 1973

Audited by a Major Public Accounting Firm

Current assets			
Cash		$ 109,080	
Accounts receivable		362,125	
Inventories			
Finished goods for contract sales	120,000		
Finished goods for amateur radio sales	200,000		
Raw materials and goods in process	242,055		
Total inventories		562,055	
Total current assets			1,033,260
Fixed assets			
Property, plant, and equipment, less yearly, straight-line depreciation of $50,000 per year		2,000,000	
Total fixed assets			2,000,000
Total assets			$3,033,260

EXHIBIT I (Cont'd)

Current liabilities

Accounts payable	600,000	
Current portion of long-term debt	250,000	
Accruals	50,000	
Total current liabilities		900,000

Long-term debt

Due banks (secured by all assets)	1,000,000	
Total long-term debt		1,000,000

Owners' equity

Net worth	1,133,260	
Total owners' equity		1,133,260
Total liabilities and owners' equity		$3,033,260

EXHIBIT 2

Income Statement of Arizona Antennas
for year ending December 31, 1973

Audited by a Major Public Accounting Firm

Sales	$2,896,000
Cost of goods sold	2,027,000
Gross margin on sales	869,000
Selling and administrative expenses*	810,000
Operating profit before taxes	$ 59,000

*Includes interest expense.

EXHIBIT 3

Listing of Accounts Payable for Arizona Antennas
as of February 10, 1974

Creditor	Total Owing	Due for Current Purchases	Due for Past Purchases
Sally's Steel Pipe	$226,232	$132,685	$ 93,547
Clamp Manufacturing Corporation	156,848	57,631	99,217
Aluminum Angle Associates	112,727	26,849	85,878
Moxie Molders Incorporated	60,281	19,632	40,649
Stan's Welding Supply	5,200	0	5,200
Sparts, Inc.	6,700	100	6,600
Dan's Office Supply	6,500	0	6,500
All other small suppliers	25,512	6,300	19,212
Totals	$600,000	$243,197	$356,803

Questions

1. List possible, near-term sources of funds for Arizona's payout of creditors, based on the financial statement and the case. Assume that the firm needs 45 days' sales of amateur radio, finished-goods inventories. Prepare a chart of fund flows available in future periods, with associated probabilities, assuming that Arizona's recent, extraordinary losses will shield income from taxes for the next five years. State any other assumptions.

2. Should the claims of the smaller creditors be liquidated, immediately, or should Knight attempt to include them in a payout schedule?

3. Debtor proposals sometimes consist of an initial, percent liquidation of past-due debt, with the remainder of the balances due creditors being paid out in equal-percent increments, over a period of years, at no interest. In your opinion, what sort of schedule should Knight offer creditors, initially, given that the primary goal is Arizona's survival? Assume that any agreement includes the standard "accelerator clause", so that the debtor is considered in default (and the entire balance becomes due), if any scheduled payment is missed. Do you think creditors will accept this offer?

4. An alternate type of payout schedule includes a smaller, initial payout, with rising payments over the schedule. Discuss the advantages and disadvantages of this to the firm, and to the creditors.

5. As a privately held firm, Arizona Antennas does not publish financial statements, and none of the creditors have obtained these from the firm. What figures should Knight present to the creditors' meeting?

6. If you were a creditor, could the payout acceptance decision be treated as a capital budgeting problem? Could the plan be treated in this manner from Mr. Knight's standpoint? What essential pieces of information appear to be missing?

Case 28

INNOVATIONS FOR RECREATION, INC.

FINANCING THROUGH FACTORING

Innovations for Recreation, Inc. of El Paso, Texas, was started in 1954 by Paul Louis. Originally incorporated as Louis Sporting Goods, the firm, for many years, concentrated its manufacturing and marketing efforts on producing and selling inexpensive, standard sporting goods in the Southwest. In order to participate in a market-place dominated by better-known, name-brand goods, the firm had to sell its products to retailers and wholesalers at comparatively-lower prices. Margins were low (4 percent of sales before tax), and the company seemed to be going nowhere. This, however, did not particularly disturb the Louis family. Most of the family worked for the firm, and salaries were adequate to meet their needs. Paul Louis distributed small amounts of stock, as his children matured, but no cash dividends were paid. The firm had been very conservative from a business and financial standpoint.

Early 1972 brought many changes to the old Louis Sporting Goods firm. Paul Louis, who by this time had reached his late 50's, decided that equity had built to the point where the firm could begin taking some risks, without jeopardizing the family's jobs. He hired two, bright, young engineers from Texas Tech, and set up a small laboratory for them in a corner of the main plant. Some minor expenses were incurred, and 1972's profit was not as high as usual.

In 1973, the two engineers did not contribute much to the firm, except expenses. Their attempts at designing new outdoor games, which could be produced on the Louis Sporting Goods' manufacturing equipment, were not successful. Paul Louis spent a lot of time with them during this period. The firm's name was changed to Innovations for Recreation, Inc. Near the end of the year, a number of new products were patented and test-marketed.

The next year, 1974, produced huge sales and profits increases. The firm's financial statements are shown as Exhibits 1 and 2, pages 154–155. The new products had been successful, and the firm's dollar sales increased rapidly. Additional shifts and overtime became common. Projected sales figures are shown in Exhibit 3. Paul Louis began thinking about paying dividends to disburse the extra profits.

He knew that these profits were not permanent—the new products were strictly "fad" items. In a year, they would be supplanted in the volatile market place.

Other problems had arisen, however. Very soon after the first of the year, two of Paul's sons came into the office. Paul, Junior, who served the firm as treasurer, spoke first.

"Dad, things are going great from a profits standpoint. The margins on those new products aren't even as high as our old ones, but they certainly do generate sales volume. The trouble is, the sales volume generates more liabilities than our equity base can handle. Also, to generate these sales, we've had to allow an extra 30 days for our customers to pay, and our receivables have slowed; we're going to have to hire another credit man. Our current position has deteriorated. Our payments to suppliers have slowed and our credit rating has fallen. We need some way to generate cash that will not tie us up with long-term debt. These extra sales are a temporary thing. I doubt that the banks would lend us anything on a long-term basis; we don't have the fixed assets to support it, and our debt-to-worth ratio is too high, anyway. The family doesn't have the money to make an equity contribution, and we don't want to dilute our position by letting in an outsider."

"That's right, Dad," said Steve Louis, who served the firm as purchasing agent. "Besides, one of the reasons our margins are low is due to our cash problems. Our raw materials are 50 percent of cost of goods sold; direct labor is the remainder. Our suppliers offer a 2 percent discount for 30-day payments, and we've been losing those. Because of our slow payments, I've lost a good deal of leverage with these people. We haven't been able to get contracts for purchases the way we used to; I've had to buy on a spot basis. We're paying 3 percent more for raw materials, before cash discounts, than contract customers. If we could clear up our past-due balances with suppliers, I could negotiate contracts, starting with February purchases."

Paul Junior spoke again, "I've contacted three sources of financing to try to arrange what we need. I've summarized their proposals and the effects each would have on other costs and revenues (the three plans are shown in Exhibit 4). I'd like you to take a look and see what we should do. There are some other facts you should know. We expect our margins to remain at last year's levels, not including the factors Steve mentioned. Raw materials and direct labor should be the same percent of C.G.S. Our selling, administrative, and overhead expenses, and our research and development expenses will be the same in dollars, excluding any changes due to the new credit man or due to the financing plans. These expenses, like direct labor, are paid in the month incurred. I think our minimum safe cash balance is the present level. Our bad debts are generally realized in the same month the sale is made, at the reserve rate. Our customers are paying in about 60 days. Our level of accruals will stay the same throughout the year. The interest and principal on our long-term debt is due in December. See what you can do—I'm at a loss."

EXHIBIT 1

Innovations for Recreation, Inc.

Balance Sheet as of December 31, 1974

(audited; rounded thousands of dollars)

Cash	$ 225
Accounts receivable (net of reserve for bad debt)	3,128
Inventories	1,023
Other current assets	109
Total current assets	4,485
Fixed assets less depreciation	903
Total assets	$5,388
Accounts payable	
From 12/72 on 2% 30 terms	$ 731
From prior months	1,170
Current portion of long-term debt	90
Accruals	201
Accrued taxes	149
Total current liabilities	2,341
Long-term debt	869
Stock	500
Retained earnings	1,678
Total owners' equity	2,178
Total liabilities and owners' equity	$5,388

EXHIBIT 2

Innovations for Recreation, Inc.

Profit and Loss Statement for the Fiscal Year Ending December 31, 1974

(audited; rounded thousands of dollars)

Gross sales	$17,986
Less: reserve for bad debt	90
Net sales	17,896
Cost of goods sold	15,212
Gross margin on sales	2,684
Selling, administrative, and overhead expenses	1,866
Research and development expenses	80
Interest expense	70
Profit before taxes	668
Taxes (50% of above line)	334
Profit after tax	$ 334

EXHIBIT 3

Innovations for Recreation, Inc.

Sales Projections: November, 1974 to December, 1975

(rounded thousands of dollars)

Month	Gross Sales	Net Sales
11/74 (actual figure)	$1,414	$1,407
12/74 (actual figure)	1,730	1,721
1/75	1,809	1,800
2/75	1,910	1,900
3/75	2,010	2,000
4/75	2,111	2,100
5/75	2,010	2,000
6/75	1,910	1,900
7/75	1,809	1,800
8/75	1,608	1,600
9/75	1,508	1,500
10/75	1,357	1,350
11/75	1,206	1,200
12/75	704*	700*

* This is the normal sales level, without new items.

EXHIBIT 4

Innovations for Recreation, Inc.

Summaries of Three Financing Plans

Plan A—Unsecured Line of Credit with a Bank

Under this plan, the company would have to pay a $20,000 commitment fee, payable immediately, to set up the line of credit. The company could then draw on the line of credit, at will, for the amounts needed. The interest rate on this line would be 1 percent per month, payable on the balance outstanding in the previous month, at the beginning of the next month. The current prime rate is 7 percent, and the firm's existing, long-term debt is financed at 8 percent at the bank making this proposal.

Plan B—Specific Accounts-Receivable Financing through a Major Commercial-lending Firm

Under this plan, the company would pledge specific accounts receivable to the lender, but would control the credit and collection functions. The company would be able to borrow up to 90 percent of the amount of gross sales pledged. Bad debts would be deducted from the amount pledged. The company would get the 10 percent reserve back when the invoices are paid. This plan would involve considerable paperwork for both the commercial lender and the company. Everyday, the company would have to prepare a schedule of the gross sales recorded that it wanted to assign, a schedule of collections made against assigned accounts (the company would apply the checks and endorse them over to the finance company), and a daily report showing the availability of funds and the amount the company wanted to draw. These statements and records would have to be taken downtown, to the office of the lender, and they would have to be presented with copies of invoices and shipping documents. The lender would then draw a check; this check would have to be taken to the company's bank and deposited. The company would have to hire a clerk at $8,000 per year to do this paperwork and an additional credit man. The credit man's salary would be $12,000 per year, under the standard employment contract. The company would retain their accounts-receivable and cash-application departments, which now cost $12,000 to run. The company would pay a flat rate of 1/40 percent per day on the monthly balance outstanding, payable at the beginning of the next month.

Plan C—Factoring of Accounts Receivable

Under this plan, the company would pay two fees. In return for doing all of the credit and collections work, applying the cash, assuming all bad-debt losses, and handling all the paperwork, the factor will charge 1.25 percent of gross sales. This will be deducted from the sales the company gives the factor. The company would have to provide the same documentation as in Plan B. The company would transfer the present credit man to the opening in the cost-accounting department, and save $16,000 by not having to hire another man. The company could either allow the factor to pay the company the collections from accounts receivable, on the due date of the invoices, or it could draw against the amount of receivables outstanding; the company would then pay interest from the day it drew against the receivables-outstanding amount until the invoice due date, at 8 percent per year. However, it would have to sign a contract, for service on a yearly basis, for all of its receivables; it could not assign only specific invoices. Since November, 1974 receipts have already been collected, the factoring contract would cover sales from December, 1974 to November, 1975. Interest on the amount drawn is payable on the first of the month, for the previous month's balance.

Questions

1. Derive a monthly cash forecast for the firm for 1975. Ignore tax payments and the effect of taxes. Assume no changes in assets and liabilities, except for those specified in the case. Assume that the firm adopts one of the three financing plans, pays off the past-due accounts payable, immediately, and adheres to suppliers' terms, thereafter. A payment of $160,000 is due on long-term debt on December, 1975; this includes the principal, plus interest to be accrued during 1975. Assume that all transactions take place on the first of the month, and that all months have 30 days. Assume that the additional credit man will be hired. Exclude from your original forecast, interest charges and other changes in cash disbursements and receipts associated with each financing plan. Assume that January's receipts are already collected, but that current payables can still be discounted.

2. Modify your answer to Question 1 to include interest charges and other changes in cash transactions associated with each financing plan. Show the amount owed to the lender at the beginning of each month.

3. Create a profit and loss statement for 1975 for each of the three financing plans, showing the increase or decrease in yearly, before-tax profit associated with the adoption of each plan. Which plan is superior by this method of decision?

4. The method of decision used in Question 3 ignores the time value of money by summing, not discounting, the monthly cash flows. When cash flows are similar over time among projects, and the time period under consideration is short, this method is often used by corporations. Is it also possible to use net present value to compare the financing plans? If the appropriate rate of discount is 1 percent per month, what is the net present value of financing Plan A for 1975? Why (aside from the discount factor) is this answer different from the profit and loss figure for Plan A?

Case 29

DETROIT SCIENTIFIC, INC.

LEASE VERSUS BORROW AND BUY

In June 1977, the automotive division of Detroit Scientific, Inc. was faced with the problem of upgrading its parts-delivery system. An economic analysis indicated that strategic utilization of an efficient teletype system would serve to improve customer service levels, significantly. A related question was whether the equipment should be leased or purchased. Ms. Sandra Lewis, a financial and cost analyst with the automotive division, was assigned the task of preparing a lease or purchase analysis for review by the division manager. While the division was planning to outfit a substantial number of locations with the teletype equipment, Ms. Lewis felt that results from the analysis of a single teletype installation could be readily extrapolated to multiple installations.

Detroit Scientific, Inc. is located in Detroit and is a supplier to the automotive manufacturers in Detroit. The automotive division is a manufacturer of automobile cooling-system thermostats, air valves, gaskets, switches, electrical connectors, and radiators. In recent years, the division has been making strong gains in selling these products in the replacement market, also.

Each teletype installation would require one teletype unit, one acoustic coupler, one software system, and one peripheral hardware system. The teletype may be purchased for $1,090. It has an expected useful life of 3 years, with an expected salvage value of $130. It may be rented for $696 per year for three years. If the automotive division decides to purchase the teletype, it would also purchase a maintenance contract for $180 per year. The rental plan includes equipment maintenance. The acoustic coupler may be purchased for $365, or leased for $156 per year for three years. If it is purchased, it would have an expected salvage value of $65 after three years. The coupler would come with an unconditional, one-year guarantee. The second-year's maintenance expense would be $25, and would be $30 for the third year. The software and hardware systems can be purchased for $1,280 and $1,800, respectively. However, due to rapid changes in technology, it was felt that, regardless of the decision to lease or purchase, the software

159

and hardware systems would be leased. That is, the lease or pur-chase analysis is applicable only to the teletype and the coupler. The cost figures are summarized in Exhibit 1.

After completing her analysis, Ms. Lewis decided to emphasize the following points in her written report to the division manager.

(a) Salvage values are based on estimates of useful lives, experience with similar lines of equipment, elsewhere, and a recent report on technological innovations in the teletype market. Because of the relatively rapid rate of change in teletype technology, there is a significant chance that the teletype salvage value will be lower than $130. Secondly, the acoustical-coupler market is being greatly influenced by recent electronic advances. It is entirely feasible that the couplers will be technologically obsolete within four years.

(b) Detroit Scientific enjoys an excellent relationship with the Motor City Bank. The bank would be willing to provide an intermediate term loan to finance the purchase of the equipment. The bank's yield on the loan would be 8.33 percent. The loan would be repaid in three equal in-stallments of principal and interest, which would be due annually. The loan-repayment schedule for a teletype and coupler is shown in Exhibit 2.

(c) With a 48-percent tax rate, Detroit Scientific's aftertax, cost of debt is 4 percent. Its cost of equity is 13 percent, and its marginal cost of capital is 11 percent. Ms. Lewis felt that, given the magnitude and volatility of cash flows, either of the above rates could be used for dis-counting the cash flows. In any case, she wanted to be sure that her report included sufficient justification for the discount rate or rates used.

(d) For purposes of analysis, the equipment would be depreciated over three years by using the straight-line method.

(e) Any investment tax credit available would be passed on by the lessor to Detroit Scientific.

EXHIBIT 1

Detroit Scientific, Inc.

Cost Data for Teletype Installation

Item	Price	Annual Maintenance	Salvage	Annual Lease
Teletype	$1,090	$180	$130	$ 696
Coupler	365	$25 and $30*	65	156
Software	1,280	–	–	660
Hardware	1,800	30	–	1,080

* Second and third years, respectively.

EXHIBIT 2

Detroit Scientific, Inc.

Loan Repayment Schedule

Year 1	Beginning Balance 2	Payment 3	Interest 4	Principal Payment 5=3–4	Remaining Balance 2–5
1	$1,455.00	$567.95	$121.20	$446.75	$1,008.25
2	1,008.25	567.95	83.99	483.96	524.29
3	524.29	567.96	43.67	524.29	0.00

Questions

1. Which discount rate (or rates) is (are) most appropriate for discounting the net cash flows? Why?

2. Evaluate, on a present net value basis, the cost of leasing versus the cost of borrowing the funds to purchase.

3. What could you do to examine how sensitive your decision is to changes in the discount rate used? What conclusions can you draw, after performing the analysis by using a discount rate different than the one you used originally?

4. What would you recommend that Detroit Scientific do?

Case 30

ATLANTIC OIL COMPANY

LEASE VERSUS BORROW AND BUY

In December, 1976, Mr. John Schafer, financial vice president of the Atlantic Oil Company, was considering the relative merits of various capital-investment proposals. One of these had been submitted by the data processing division, which had made a recommendation for upgrading the existing computer hardware facilities. After evaluating the proposal, there was no doubt in Mr. Schafer's mind that, not only was a better computer system needed, but that the proposed replacement was also very economically feasible—the proposal had a high internal rate of return. The data processing division had recommended that the existing IBM computer be replaced with an IBM 370/168, Model 3 with four megabytes CPU memory. In addition, one IBM 2860 Selector Channel, two IBM 2880 Block Multiplexors, and one IBM 2870 Multiplexor Channel were needed. No additional changes in the existing I/O devices, peripheral equipment and software configurations were required.

Upon approving the project, Mr. Schafer requested additional information on the various leasing arrangements that were available through either IBM, or a third party. By the end of the week, the data processing division had supplied Mr. Schafer with the information he needed. The first alternative was to purchase the equipment from IBM. The second alternative was to lease the equipment from IBM, and the third alternative was to lease the equipment from the General Computer Leasing Company (GCLC).

If Atlantic decided to purchase the equipment from IBM, the total purchase price would be $4,827,970. Specifics are provided in Exhibit 1, page 164. IBM would provide the maintenance, free of charge, for the first year. Beyond the first year, the annual maintenance charges would be $84,000. Atlantic would be able to finance the purchase of the equipment through a bank loan, at an interest rate of 8.3 percent per annum. The loan would be amortized over five years. The data processing division had estimated that the useful life of the equipment was five years. Neither IBM nor the data processing division personnel could provide an exact figure for the salvage value of the equipment. They indicated, however, that based upon factors such as the economic and technological environments, the actual salvage value after five years could vary between 5 percent and 20 percent of the original purchase price, with an expected salvage value of 10 percent of the original price. For analytical purposes, Mr. Schafer decided to use straight-line depreciation.

The second alternative, direct leasing from IBM, carried a different set of implications. The total, annual leasing charge would be $1,351,248. Specifics are shown in Exhibit 1. This rental charge includes all maintenance costs. Furthermore, the lease arrangement entitled Atlantic to 176 hours of computer time use per month, with additional usage, above 176 hours per month, to be billed according to the following formula:

$$\frac{\text{Additional monthly}}{\text{usage charges}} = \frac{\text{Monthly base}}{\text{lease payment}} \times \frac{1}{176} \times \frac{\text{additional computer}}{\text{hours used in month}} \times .10$$

The data processing division had estimated that the new equipment would be used 24 hours a day, seven days a week. Allowing for downtime, it was estimated that average, monthly usage would be close to 700 hours.

Under the third alternative, leasing the equipment from the General Computer Leasing Company (GCLC), the annual leasing charges would be $945,628 per year. The GCLC lease did not provide for maintenance, and Atlantic would have to buy a five-year maintenance contract from the Service Bureau Corporation at a cost of $7,000 per month for five years. Based upon an average, monthly usage of 700 hours, the GCLC lease would require additional payments of $218,628 annually.

Existing tax regulations permitted Atlantic to claim an investment tax credit, which varied according to the depreciable life of the assets. According to current regulations, the purchasor is entitled to an investment tax credit totaling 10 percent of the asset purchase value. This credit is applicable during the first year of the asset's life, and carries with it the restriction that the asset be held for at least five years. Atlantic Oil Company's balance sheet is provided in Exhibit 2. Mr. Schafer had estimated that Atlantic's aftertax marginal cost of capital was 12 percent, and its marginal tax rate was 52 percent.

EXHIBIT 1

Atlantic Oil Company

Purchase and Lease Data

Item	Purchase Costs	IBM Lease; annual charges	GCLC Lease; annual charges
IBM 370/168 Model 3	$4,168,200	$1,152,768	$807,000
IBM 2860 Selector Channel	159,600	41,040	28,728
IBM 2880 Block Multiplexors (2)	371,480	127,440	89,208
IBM 2870 Multiplexors Channel	128,690	30,999	21,000
Total	$4,827,970	$1,351,248	$945,936

EXHIBIT 2

Atlantic Oil Company

Balance Sheet, September 30, 1976

(rounded thousands of dollars)

Assets		Liabilities and Equity	
Cash	$ 4,736	Notes payable	$ 2,860
Marketable securities	8,256	Other short-term debt	1,355
Accounts receivable	30,960	Accounts payable	41,965
Inventories	26,590	Accruals	20,610
Total current assets	70,542	Total current liabilities	66,790
Investments in subsidiaries	5,400	Long-term debt	24,950
Net properties	120,954	Proceeds from future production	2,981
Deferred charges	2,600	Deferred income taxes	6,290
Other assets	1,161	Total liabilities	101,011
Total assets	$200,657	Common stock	39,060
		Retained earnings	60,586
		Total liabilities and equity	$200,657

Questions

1. What is (are) the most appropriate discount rate(s) to use in this analysis? Why?

2. Which financing alternative should Atlantic Oil Company utilize

in acquiring the use of the computer system?   Show your calculations to justify your answer.

3. If you were to use an accelerated depreciation procedure, such as sum-of-the-years digits or double-declining balance, what impact would this have on your results?   A descriptive answer will suffice.

4. What impact does purchasing the equipment have on the leverage ratio (total debt/total assets) for Atlantic?   How about leasing? If Atlantic were to lease, say $40 million of tank cars, what would a financial analyst need to do in order to identify Atlantic's financial risk more precisely?

PART VI

Long-Term
Financing

Case 31

BELL MATERIALS CORPORATION

BOND REFUNDING

On January 4, 1977, Mr. William Jordan, vice president of finance for the Bell Materials Corporation, met with Mr. Allan Solomon, representative of Farmer, Hutton and Barron, Inc., an investment banking firm. Also attending the meeting was Mr. Mansoor Moosa, an economist for Bell Materials. The purpose of the meeting was twofold: first, to finalize the details of Bell's offering of $20 million in new bonds; second, to determine if it would be economically feasible to refund Bell's already-outstanding bonds, which had a face value of $30 million.

The Bell Materials Corporation is a manufacturer of construction materials, chemicals and metals. Its construction materials division will account for 50 percent of the firm's 1976 estimated total sales of $332 million, and 70 percent of its total net income of $55 million. The division produces crushed stone, blast furnace slag, lightweight shale and ready-mixed concrete. Division sales, by end users, are as follows:

Road construction	50 percent
Commercial buildings	20 percent
Residential buildings	20 percent
Dams, sewers, miscellaneous	10 percent

The chemical division, accounting for 20 percent of both total 1976 estimated sales and net income, produces basic chemicals, such as ethylene dichloride, anhydrous hydrogen chloride, ammonia, beaded caustic soda, muriatic acid and chloromethanes. Agricultural chemicals account for 50 percent of end use, while sales for the production of other chemicals account for the remaining 50 percent. During 1977, the division planned to start the manufacture of chloroform and other chlorinated hydrocarbons.

The metals division is expected to generate 30 percent of the total sales and 10 percent of the net income for 1976. The division is actively involved in the recycling of scrap aluminum. The division feels that its recycling activities are an important factor in energy conservation, since the energy requirements for producing secondary aluminum are only a fraction of those required for producing primary aluminum. It also recycles tin, and utilizes its detinned steel to produce precipitation steel for use in the copper industry. The profit picture of the division is somewhat murky, due to the dynamics of the scrap metals marketplace.

As Mr. Jordan started expressing his thoughts on refunding the existing bonds, he could detect a certain amount of apprehension in Mr. Solomon. The bonds in question had been issued in January, 1972. The total dollar amount of the issue was $30 million. Mr. Jordan had wanted to issue them in 1970, but upon Mr. Moosa's advice, had postponed issuing them until a more appropriate time. By late 1971, interest rates had declined from the highs of 1970, and Mr. Moosa recommended that Bell go ahead with issuing the bonds in late 1971 or early 1972. Mr. Jordan, at that time, had felt that interest rates might decline another 200 basis points, but had been convinced by Mr. Moosa's contention that the days of a 4.5-percent yield on AAA's were gone for good. When the bonds were issued in January, 1972, they carried a rating of AA, and a coupon rate of 8.6 percent. Mr. Jordan had insisted that the bonds carry a call privilege. The 8.6-percent coupon rate partially represents a premium for the call privilege.

The bonds already outstanding were 8.6 percent, 30-year bonds, with a call price of 110 percent of face value the first year, with the call premium subsequently declining by 1 percentage point every year. That is, in early 1977, they would be callable at 105 percent of face value. Bell had received net proceeds equal to the face value, and had incurred flotation expenses equalling $480,000.

In Mr. Jordan's opinion, it would be ideal to replace the "high-cost" bonds with new ones, which would bear a coupon rate of 7.84 percent. Mr. Jordan stated, "Each basis point is worth 75 bills over the 25-year haul, and with over 70 basis points savings in interest, Bell is going to come out more than 5 million bucks ahead of the ball game. We can't afford to ignore these numbers." Mr. Solomon responded, "I understand your feelings very well, Bill. It is highly possible that, in the *short* term, Bell may be ahead of the ball game. However, in these days of tight money supply and jitterish investors, it would be nice to maintain good working relations with investors. Who knows when you may have to go and sell a new common-stock issue, or perhaps raise funds to finance an acquisition. These investors may not forget that you replaced their 8.6 percent bonds with 7.84 percent bonds. I don't think they would be very happy about it."

Despite his stated reservations about refunding the bond issue, Mr. Solomon provided Mr. Jordan with the necessary details. For the total $50 million issue, the flotation costs for the new 25-year, 7.84 percent bonds would be $900,000. The bonds would be sold to net Bell Materials the face value. Finally, because of "friction" in the market, the new bonds would be issued, first, and then the old ones would be called. Therefore, Bell would incur one month's interest, simultaneously, on both the new and the old bonds.

Mr. Jordan was very interested in knowing how Mr. Moosa felt about the trend in interest rates. Mr. Moosa stated, "As you know, the interest rates have declined considerably in the last few months. Whether they decline any further is dependent upon president-elect Carter's economic policies, whose specifics are largely unknown at the present time. My own feeling is that some sort of tax rebates are in the works. Additional stimulation to the economy to reduce unemployment could increase capital expenditures and the demand for money. I would say that interest rates have or are about to bottom out."

With this information, Mr. Jordan had to decide whether the refund decision was economically feasible, and if so, whether Bell should go ahead with refunding the old bonds. Bell Materials' marginal cost of capital is 10 percent, and its marginal tax rate is 49 percent.

Questions

1. Are Mr. Solomon's reservations justified? That is, if the refund is economically viable, should Bell Materials proceed with the refund? Explain.

2. In the refund analysis, what discount rate should be used? Why?

3. Calculate the net present value of the decision to refund. What would you recommend to Mr. Jordan?

Case 32

RESTON ENGINEERING CORPORATION *

DEEP-DISCOUNT BOND FINANCING

In April, 1977, the finance committee of the Reston Engineering Corporation was investigating various alternatives for raising approximately $20 million. Mr. Richard Schroeder, in the treasurer's office, was assigned the task of evaluating the various alternatives and contracting underwriters for preliminary discussions related to issuance of the appropriate financing instruments.

The Reston Engineering Corporation, based in Boston, is a major producer of electronic equipment and testing devices. Started in the mid-forties as a manufacturer of switch and signal testors, Reston was constantly on the lookout for new marketing opportunities, where its technological competence could be effectively utilized. The senior management at Reston had worked closely with each other for several years. They shared the goal of building "value" into the company's products. The net result of the interaction of the company's technical competence and managerial philosophy had been high-quality products, which were always well received by the market. Mr. Frank Reston, president of Reston Engineering, feels that the company's high-quality products makes it far less vulnerable to competitive and economic pressures.

As Mr. Schroeder started to look at the alternatives available, he was struck at once by the financial strength of Reston's balance sheet—the company virtually had no long-term debt (see Exhibit 1). Talks with underwriters confirmed his intuitive feelings that Reston should issue long-term bonds to raise the $20 million. A number of underwriters expressed strong interest in bringing out the bond issue. The underwriting firm of Goodman, Solomon informed Mr. Schroeder that it would underwrite the bonds to raise $20 million for an underwriting fee of $400,000. These bonds would be sold as 25-year bonds at face value, and would carry a coupon note of 8.5 percent.

Mr. Schroeder had recently read an article that advocated a closer look at "deep-discount bonds."** Typical bond issues are priced

* This case was written in collaboration with Jonathan M. Westin, Graduate School of Business, University of Pittsburgh.

**William K. Harper, P.D. Berger and E.M. Foster, "How About Original Issue, Deep-Discount Bonds?" *Harvard Business Review,* September—October 1975, pp. 8, 12, 16.

so that coupon rate, current yield and yield to maturity are almost identical. A deep-discount bond is one which, at issuance time, carries a coupon rate considerably below current yield and yield to maturity. Because the coupon rate is considerably below the market expectations of current yield and yield to maturity, the bonds are sold at a "deep-discount" from the face value. Deep-discount bonds do not require large cash outlays each year. Secondly, the discount can be amortized and written off against income each year. Finally, deep-discount bonds have a tendency to fluctuate widely, and as a result, provide the issuer the opportunity to retire a portion of them by purchases in the open market. After considering all the pros and cons of deep-discount bonds, Mr. Schroeder contacted Goodman, Solomon, and asked particulars about issuing deep-discount bonds. After a couple of days, the Goodman, Solomon representative contacted Mr. Schroeder, and informed him that $94 million of 25-year, 2-percent, noncallable, original-issue, deep-discount bonds could be issued to provide Reston with $20 million. Flotation costs would be $500,000, which Reston would amortize over the life of the bonds. The net proceeds of the issue to Reston would be $19.5 million.

At the next meeting of the finance committee, Mr. Schroeder presented the details of the two, bond-financing alternatives. Mr. Reston said at once, "$200, now, for $940 of Reston's money, later on, is outrageous. If my arithmetic is correct, that's 9.4 percent (2 percent times $94 million over $20 million) for current yield. In addition, when we factor in the bond amortization, we are paying an interest rate substantially in excess of 8.5 percent. Why should we even consider the deep-discount bonds, when straight-debt financing is so much cheaper?" Mr. Reston, as well as a couple of the other finance committee members, felt that deep-discount bond financing carried excessive costs. On the other hand, Mr. Schroeder and the controller felt that the two factors of importance in analyzing deep-discount bonds were (1) the yield to maturity and (2) the deferment of certain cash outflows. The net result of the discussions by the finance committee was to postpone the financing decision for one week. During this time, Mr. Schroeder was to identify another alternative that would constitute a semi-deep-discount bond. In addition, he was to generate the appropriate cash-flow figures for consideration by the finance commmittee.

Mr. Schroeder duly transmitted to Goodman, Solomon, the gist of the discussions that transpired in the finance committee meeting. Shortly thereafter, the Goodman, Solomon representative contacted

Mr. Schroeder, and presented an alternative bond package. This alternative bond package called for issuing $39 million of 25-year, 4.5 percent noncallable bonds at 51.282 percent of par value. Reston would receive $20 million, before underwriting costs of $500,000.

Mr. Schroeder felt that he had sufficient information now to prepare the analysis requested by the finance committee. Mr. Schroeder knew that the firm's marginal tax rate was 48 percent. The firm had been consistently profitable over the past few years. Mr. Schroeder felt that, while Reston's chances of continuing its profitable operations were good, there was a small possibility of incurring losses on rare occasions in the future. Mr. Schroeder identified Reston's aftertax investment opportunity at 12 percent.

EXHIBIT 1

Reston Engineering Corporation

Balance Sheet, January 31, 1977

(in millions of dollars)

Current assets		Current liabilities	
Cash	$ 4.5	Accounts payable	$ 13.0
Accounts receivable less allowances	10.0	Contract payments received	
Marketable securities	5.5	in advance	2.0
Inventories	30.0	Income taxes payable	3.0
Prepaid expenses	2.0	Dividends payable	1.0
Total current assets	52.0	Total current liabilities	19.0
Plant property, and equipment			
Machinery and other equipment	58.0	Long-term debt	–0–
Buildings and improvements	98.0		
	156.0	Owner's equity	
Less accumulated depreciation	108.0		
Total plant property and equipment	48.0	Common stock–$100 par value	.8
Other assets			
Patents, drawings, and manufacturing rights at cost less accumulated amortization of $60,000	1.0	Additional contributed capital	1.2
Notes receivable from customer– non current portion	3.0	Retained earnings	83.0
		Total owner's equity	85.0
Total other assets	4.0	Total liabilities	
Total assets	$104.0	and equity	$104.0

Questions

1. On a descriptive basis, and from the firm's as well as the investor's viewpoint, evaluate the potential advantages and disadvantages of using deep-discount bonds for financing.

2. What is the proper accounting entry for showing bonds sold at a discount from par value on the firm's blance sheet. What effect would the three financing alternatives have on Reston's total-debt-to-total-assets ratio?

3. The following expression provides a good approximation for determining the effective after-tax cost of debt financing, when debt is issued above or below par value:

$$k_d = \frac{(1-t)(1+\frac{P-S}{n})}{\frac{P+S}{2}}$$

where

k_d	=	Aftertax cost of debt
t	=	Tax rate
I	=	Annual interest per bond
P	=	Par value of a bond
S	=	Selling price of a bond
n	=	Life of bonds

Use the above expression to calculate the approximate, effective aftertax cost of each of the financing alternatives. Which alternative is the best one? Assume that interest is paid annually. Ignore flotation costs, for the present. (Hint: selling price of the 2 percent bond would be $(20/94) \times 1000 = \$212.77$.)

4. Taking into consideration the timing and magnitude of the initial receipt, annual interest payments, annual amortization of flotation costs and bond discounts, and redemption of bonds after 25 years, calculate the yield to maturity for each alternative.

5. What should the Reston Engineering Corporation do?

Case 33

JOHNSON STEEL COMPANY

STOCKS VERSUS BONDS

In Spring, 1977 Mr. Ramon Malnik, treasurer of the Johnson Steel Company, was considering the alternative methods of raising $40 million. Mr. Malnik was to prepare a comprehensive report for review by Mr. Wes Johnson, vice president of finance for the Johnson Steel Company.

The Johnson Steel Company is a medium-sized producer of finished and semifinished steel. It produces numerous carbon grades of steel, some stainless steel and, on occasion, has engaged in the production of certain types of specialty and exotic steels. Its steel is sold in ingots, slabs, bars, sheets—hot and cold rolled, pipe, tubing, and galvanized sheets. The Johnson Steel Company also owns a raw-materials transportation company, whose assets include tugs and barges. While the principal function of the transportation company is to transport coal and ore for the Johnson Steel Company, on rare occasions, it has provided transportation services for other basic materials producers, located on its principal inland water route.

In recent years, keeping in mind the influx of foreign bar and specialty steels, Johnson Steel has started a program to expand its capabilities to plastic molding bases. Plastic products are typically, injection, transfer or compression molded. For injection molding, the molten resin is injected into a steel mold to form the finished plastic product. Johnson Steel provides steel molds, as well as mold bases, to plastic product manufacturers. This area of Johnson's endeavors has proven to be a rapidly growing one.

In the past five years, Johnson's sales have grown from $250 million to $412 million. For the most recent year, sales had declined from the previous year's level, due to a rare combination of adverse factors. A summary of income statements for the past five years is shown in Exhibit 1, page 178. Johnson was able to generate its 1976 sales on a total assets base of $370 million. The 1976 balance sheet is shown in Exhibit 2. The finance committee, headed by Mr. Johnson, had felt that, in order to capitalize certain current liabilities, to increase working capital, and to fund forthcoming plant expansions, the company needed to raise $40 million over and above the funds being generated internally.

As a preliminary to his report, Mr. Malnik had scheduled a meeting with Mr. George Neff, partner in the company's investment banking firm of Neff, Neff and Osborn, Inc. Mr. Malnik proceeded to summarize some of the financial information that would likely be needed at the meeting. The summary of the financial information is shown in Exhibit 3. In addition to summarizing the financial information, Mr. Malnik also prepared a table showing the operating income for various levels of 1977 sales and operating margins (operating income/sales). Based upon estimates of the sales department, Mr. Malnik thought that Johnson's 1977 sales could vary from $440 million to $460 million. Operating margins had been around 14 percent, recently. Mr. Malnik used 13 to 15 percent as his range for the operating margin. His table is reproduced in Exhibit 4. Finally, Mr. Malnik also summarized key financial ratios for the industry and for Johnson Steel. These ratios are shown in Exhibit 5.

At their scheduled meeting, Mr. Malnik said to Mr. Neff, "George, as you can see from the tables that I have prepared, Johnson Steel has been able to consistently maintain operating margins of around 14 percent. Even in 1976, when our sales declined, we were able to tighten the belt at headquarters and maintain the margin. For 1977, our sales could easily be at the $460 million level, and with increased operating efficiencies, our operating income should be close to $69 million. We plan to use approximately $20 million for new expansion, and the remaining $20 million to repay the current portion of long-term debt, and to add to working capital. Our profitability ratios are better than the industry average, and the market evaluation of our performance has resulted in a higher P/E ratio than the industry figure. Finally, our leverage ratios are lower than the industry average, and I think that we can take on additional debt. What do you think?"

Mr. Neff indicated that his assessment of the firm's performance was in general agreement with Mr. Malnik's. He briefly explained his perception of "increased operating efficiencies," and indicated to Mr. Malnik that the $69 million estimate for 1977 operating income might prove to be conservative, but nevertheless, was an excellent estimate with which to work. Mr. Neff, however, had reservations about using bond financing. He explained, "It is quite true that, at the present time, Johnson Steel is underlevered. And that may be precisely the reason why the market assigns a higher P/E ratio to Johnson Steel. By issuing bonds now, Johnson is using up its borrowing power and would have to resort to common-stock financing, later on. As you know, the present book value of Johnson Steel is $55 per share. Should you issue bonds now and the P/E declines, at a later date, you may find that you can only raise equity funds by selling stock below book value. This alternative may not be acceptable to Mr. Johnson, personally. All in all, I think that the $40 million should be raised by issuing common stock. Neff, Neff and Osborn would be delighted to put together a syndicate to help with the issuance of the new common. Johnson Steel should expect net proceeds of $60 per share." Upon further questioning, Mr. Malnik was able to solicit from Mr. Neff the additional information that bonds could be sold with a coupon rate of 8.5 percent to net Johnson Steel their face value. Mr. Malnik promised to get back to Mr. Neff in the near future, and started to prepare his analysis of the two alternatives for raising the $40 million.

EXHIBIT 1

Johnson Steel Company

Income Statements, Years Ending December 31

(in millions of dollars)

	1976	*1975*	*1974*	*1973*	*1972*
Sales	$412.9	$438.7	$356.2	$291.1	$257.3
Cost of goods sold	309.0	329.2	259.1	232.9	193.0
General and selling expenses	45.3	48.1	47.9	45.1	41.7
Operating income	57.7	61.4	49.2	13.1	22.6
Interest	8.0	8.0	8.0	3.5	3.5
Income before tax	49.7	53.4	41.2	9.6	19.1
Tax	24.9	26.7	20.6	4.8	9.6
Net income	24.8	26.7	20.6	4.8	9.5

EXHIBIT 2

Johnson Steel Company

Balance Sheet, December 31, 1976
(in millions of dollars)

Cash and equivalent	$ 17.6
Receivables	25.1
Inventory	61.2
Total current assets	103.9
Net plant	240.7
Other assets	25.4
Total assets	370.0
Total current liabilities*	54.7
Long-term debt, 8%	90.0
Other LTD	5.0
Total debt	149.7
Common stock	100.0
Retained earnings	120.3
Total liabilities + equity	$370.0

*Includes $10-million current portion of long-term debt.

EXHIBIT 3

Johnson Steel Company

Summary of Financial Information

	1976	1975	1974	1973	1972
Sales (in millions)	$412.0	$438.7	$356.2	$291.1	$257.3
Net income (in millions)	24.8	26.7	20.6	4.8	9.5
Earnings/share	6.20	6.67	5.15	1.20	2.37
Dividends/share	3.00	3.00	2.50	1.92	1.92
Average price	64.00	53.00	27.00	19.00	24.00

EXHIBIT 4

Johnson Steel Company

1977 Estimated Sales, Operating Margins Table
(in millions of dollars)

Sales	$440	$450	$460
Op margins			
13%	$57.2	$58.5	$59.8
14%	61.6	63.0	64.4
15%	66.0	67.5	69.0

EXHIBIT 5

Johnson Steel Company

Comparative Industry Financial Ratios

	Industry	Johnson Steel
Current ratio	2.2	1.9
Profit margins	4.4%	6.0%
Return on net worth	10.2%	11.3%
Return on total assets	5.7%	6.7%
Total debt/net worth	79 %	68 %
Total debt/total assets	44 %	40 %
Inventory turnover	8.1	6.7
Total assets turnover	1.3	1.1
Collection period	47 days	22 days
Price/earnings	8	10

Questions

1. Mr. Malnik and Mr. Neff referred to "increased operating efficiencies" resulting in higher operating income. Are their estimates, for sales and operating income, reasonable? Explain, by referring to industry and Johnson Steel ratios.

2. Calculate earnings per share for 1977, under each of the financing alternatives.

3. Calculate the two leverage ratios—total debt to net worth, and total debt to total assets—for both stock and bond financing. Base your calculations on the total assets and total debt figures, which exist after raising and applying the funds, and not on year-end 1977 figures.

4. Which alternative appears to be the better one? Why? Evaluate Mr. Neff's statement that issuing bonds now would cause Johnson Steel to use up its borrowing power.

Case 34

PAXTON COMPANY

FINANCING WITH CONVERTIBLES

Mr. David Lloyd, treasurer of the Paxton Company, looked at his watch and noted that Jack Henning was seven minutes late for his appointment. It was not like Henning, senior vice president, of Wilshire Securities, to be late for an appointment, especially when this one might lead to Wilshire Securities' first, major, underwriting endeavor.

It was Spring, 1978, and the Paxton Company was looking at alternate sources to raise $80 million. Mr. Lloyd had contacted a prestigious, New York investment banking firm to explore the possibility of retaining it as an underwriter. Henning had found out about the underwriting opportunity through a well-connected golfing partner, and for the past few weeks, had been aggressively pursuing the underwriting job. On this particular day, he was to present his final analysis on the available alternatives, and to enter Wilshire Securities' bid to land the underwriting job.

In the late nineteenth century, T. Walter Paxton, a fisherman by avocation and a food conservationist by necessity, started smoking and storing fish fillets. Much to his delight, he found out that his excess supply of smoked fish was easily sold to friends and neighbors. In fact, the demand for his smoked fish was so great that he decided to concentrate, full-time, on processing and selling smoked fish. By the turn of the century, his proprietorship had grown, substantially, had been incorporated as Paxton Company, and was under the managerial control of T. W. Paxton, Jr.

In recent years, management of the Paxton Company had passed into the hands of managers who were not related to the Paxton family, and who did not control any significant portion of Paxton's stock. Partially to preserve the company's independence, they had embarked—rather successfully—on an ambitious expansion program. By early 1978, the Paxton Company had become a diversified manufacturer of a very broad line of processed foods. The product line includes processed and packaged beef, lamb, fish, and vegetables for human consumption. It also manufactures cat and dog foods, sold principally through supermarkets. Paxton has been able to effectively utilize its excess plant capacity by filling private-label orders. Paxton's most recent income statement and balance sheet are shown in Exhibits 1 and 2.

Mr. Lloyd's phone rang, and his secretary announced the arrival of Mr. Henning. As Mr. Henning was ushered in, he anticipated Mr. Lloyd's frown and said, "I apologize for being late, Dave. I had not realized that your security personnel do such a thorough screening job before permitting anyone beyond the lobby. I have identified two, very viable, financing alternatives for Paxton. As you know, Paxton's ratio of total debt to total assets—leverage ratio—is not out of line with the industry average of 42 percent. The leverage-ratio range, for most of the major firms, varies from 38 to 52 percent. Secondly, Paxton, with 1977 earnings per share of $2.59 and a $29 price, shows a higher P/E ratio than the industry average of 10. Third, you indicated that, without additional new financing, Paxton anticipated reaching a sales volume of $1.4 billion. If we assume that operating income from the existing business will increase proportionately, deployment of the new funds would further increase operating income by $4 million and raise depreciation to $26.10 million, we can calculate *pro forma* earnings per share for 1978. Fourth, given management's desire to minimize equity dilution, we are provided with two, very viable alternatives. One is to issue mortgage bonds. We could issue mortgage bonds, with a face value of $80 million, at $101.10 to net Paxton $80 million. The bonds would be 30-year, callable bonds, with a coupon rate of 8.8 percent. The second alternative is to issue convertible debentures. We could issue $80 million of these "debbies" at $101.35 to net Paxton $80 million. The debentures would be convertible into common at $33.33 a share. Given the recent market price of $29, the conversion premium is relatively modest. Therefore, I feel that we could get by with a coupon rate of 6.5 percent. I have worked out the numbers, here. This chart shows the effect of the two financing alternatives on earnings per share. As you can see, one of these alternatives appears to be more desirable from Paxton's viewpoint. We, at Wilshire, are equipped to . . ." As Mr. Henning started to make a pitch on behalf of Wilshire Securities, Mr. Lloyd's attention turned to the two financing alternatives that he had been presented.

EXHIBIT 1

Paxton Company

Income Statement, Year Ending December 31, 1977

(in millions of dollars)

Net sales	$1,289.72
Expenses	1,171.23
Operating income	118.49
Depreciation	22.78
Interest	16.01
Income before taxes	79.70
Taxes	38.25
Net income	41.45
Dividends	16.00
Returned earnings	$ 25.45

EXHIBIT 2

Paxton Company

Balance Sheet, December 31, 1977

(in millions of dollars)

Cash	$ 87.67
Receivables	116.44
Inventories	301.21
Other current assets	13.71
Total current assets	519.03
Net property	230.80
Investments	39.64
Total assets	$789.47
Short-term notes	$ 51.37
Accounts payable	147.26
Income taxes	26.71
Total current liabilities	225.34
Long-term debt	137.00
Other long-term debt	21.23
Total liabilities	383.57
Common stock, par $1	16.00
Retained earnings	389.90
Total liabilities and equity	$789.47

Questions

1. Calculate earnings per share for 1978, under each of the two financing alternatives. Assume that interest is payable for only 8 months on either of the two debt issues. Also assume that "old" interest remains at the 1977 level.

2. Calculate the 1978 year-end ratio of total debt to total assets for Paxton, under both financing alternatives. Assume that from 1977 to 1978 dividends per share remain constant.

3. Assuming that all convertible debentures are converted into common *before* payment of any applicable interest on debentures in 1978, answer Questions 1 and 2.

4. What would be the most appropriate financing alternative for Paxton? Why?

Case 35

UNITED PAPER CORPORATION (B)

CAPITAL STRUCTURE AND FINANCING ALTERNATIVES

In Spring, 1977, the executive committee of the United Paper Corporation met to consider various financing alternatives for United's planned expansion program. United had begun a very ambitious expansion program, and needed to raise $40 million to help finance its new plans. As the meeting began, Mr. John Craven, president, leaned towards Mr. Charles Miller, group vice president, and said, "Well Chip, I think that by now you have obtained all the necessary information for our external financing. Do you have your presentation on financing alternatives and your recommendation ready? I am going to turn the floor over to you, so you can proceed with your presentation."

The United Paper Corporation is a diversified firm, manufacturing wood-based and other industrial products, and mining and selling coal. In the year ended December 31, 1976, United earned $33.7 million on sales of $917.6 million. A consolidated statement of earnings is shown in Exhibit 1, page 188. At year-end 1976, United had total assets of $667 million (see Exhibit 2). The company is organized in four divisions. The fiber paper division makes writing paper, commercial/newsprint paper and specialty paper. Near-term prospects for the industry look good. It is anticipated that price boosts of about 5 percent will be instituted. The industry performance is being influenced by a number of factors, including a shortage of suitable mill sites, pollution-control requirements for existing mills, and environmental impact statements for proposed new mills. The division is the largest in terms of sales volume, contributing 35.4 percent of 1976 net sales. However, its contribution to pre-tax earnings was 18.1 percent (Exhibit 3).

The paperboard division produces a wide variety of paperboards with different chemical and physical performance characteristics. Within the division, the products fall in two broad categories: containerboard and boxboard. Containerboard products include corrugated containers, corrugating material and chipboards. Demand has been somewhat sluggish, although long-term prospects look good. Boxboards products are used for packaging consumer goods and, therefore, need to be lightweight and strong. The division has an excellent reputation in the trade for manufacturing boxboard suitable for high-fidelity, graphic reproduction. However, the industry has been demonstrating a slow growth rate. The paperboard division has had to make pollution-control expenditures on some of its mills in recent years. In 1976, the division contributed 24.9 percent of sales and 11.5 percent of pretax earnings.

The industrial products division makes castings, cement and metal pipes, gaskets and valves, and small tools for use in the coal mining industry. Intermediate and long-term growth prospects are good. The division contributed 27.7 percent of 1976 sales and 25.6 percent of pretax earnings. The smallest division in terms of sales is the mineral resources division, whose primary business is to mine and sell metallurgical coal. The division owns coal mines in Kentucky, Pennsylvania, and West Virginia. In recent years, the division has become extremely profitable, contributing 30.1 percent of pretax profits and 12 percent of sales. By coal industry standards, the division is very small, mining just over 2 million tons of coal. The division is interested in acquiring additional mines to operate.

Mr. Miller started his presentation to the executive committee, which, in addition to Mr. Craven, also included United's controller and the four division vice presidents, "I have carefully examined the alternatives open to United. Our present financing involves $326.8 million of short- and long-term debt, or 49 percent of total financing. The $20 million in preferred stock provides 3 percent of financing, and equity provides the remaining 48 percent of financing. From my viewpoint, all three of these alternatives are possible choices. That is, we can raise the $40 million by using either common stock, preferred stock, or bonds. If we decide to go with bonds, which we can by having a coupon rate of 8.2 percent, our leverage ratio would not change that much. We would net face value with the 8.2 percent interest rate. The bonds would be noncallable. We could issue preferred stock with $100 par value and a dividend rate of $9 per share. We would sell the preferred at par, and would net $98 per share. Finally, we could also issue common stock. We should expect net proceeds of $22.60 per share, which would be high enough to prevent dilution of the existing book value per share. Do you have any comments concerning which of the financing alternatives might be most desirable?"

Mr. Robey, vice president of the fiber paper division, spoke first, "I don't see where we have any choice but to issue bonds. The wood products industry has been in the doldrums for the past four years. Just about the time we see any signs of recovery, the E.P.A. starts requiring the addition of nonproductive pollution-control equipment to our existing facilities, and what few choices we have for new mills, have to pass environmental impact studies before construction can begin. In fact, I have a good hunch that we will have to shut down our South Carolina mill, because the cost of conforming to E.P.A. standards is going to exceed our returns from that mill. The net result of market and environmental factors has been to reduce United's price to close to book value. I am afraid that any new issue would only serve to depress market prices further. Furthermore, all of us have stock options, and what good will they be if United's common stock price is further depressed. I say that we go with bonds. The increased leverage is not substantial. Besides, bonds are the cheapest source of funds and isn't that what we should use to minimize costs?"

Mr. Murphy, who started with United as a cost accountant, 38 years ago, moved to internal auditing, and became controller, seven years ago, spoke next, "I am not so sure that bonds are the best alternative. First of all, I think that we are already over-leveraged at 52 percent compared to the industry average future of 46 percent. I am, of course, including preferred stock in my numerator, since preferred dividends do constitute fixed charges. Secondly, if we are interested in reducing the common stockholders' exposure to risk, then we are not going to accomplish it by issuing debt which will increase the amount of fixed charges that have to be paid. Finally, our stock price has recovered quite a bit from its level of sixteen months ago. I think that is a good sign of the market's willingness to absorb additional new common of United. I think we should not only issue new common to finance our expansion, but also raise the dividend to $1.10 per share."

Mr. Kelly, vice president of the mineral resources division spoke next, "You know, I am a production man and all of this high finance is beyond me. One thing I am sure of. We keep referring to United as a wood-products company and it is true that 60.3 percent of sales come from wood-related products. But if you look at the profit side, the two wood divisions are contributing only 29.6 percent of pretax earnings, whereas the two nonforest products divisions are contributing 55.7 percent of pretax profits. I think that it is time we think of United as a broadly diversified firm, rather than a wood-products firm. I can see that, to a considerable extent, United's future growth is going to come from the industrial products and mineral resources divisions. Keeping this factor in mind, I can see the advantages and disadvantages of both stock and bonds. I think that issuing preferred is a good compromise solution."

Mr. Miller spoke again, "I am glad to hear your comments. In fact, I had anticipated the types of questions you are raising. While I cannot resolve the issues related to stock, preferred, or bond financing, I have compiled some statistics on industries that are related to our endeavors. The information on this sheet (see Exhibit 4) indicates that, for example, the industry where our fiber paper division would belong, has a leverage ratio of 49 percent. The "industrial products" industry is a composite one, where firms are comparative to our industrial products division. Finally, there are very few, independent coal companies these days. A number of energy-resource firms have acquired coal companies in recent years. Therefore, the ratios for the coal industry are based on a relatively small sample."

As the deliberations of the executive committee concerning financing alternatives continued into the late afternoon, a number of factors became apparent: (a) It was not immediately apparent that United was a wood-products company; (b) related to United's diverse activities, was the question of optimal leverage ratio; (c) all financing alternatives appeared to have associated advantages and disadvantages; (d) any debt financing would have to be callable bonds, which would carry an interest premium of .5 percent over noncallable bonds.

EXHIBIT 1

United Paper Corporation

Consolidated Earnings Statement, Year Ending December 31, 1976

(in millions of dollars)

Net sales	$917.6
Cost of goods sold	751.8
Selling and administrative expense	98.1
Interest expense	13.3
Operating income	54.4
Income equity in jointly owned corporations	9.4
Income before taxes	63.8

EXHIBIT I (Cont'd)

Income taxes	29.1
Net income before preferred dividends	34.7
Preferred dividends	1.0
Net income	33.7
Common dividends	14.5
Retained earnings	19.2

EXHIBIT 2

United Paper Corporation

Consolidated Balance Sheet, December 31, 1976

(in millions of dollars)

Cash	$ 21.2
Net receivables	105.7
Inventory	107.1
Total current assets	234.0
Land and Mineral	52.5
Buildings, plant, net	254.1
Equity in jointly-owned corporations	126.4
	$667.0
Accounts payable	60.2
Accrued liabilities	39.1
Other liabilities	4.9
Total current liabilities	104.2
Deferred taxes	30.1
Long-term debt	192.5
Total liabilities	326.8
Preferred stock, $5	20.0
Common, $1 par	14.5
Paid-in capital	90.5
Retained earnings	215.2
	$667.0

EXHIBIT 3

United Paper Corporation

Sales and Earnings by Divisions

	% of sales	% of earnings[*]
Fiber paper division	35.4	18.1
Paperboard division	24.9	11.5
Industrial products division	27.7	25.6
Mineral resources division	12.0	30.1
Jointly owned corporations	–	14.7
	100.0	100.0

[*]Based on pretax income of $63.8 million.

EXHIBIT 4

United Paper Corporation

Selected Statistics from Related Industries[*]

Industry	TD/TA ratio	NI/sales	Price/EPS	Div. yield
Paper	49%	6.7%	11	3.4%
Paperboard	46%	6.2%	10	3.3%
Industrial products	42%	7.7%	8	4.0%
Coal	38%	10.0%	9	2.5%

[*]The ratios are normalized, long-term estimates.

Questions

1. Calculate United's leverage ratio and net income/sales ratio based upon data in Exhibits 1 and 2. Based upon United's current price of $23.25, calculate a P/E ratio and dividend yield for it. Using data from Exhibit 3, calaculate net income/sales ratios for each division. Use this information and that in Exhibit 4 to estimate and justify an appropriate leverage ratio for United.

2. Assume that, for 1977, United's operating income before interest expense ($67.7 million) increases by 8 percent, that income-equity in jointly owned companies increases by 9 percent, and that employment of the new $40 million will increase operating income before interest by an additional $3 million. Assume that

net current liabilities increase by $4 million by year end 1977. Calculate earnings per share and leverage ratio for United. (For bond financing, assume that interest is paid for the total year. For preferred financing, assume dividends are paid for the total year.)

3. Discuss the advantages and disadvantages of each of the three financing methods. To answer this question, you will need to calculate 1976 and 1977 fixed-charge coverage (earnings before interest and taxes divided by the sum of interest expense and pretax preferred dividends).

4. Which financing method appears to be the most appropriate for United? Why?

5. Assume that, in the December 31, 1976 long-term debt figure of $192.5 million, is a bank note of $50 million, either payable on December 21, 1979, or convertible on that date into a term note, repayable in 10 equal installments of principal and interest. Does your answer to Question 4 change? Why or why not?

Case 36

INTERNATIONAL METALS CORPORATION

COMPREHENSIVE FINANCING CONSIDERATIONS

In January, 1977, the International Metals Corporation was evaluating various alternatives to raise $100 million. Mr. Kenneth McMillan, financial vice president of International Metals Corporation (IMC), and a member of the board of directors of IMC, had retained Mr. Dan Solomon, senior partner with the investment banking firm of Goldblum, Solomon, Inc., as a paid consultant to advise on various financing alternatives open to IMC. (Keeping in mind recent lawsuits against some boards of directors by stockholders, Mr. McMillan had decided to retain Mr. Solomon as a paid consultant. The actual underwriter would be chosen by competitive bidding.) Since the IMC board of directors was scheduled to convene in two weeks. Mr. McMillan had seen to it that the issue of raising the $100 million external capital be placed on the board's agenda for the forthcoming meeting. Mr. McMillan wanted to make sure that all analyses and information were available for the board's review to enable them to make a decision. From past experience with the external members of the board of directors, Mr. McMillan knew that they would be most interested in the potential impact of the financing alternatives on short and intermediate term profits, and price of IMC common stock. (In the past, because of capital markets dynamics and IMC's frequent financing needs, the board members had not expressed any particular interest in long-term impact.)

The International Metals Corporation (IMC) is a relatively large producer and fabricator of nonferrous metals, such as aluminum, lead, titanium, and zinc. Since early 1974, IMC's sales and earnings have been growing rapidly. Two factors have accounted for this trend: one was the end of price controls in April, 1974; the second is a worldwide shortage of aluminum, which is expected to last for several years. Use of aluminum has been rising steadily in the building, transportation, electrical and consumer goods industries, and the trend is expected to continue. Demand for lead, too, has been firm recently. The primary use of lead has been in making storage batteries. The research on electric-powered automobiles adds to the long-range growth prospects for this aspect of IMC's business. Titanium and zinc are minor factors in IMC's production operations. However, they do assure IMC of a source of raw materials supplies in its manufacture of titanium forgings and brass products. In addition to aluminum sheets, ingots, bars, tubings, and so on, IMC also manufactures aluminum foil, pots and pans, siding, and other building products requiring the use of aluminum.

Unaudited figures for 1976 (Exhibits 1 and 2, pages 194-195) show that IMC, with a total asset base of $970 million, earned 58.8 million on total sales of $775 million. IMC paid $24.9 million in dividends, and added $33.9 million to retained earnings. IMC's targeted dividend payout is 45 percent of net income available to common. Mr. McMillan felt that this payout would be continued in the foreseeable future.

After discussions with Mr. Solomon, Mr. McMillan came to the conclusion that IMC could consider six different financing alternatives. They are detailed below:

1. Common stock. IMC could issue common stock to net $38 per share.

2. Preferred. IMC could issue $8.50 preferred, par $100 stock, at par value, and would net $98 per preferred share.

3. Bonds. Straight debt could be issued, which would carry a coupon rate of 9 percent and net the firm face value.

4. IMC could issue convertible debentures, with a coupon rate of 6.5 percent to net face value. Each debenture would be convertible into 20 shares of common stock through maturity. The debentures would be callable at 105 percent of face value, and the conversion privilege would be protected against dilution.

5. IMC could issue convertible debentures with a coupon rate of 8 percent to net face value. Each debenture would be convertible into common at $60 per share through maturity. The aforementioned call and dilution covenants would apply.

6. IMC could issue bonds with warrants. The bonds would carry a coupon rate of 7 percent, and would be sold to net IMC face value. Each bond would have 20 warrants attached, each warrant entitling the holder to *acquire* one common share for $50.00. The warrants would not be exercisable after December 31, 1984, and would be detachable. Finally, the holder would be able to exercise the warrants by paying cash *or* tendering the 7 percent bond at face value.

Comparative industry ratios for IMC are provided in Exhibit 3. In his last meeting with Mr. Solomon, Mr. McMillan could vividly recall Mr. Solomon's statement regarding IMC's market evaluation: ". . . In the opinion of our analysts who follow the nonferrous metals manufacturers and fabricators, IMC's risk and return puts it in the 10 percent market capitalization rate group. In addition, our econometric group has forecasted IMC's 1977 dividend payments, normalized to year-end payment, at the $1.60 level." Based upon Mr. Solomon's statement, and IMC's current price of about $40 a share, Mr. McMillan calculated the capital market growth rate expectations of IMC. He found it interesting that, under the assumption of a stable operating margin, this rate was just about the same as the long-term growth rate he had estimated for IMC's operating income. To estimate 1977 operating income, Mr. McMillan applied the growth rate to the 1976 operating income figure of $133.9 million and, due to the deployment of higher-than-usual incremental assets to be acquired through the new financing, added an additional $12 million to the estimated amount.

Mr. Solomon had told Mr. McMillan that, at the present time, the market would be receptive to any of the six financing alternatives. The probability of interest rates declining from present levels was small, and the current market price of IMC's common stock, while not near its all-time high, was nevertheless not "depressed", by any measure. Mr. McMillan felt confident that he had sufficient information on hand now to prepare a thorough analysis of the financing options open to IMC.

EXHIBIT 1

International Metals Corporation

Balance Sheet (December 31, 1976)

(in millions of dollars; unaudited)

Cash and equivalent	$ 23.5
Receivables	121.1
Inventory	211.7
Total current assets	356.3
Net plant	602.7
Other fixed assets	11.0
Total assets	$970.0

EXHIBIT 1 (Cont'd)

Accounts payable	65.2
Current portion of LTD[*]	15.5
Taxes payable	30.3
Accruals	20.0
Total current liabilities	131.0
Long-term debt[*]	237.5
$4.00 preferred, par $100	30.0
Common stock, par $2	33.2
Paid-in surplus	136.8
Ratained earnings	401.5
Total liability and equity	$970.0

[*]Total interest-bearing debt on January 1, 1976 was $253 million.   Current portion of LTD is payable December 31, 1977.

EXHIBIT 2

International Metals Corporation

Income Statement, Year Ended December 31, 1976

(in millions of dollars; unaudited)

Net sales	$775.0
Cost of goods sold	586.9
Selling, general expenses	54.2
Operating income	133.9
Interest expense	13.9
Income before taxes	120.0
Taxes	60.0
Net income	60.0
Preferred dividends	1.2
Available to common	58.8
Common dividends	24.9
Retained earnings	$ 33.9

EXHIBIT 3

International Metals Corporation

Comparative Industry Ratios

Profit margins	6.1 percent
Dividend payout	41.0 percent
P/E ratio	9.5
Total debt/assets[*]	40 percent

[*]Total debt does not include preferred stock.

Questions

1. Replicate Mr. McMillan's operating income forecasts for 1977 through 1982. What assumptions did you make in forecasting operating income?

2. Based upon your 1977 year-end operating income forecast, calculate EPS and leverage ratio (total debt to total assets, not including preferred stock in total debt) for IMC for each of the six alternatives mentioned in the case. Assume that the expansion has resulted in a net increase in current liabilities equal to $8 million. That is, December 31, 1977 current liabilities are $139 million. Also, assume that common stock dividends paid in 1977 equal $1.60 per share.

3. Calculate a potential price for IMC on December 31, 1977 for each of the alternatives. Assume that, for up to each 5 percentage points increase, only, in leverage over the industry average, P/E would decline by one. That is, if before financing, IMC's leverage was 37% and P/E 10, and after financing, leverage was 48 percent, then IMC's P/E would decline to 8.

4. Based upon your December 31, 1982 forecast of operating income, calculate EPS and leverage ratio for IMC for all of the alternatives mentioned in the case. The relationship between additions to retained earnings and financing alternatives is a dynamic one. However, assume that between January 1, 1978 and December 31, 1982, cumulative marginal increases in retained earnings equaled $227 million. Assume that December 31, 1982 current liabilities are $186 million, and that long-term debt is the same as on January 1, 1978; that is, $237.5 million. The interest rate implicit in Exhibits 1 and 2 is also applicable here. Also, assume that for Alternatives 4–6, conversion (or exercise) of the total issue (all warrants) occurs at the beginning of the following year, if price of common is 6 percent or more above the conversion (exercise) price. Finally, for Alternative 6, assume that if warrants are exercised, one half of the holders pay cash; the other half, tender the 7 percent bonds.

5. Calculate a potential price for IMC for December 31, 1982 for each of the alternatives. Assumption of Question 3 applies here, also.

6. Mr. McMillan anticipated that some board members would want to know why the call and dilution features in Alternatives 4–6 were necessary, and at what cost. How would you respond?

7. Mr. McMillan felt that at least one board member would want to know why Alternative 6 was being considered, since it is identical to Alternative 4, except for the higher interest rate. How would you respond.

8. From your viewpoint, which alternative is the most desirable? Why?

PART VII

Acquisitions, Reorganization and Liquidation

Case 37

ITEL CORPORATION[1]

ACQUISITION OF CENTRAL DATA SYSTEMS, INC.

In June, 1975, the Itel Corporation reached an agreement in principle to acquire Central Data Systems, Inc. (CDSI). The terms of the agreement called for the holders of 277,600 common shares of CDSI to receive $7.64 per share in cash and notes. The holders of the remaining 180,548 shares of CDSI would receive $7.64 per share in cash. Itel's total purchase price, included cash and notes, would be approximately $3.5 million.

Central Data Systems, Inc.

For information on Central Data Systems, Inc. (CDSI), see Case 4 in this book.

Itel Corporation

The Itel Corporation, based in San Francisco, provides financial services, which include leasing capital equipment and reinsurance, and data processing. Itel is active in leasing railroad cars and cargo ship containers. By providing savings in labor, handling and terminal costs, and reductions in pilferage, damage and work-force accident rates, containers are becoming increasingly popular. Firms engaged in leasing them anticipate a high growth rate in the near- and intermediate-term future. Its insurance subsidiary writes property and liability insurance. The data products division leases IBM computers to users, and is going to sell a line of computers made by National Semiconductor. The company has also been active in acquiring firms. The proposed merger with CDSI would extend Itel's activities to providing data-processing services in the midwestern market.

Itel derives the bulk of its revenues from leasing activities. The leasing industry is part of the financial services industry. The performance of the financial services industry is greatly affected by economic activity, interest rates and product policies of manufacturers whose equipment is subject to third-party leasing. In its

---

[1] This case was prepared from public information. It is designed for educational purposes, and not for the purposes of research or to illustrate correct or incorrect handling of administrative practices.

1975 annual report, Itel identifies the following economic and business factors that affect its operations:

Capital Spending. Capital spending as a variable primarily relates to Itel's leveraged leasing activities. In this area, Itel serves to develop the necessary availability of capital to meet the spending plans of corporations. As capital spending increases, the number of transactions completed by Itel also tends to increase.

Interest Rates. Interest rates affect Itel in its operating leasing activities and to a lesser degree in its leveraged leasing transactions. While much of Itel's senior debt is tied to the prime lending rate, historically the demand for operating leases increases as interest rates rise.

Interest rates also affect the level of income reported by Itel from its residual values. The expected values of the Company's residuals are discounted at the interest rates contained in the debt portion of leveraged lease transactions. On the other hand, it is the impact of inflation which directly affects the value of the used equipment, and, therefore, the cash Itel will receive through the disposition of the equipment at lease termination.

General Economy. The general level of activity in the economy moderately affects all of Itel because it reflects the level of corporate demand for the services which the Company provides. This is somewhat more evident in Itel's operating leasing activities where the Company provides corporations with transportation equipment and in its data-services area where the number of client transactions is related to the general economy.

World Trade. World trade primarily impacts the demand for the ships and containers of Itel's SSI Navigation and Container subsidiaries. Here, a high level of world trade requires increased transportation of goods.

Tax Environment. A favorable tax environment is another critical factor in Itel's leveraged leasing operations. Companies which cannot immediately utilize the investment tax credit and accelerated depreciation, find leveraged leasing the lowest cost form of financing available. Lessees are generally able to share such benefits through lower lease rates.

Accounting Standards. Itel's leasing activities could also be affected by significant changes in the present accounting treatment for leases.

IBM Product Announcements.   The timing and pricing of IBM products are other variables which can impact Itel's businesses. The two operations of the Company which would be affected by such announcements are Itel's leveraged leasing of computer equipment and our product marketing of independent IBM compatible peripherals. [2]

Itel's income statements for recent years are shown in Exhibit 1. With 1972 as the base year, Itel's revenues increased almost 100 percent by 1975. Net income increased from $0.5 million in 1972 to $10.7 million in 1975.

Itel Corporation's balance sheets for the past four years are shown in Exhibit 2.   Total assets increased from $260.81 million in 1972 to $378.718 million in 1975.   Additional per-share statistics are shown in Exhibit 3.

The interest rate on senior debt varies, depending on the prime rate.   Itel's annual report indicates that the applicable interest rate in 1975, on the average, was 9.5 percent.   The subordinated debt consists of convertible debentures. It would be reasonable to assume that the current applicable interest rate is around 11 percent. These costs and related items for calculating Itel's cost of capital are summarized in Exhibit 4.

EXHIBIT 1

Itel Corporation

Income Statements, Years Ending
December 31, 1972–December 31, 1975 *

(in thousands of dollars)

	1972	*1973*	*1974*	*1975*
Revenues	$100,100	$108,500	$143,500.	$204,000
Expenses	100,490	93,100	124,700	184,900

[2] Itel Corporation, 1975 Annual Report, page 10.

EXHIBIT 1 (Cont'd)

Nonoperating income	1,100	(2,600)	–	–
Income before tax	710	12,800	18,800	19,100
Taxes	210	7,200	9,024	8,400
Net income	$ 500	$ 5,600	$ 9,776	$ 10,700

*Average number of shares outstanding: 1972–7.3 million; 1973–7.56 million; 1974–7.64 million; 1975–6.82 million.

EXHIBIT 2

Itel Corporation

Balance Sheets, December 31, 1972–December 31, 1975

(in thousands of dollars)

	1972	1973	1974	1975
Cash	$ 29,520	$ 29,500	$ 31,700	$ 33,490
Net receivables	15,256	62,600	92,400	101,950
Inventories	15,753	9,900	10,100	11,286
Other current assets	4,043	40,100	60,234	68,434
Total current assets	64,572	142,100	194,434	215,160
Net plant	187,603	92,700	122,000	155,005
Other assets	8,635	82,900	49,666	8,553
Total assets	$260,810	$317,700	$366,100	$378,718
Accounts payable (Total current liabilities)	23,454	24,100	31,200	34,786
L.T. debt*	191,043	240,700	271,900	275,414
Total liabilities	214,497	264,800	303,100	310,200
Common stock	7,406	7,500	7,600	7,780
Capital surplus	34,901	35,800	36,100	36,657
Retained earnings	4,006	9,600	19,300	24,081
Total equity	46,313	52,900	63,000	68,518
Total liabilities + equity	$260,810	$317,700	$366,100	$378,718

*Long-term debt for 1975 includes senior debt of $167.7 million, and subordinated debt of $45.7 million.

EXHIBIT 3

Itel Corporation

Selected per Share Statistics

(in dollars)

Statistic	1972	1973	1974	1975
Earnings	$ 0.07	$ 0.74	$ 1.28	$ 1.57
Dividends	–	–	–	0.05
Price–Low	7.00	3.63	2.50	3.25
Price–High	12.50	11.88	6.38	9.50

EXHIBIT 4

Itel Corporation

Selected Figures for Cost-of-Capital Calculation

	Amount	% of structure	Before-tax cost
Senior debt	$167.7	59.5	9.5%
Subordinated debt	45.7	16.2	11.0%
Common equity	68.6	24.3	*
	$282.0	100.0	

*Has to be on an after-tax basis, and is left for the student as an exercise.

Questions

1. Evaluate the performance of Central Data Systems. Also, forecast its sales and earnings for 1975 and 1976. This question is equivalent to solving Case 4.

2. Evaluate the performance of Itel Corporation.

3. Forecast Itel's sales and earnings per share for 1976.

4. Calculate the marginal cost of capital of Itel. Use it to evaluate the worth of CDSI to Itel.

5. For 1976, and on a *pro forma* basis, examine the effects of the merger on Itel's sales and earnings per share.

6. What additional factors need to be considered in evaluating the merger?

7. Was the merger beneficial to stockholders of both Itel and CDSI? Explain.

Case 38

REVLON, INC.[1]

ACQUISITION OF BARNES-HIND PHARMACEUTICALS

On June 14, 1976, it was announced that Revlon, Inc. was going to acquire all 812,901 shares outstanding of Barnes-Hind Pharmaceuticals. Each share of Barnes-Hind common would be exchanged for 0.7333 Revlon common. Revlon is the second largest firm in the cosmetics/toiletries industry (see Exhibit 1, page 210). Barnes-Hind is a small manufacturer of ophthalmic products in the multibillion-dollar drug industry.

Cosmetics/Toiletries Industry

The cosmetics/toiletries industry is one characterized by strong competition. Total industry sales for 1975 were estimated to be around $6.5 billion, with independent firms in the industry accounting for 82 percent of sales. Avon is the industry giant, with an approximately 20 percent share of the market, followed by Revlon with 13 percent, and Max Factor with 5 percent. The industry has literally hundreds of small firms in it, primarily because, based on initial capital requirements, entry is relatively easy. However, establishing a brand name and acquiring shelf space is an extremely difficult task. Cosmetics firms have to mount massive promotional campaigns to gain shelf space.

While industry sales tend to be somewhat recession-resistant, there is some indication that consumers are becoming more price conscious, while still expecting a high-quality product. The Food and Drug Administration has recently proposed a ban on the use of fluorocarbons as propellents in spray cans. Various toiletry items, such as hair sprays, deodorants, and so on, would be affected. However, the industry is making a transition to nonaerosol packaging, and the effects of the FDA ban would be minimal.

While industry sales have been growing the last few years, profit margins have been steadily declining. Certain industry figures are provided in Exhibit 2.

The industry appears to be undergoing a change. Industry leaders, such as Helena Rubinstein, Charles Revson, and Elizabeth Arden, are gone now, and many industry experts feel that the creative

[1] This case was prepared from public information. It is designed for educational purposes and not for purposes of research nor to illustrate either correct or incorrect handling of administrative practices. This case is an abbreviated version of Revlon, Inc. © 1977 by Iqbal Mathur.

marketing expertise diminished with their departure. They are being replaced by professional managers, such as Samuel Kalish at Max Factor, Michel Bergerac at Revlon, and Martin Schmidt at Lanvin-Charles of the Ritz, who are applying financial controls and budgeting to improve short- and intermediate-term profits, and are implementing long-range plans to hold or improve market share. There also has been a trend towards mergers between drug firms and cosmetics firms: Eli Lilly acquired Elizabeth Arden, Norton Simon acquired Max Factor, Helena Rubinstein was merged into Colgate-Palmolive, Squibb acquired Lanvin-Charles of the Ritz, and Coty was acquired by Chas. Pfizer.

Over the near term, industry experts feel that firms in the industry will resort to tighter inventory control, fewer varieties within a branded product line, and mass merchandising. Recent selected industry ratios are given in Exhibit 3.

Revlon, Inc.

Revlon, Inc. is the nation's second-largest cosmetics firm, with 1975 net sales of $749.8 million (see Exhibits 4 and 5 for Revlon's financial statements). In 1976 the sales are expected to be $900 million, with 1977 sales expected to be in excess of one billion dollars. Cosmetics generate 75 percent of sales, pharmaceuticals 17 percent, health services 4 percent, and proprietary drugs 4 percent.

Included in Revlon's *cosmetics* products are lipstick, eye and facial makeup, deodorants, hair and skin care products, perfumes and colognes, manicure products, and wigs. Revlon markets these products under such well-advertised brand names as Revlon, Ultima II, Charlie, Moondrops, Replique, Princess Marcella Borghese and Norell. Its toiletry items for men include the brand names: Bragg, Royal Pub, Principe and Monsieur Balmain. Revlon also sells shampoos, hair relaxers and other hair care products to beauty salons. Revlon's pharmaceutical products include antihypertensives and psychotherapeutic preparations. Its *health services* division operates a dozen clinical-testing laboratories. Revlon's *proprietary* (non-prescription) preparations include Mitchum, skin-toning cream, asthma-relief drugs, and antipsoriasis soaps.

In the last few years, Revlon has acquired a number of firms. In 1965, it acquired the assets of Amerline Corporation. Four years later, the Amerline assets were sold to Centron Corporation. In 1965, Revlon divested itself of its 27.5 percent ownership of Schick Electric, Inc. In 1966, Revlon acquired the U. S. Vitamin and

Pharmaceutical Corporation.   In 1967, Revlon acquired Nysco Laboratories, Inc., and Laboratories Grossman S.A., among others. In 1968, it acquired the Standard Beauty Supply Co., Inc. In 1970, Revlon acquired the Mitchum Company and Alford Industries. With the arrival of Michel Bergerac in 1974, the merger pace picked up, with Revlon acquiring six firms, including ICN Pharmaceutical's German subsidiary, and Coburn Optical Industries, a manufacturer of optical equipment and supplies.

A ten-year summary of Revlon's sales, earnings and dividends is given in Exhibit 6.

Drug Industry

Barnes-Hind Pharmaceuticals is a manufacturer in the multi-billion-dollar drug industry.   Selected statistics for the industry are shown in Exhibit 7.   The total United States expenditure on health care has been averaging 8 percent of the gross national product, or about $130 billion in 1976.   Of this amount, approximately 9 percent is spent on proprietary (nonprescription) and ethical (prescription) drugs.   The industry is characterized by high expenditures on research and development of new chemical compounds—it has been estimated that drug firms spend 5.5 percent of sales on R&D. Indications are that R&D activities are becoming increasingly productive.   This partially accounts for the high-profit margins enjoyed in the industry.   Approximately 40 percent of the sales are in foreign markets, which has certain implications for the industry; first, the regulatory environment in Europe is becoming more intensified; second, currency exchange losses do not appear to show any signs of abatement.

The drug regulatory environment appears to be becoming more stringent in the United States.   In late 1976, the Food and Drug Administration appeared ready to remove Syntex's new anti-inflammatory drug from the market, due to questions regarding the test data submitted by Syntex.   All of this means increased costs for the industry.   Analysts feel that margins will be maintained by raising prices.

New Financial Accounting Standards Board regulations may result in industry usage of replacement cost accounting.   However, this accounting procedure is expected to have a negligible impact on profits.   Selected ratios for the industry are shown in Exhibit 3.

Barnes-Hind Pharmaceuticals

Barnes-Hind is a small manufacturer of ophthalmic products, with fiscal 1976 sales of $22.89 million (see Exhibits 8 and 9 for financial statements).   Its product line includes therapeutic and diagnostic ophthalmic drugs, accessory items for contact-lens wearers. and radiological and dermatological products. Ophthalmic products accounted for 85 percent of sales. Products are sold to wholesalers, jobbers, hospitals, and retail drug and optical outlets. A summary of sales, earnings, and price range is given in Exhibit 10. The firm has never paid a dividend since it went public in September, 1965.

Recent Events

On March 19, 1976, it was announced that Cooper Laboratories, a drug manufacturer, increased its holdings in Barnes-Hind common from 9 percent to 25 percent. On April 29, 1976, it was announced that Barnes-Hind was going to be merged into Syntex Corporation, a drug manufacturer. On May 10, 1976, it was announced that an American unit of Syntex Corporation had purchased 30,000 shares or 3.7 percent of total outstanding of Barnes-Hind common and was contemplating additional open market purchases. By May 12, 1976, Cooper Laboratories had increased its holdings in Barnes-Hind to 27 percent, and the Syntex unit owned 56,200 shares of 6.9 percent. By May 26, 1976, Cooper Laboratories had increased its Barnes-Hind holdings to 29 percent. Also, on this day, Barnes-Hind filed a suit in Federal Court in San Francisco against Cooper Laboratories, seeking a temporary restraining order barring additional Barnes-Hind common purchases by Cooper.

On June 14, 1976, it was announced that an agreement in principal had been reached, whereby Revlon would acquire Barnes-Hind for common stock. The exchange ratio was 0.7333 common of Revlon for each share of Barnes-Hind. This agreement followed the termination, by mutual consent, of a previously-announced merger between Barnes-Hind and Syntex. Cooper, which by June 14, 1976, owned 35 percent of Barnes-Hind stock, agreed to vote its shares for the Revlon merger. Barnes-Hind agreed to dismiss its law suit against Cooper. H. H. Hind, owner of 24.8 percent of Barnes-Hind shares, also agreed to vote for the merger. On August 12, 1976, a definitive agreement on the merger was signed between Revlon and Barnes-Hind. The Barnes-Hind price of common was $46.500

on Friday, June 11, and $52.250 on June 14, 1976. Revlon's closing price on June 11 was $77.50. Monthly prices for Revlon and Barnes-Hind for 1976 are given in Exhibit 11.

EXHIBIT 1

Revlon, Inc.

Major Independent Firms in the Cosmetics Industry

Name	1975 sales in millions	Cost of goods sold (% of sales)	Selling, etc. (% of sales)	Profit Margins %	Return on Equity %
Avon Products	$1,295	35.2	42.3	10.7	27.9
Revlon, Inc.	753	35.4	46.1	8.3	18.2
Cheesebrough	675	48.2	36.1	7.1	18.0
Faberge	181	55.1	38.4	1.8	2.9
Helene Curtis	106	53.8	40.2	2.1	10.8

EXHIBIT 2

Revlon, Inc.

Selected Statistics for the Cosmetics Industry *

	1972	1973	1974	1975
Sales [†]	$3,636	$4,241	$4,788	$5,300
Net income [†]	347	392	386	411
Net cash flow [†]	409	465	474	509
LTD [†]	366	344	407	490
Net worth [†]	1,640	1,906	2,100	2,330
P/E ratio	39	35	17	16
Dividend yield %	1.3	1.3	3.1	3. 2

* Figures include data from public firms, only.

[†] In millions of dollars.

EXHIBIT 3

Revlon, Inc.

Selected Ratios in Cosmetics and Drug Industries*

	Current	Acid	Profit Margin	Profits/ TA	TD/TA	Cost GS/ Inventory	Collection Period	Sales/ TA
Cosmetics	2.9	1.0	7.7%	10.3%	42%	2.0	53	1.32
Drugs	1.8	0.8	11.6%	10.7%	40%	2.5	58	0.91

*These ratios are compiled from data from a financial data tape. To achieve better comparability, certain companies have been added or deleted from the original SIC industries.

EXHIBIT 4

Revlon, Inc.

Income Statements for Revlon for Years Ending December 31, 1974, 1975

(in thousands of dollars)

	1975	1974*
Net Sales	$749,773	$635,263
Other operating revenues	3,408	3,297
Net sales & other o.r.	753,181	638,560
Cost & expenses	614,338	525,254
Operating income	138,843	114,308
Other income	10,628	9,294
Total income	149,471	123,600
Depreciation	11,468	10,548
Other deductions	1,897	132
Interest expense	17,933	13,972
Taxable income	118,173	98,948
Taxes	55,551	44,943
Net income [†]	62,622	54,005
Common dividends	17,942	15,504
Dividends of pooled companies	778	1,231
Retained earnings	$ 43,902	$ 37,270

*Restated to reflect 1975 acquisitions.

[†]Average common and common equivalent: 14,152,000 in 1974; 14,388,000 in 1975.

EXHIBIT 5

Revlon, Inc.

Balance Sheets for Revlon, December 31, 1974, 1975

(in thousands of dollars)

Assets	*1975*	*1974*
Cash	$ 18,263	$ 17,154
Marketable securities	222,812	91,159
Receivables	157,286	156,242
Inventories	162,901	177,519
Prepayments	18,080	14,315
Total current assets	579,342	456,388
Net plant	97,052	91,868
Goodwill	36,926	24,821
Patents	19,972	21,556
Deferred charges	7,614	7,789
Other assets	11,536	9,897
Total assets	$752,442	$612,319
Liabilities and equity		
Notes payable	$ 36,500	$ 60,653
Current LTD	7,755	9,907
Accounts payable	37,529	38,328
Accruals	62,451	47,615
Income taxes	25,091	21,990
Dividend payable	4,979	3,980
Total current liabilities	174,305	182,473
Long-term debt	193,587	96,910
Deferred income tax	4,700	4,893
Total liabilities	372,592	284,276
Common stock. p. $1	14,369	14,244
Treasury stock*	d2,611	d2,611
Paid-in surplus	77,062	69,282
Retained earnings	291,030	247,128
Total liabilities & worth	$752,442	$612,319

*69,329 shares.

EXHIBIT 6

Revlon, Inc.

Revlon's Sales, Net Income, Dividends, Price Range 1966–1975

	Sales*	Net Income†	Dividends†	Price Range‡
1966	$268,291	$1.88	$0.87	$22–36
1967	283,868	2.05	0.87	30–57
1968	316,512	1.99	0.93	46–61
1969	317,552	2.11	0.93	50–72
1970	373,509	2.21	1.00	46–74
1971	394,053	2.66	1.00	54–80
1972	440,999	2.88	1.00	67–78
1973	508,908	3.30	1.08	56–75
1974	638,560	3.82	1.14	38–61
1975	749,773	4.35	1.25	47–81

*Net sales and other operating revenues are included here. In thousands of dollars.

†On a per-share basis. Adjusted for November, 1969, 3-for-2 split.

‡Low-high range rounded to nearest dollar. Adjusted for November, 1969, 3-for-2 split.

EXHIBIT 7

Revlon, Inc.

Selected Statistics for the Drug Industry*

	1972	1973	1974	1975
Sales†	$6,010	$6,850	$8,040	$8,875
Net income†	715	855	962	1,037
Net cash flow†	880	1,038	1,170	1,275
LTD†	545	545	820	1,380
Net worth†	3,820	4,375	4,995	5,820
P/E ratio	31	32	23	20
Dividend yield %	1.4	1.2	1.8	2.0

* Figures include data from public firms only.

†In millions of dollars.

EXHIBIT 8

Revlon, Inc.

Income Statements for Barnes-Hind for Years Ending June 30, 1975, 1976

(in thousands of dollars)

	1976	1975*
Net sales	$22,890	$18,436
Cost of sales		5,058
Selling, gen. & admin.		9,599
Deprec. & amort.		316
Interest, net		72
Taxable income		3,391
Income tax		1,410
Net income†	$ 2,791	$ 1,981

*On a *proforma* basis. Loss from discontinued operations, equalling $948,000, is excluded.

†Average common and common equivalent: 788,748 in 1975; 819,474 in 1976. Net income per share in 1975 from continuing operations was $2.51; from discontinued operations, $d1.20.

EXHIBIT 9

Revlon, Inc.

Balance Sheet for Barnes-Hind, June 30, 1975

(in thousands of dollars)

Assets	1975
Cash and equivalent	$ 3,059
Receivables	3,496
Inventories	3,452
Prepayments	139
Total current assets	10,146
Plant	3,467
Other Assets	312
Note receivable	175
Total assets	$14,100
Liabilities & equity	
Notes payable	$ 150
Current LTD	780

EXHIBIT 9 (Cont'd)

Accounts payalbe	732
Accruals	909
Income taxes	79
Deferred income taxes	46
Total current liabilities	2,696
Long-term debt	930
Common stock no par	859
Treasury stock	d57
Pain-in surplus	269
Retained earnings	9,403
Total liabilities & worth	$14,100

EXHIBIT 10

Revlon, Inc.

Barnes-Hind's Sales, Net Income, Price Range 1966–1976

	Sales*	Net Income ‡	Price Range**
1966	$ 5,668	$1.03	$16–36
1967	6,769	1.28	22–53
1968	7,557	1.44	35–54
1969	7,856	1.05	22–47
1970	14,343	2.10	29–51
1971	11,306 †	1.93 †	29–49
1972	12,622 †	2.04 †	33–67
1973	14,524 †	2.03 †	14–46
1974	16,218 †	2.33 †	7–19
1975	18,436 †	2.51 †	10–33
1976	22,890 †	3.41 †	–

* In thousands of dollars for fiscal year ending June 30.

† Restated to reflect discontinued operations. Reported EPS were: 1975, $1.31; 1974, $1.94; 1973, ($0.10); 1972, $1.47; 1971, $2.13.

‡ On a per-share basis for fiscal year ending June 30.

** Low-high range, rounded off to nearest dollar.

EXHIBIT 11

Revlon, Inc.

1976 Monthly Prices for Revlon and Barnes-Hind [*]

	January	February	March	April	May
Revlon	75–80	72–79	70–75	73–78	74–77
Barnes-Hind [†]	29–38	33–39	33–38	35–42	39–49

	June	July	August	September
Revlon	75–85	83–88	85–87	85–90
Barnes-Hind [†]	45–55	55–58	57–60	60–63

[*] Low-high range, rounded off to nearest dollar.

[†] Bid price.

Questions

1. Calculate the appropriate ratios for Revlon and Barnes-Hind. Discuss their performance, relative to the respective industries.

2. What may be the impact of the acquisition on Revlon's earnings per share, leverage, and growth? To answer the first two parts of this question, you may pool the financial data for 1975 provided for each company. Assume that the Revlon common share price was $80.00 at the time the merger was announced.

3. Evaluate the advantages and disadvantages of the acquisition for both firms.

4. If you were negotiating this merger for Revlon, would you consider the 0.7333 exchange ratio to be adequate or too high? That is, from your viewpoint, which would have been an appropriate exchange ratio, and how would you have determined that ratio?

Case 39

DYNAMICS CORPORATION OF AMERICA[1]

REORGANIZATION

Andrew Lozyniak is the kind of man who abhors debt, pays his bills on time, never borrows money, and even refuses to keep charge accounts. Early in his business career he wangled a transfer back to Connecticut because he disapproved of the way of life he saw in California's San Fernando Valley. Almost everyone he knew there seemed to be in hock for their ranch houses, sports cars, and furniture. And Lozyniak didn't want to rear his children in an environment where people lived beyond their means. When he moved into his present home in Westport, the living room remained bare for a year and a half until he had saved enough cash to buy furniture.

Lozyniak is a self-made man whose career was propelled by hard work. He had climbed to the office of president and chief executive of Dynamics Corp. of America, a manufacturing mini-conglomerate that ranked No. 746 on the FORTUNE Second 500. Then the roof fell in. On Friday, July 28, 1972, five banks seized all the cash Dynamics had on deposit in their vaults, in order to satisfy loans due that day, forcing the company to petition five days later for permission to reorganize under Chapter Eleven of the federal Bankruptcy Act.

It was just about the worst moment of Lozyniak's life. He knew, or soon discovered, that the odds against actually bringing off a bankruptcy reorganization are discouraging. Dynamics was among 17,490 companies that filed bankruptcy petitions of one kind or another during that fiscal year. The figure increased to 20,747 during fiscal 1974, and this year, if the bankruptcy pace of the first eight months continues, the number will rise by nearly 50 percent, to 30,600. More than nine out of ten companies that go broke simply give up, liquidate their remaining assets, and divide the proceeds among the creditors. Of those that try to fight their way back to normal operations via Chapter Eleven, only one of four succeeds.

Today, Dynamics is among the fortunate survivors. On November 27, 1974, a federal district court in Manhattan approved the

[1] The text of this case appeared as an article in *Fortune* (Eleanor J. Tracy, "Life in the Toils of the Bankruptcy Act" *Fortune*, July, 1975, pp. 142–148) and is used with permission of Time Inc.

reorganization plan, signaling the end of Lozyniak's twenty-eight-month battle with creditors, lawyers, accountants, suppliers, customers, and management consultants. The provisions of Chapter Eleven virtually guarantee wrangling. Only the company can propose a reorganization plan. But creditors have an effective veto power. During the proceedings the company suspends payment of interest on its debts; it also can break contracts, and it cannot be sued without seeking the court's permission.

But the creditors may ask the court to switch the case to the far more stringent provisions of Chapter Ten, under which the court names a trustee to take control of the company's affairs and future. If a company goes broke owing more than $3 million, the Securities and Exchange Commission by law must be consulted, further diffusing the power of the company's management.

When he chose to proceed under Chapter Eleven, Lozyniak had no inkling of how costly, time consuming, and acrimonious the struggle would be. The bills for lawyers, accountants, consultants, and court fees eventually exceeded $3 million. Forced to cope with all his adversaries simultaneously and still run his troubled enterprise, Lozyniak worked fifteen hours a day practically seven days a week; he scarcely saw his family at all. And his father, whom he revered, was slowing dying of emphysema.

An ironic name change

It was characteristic of Lozyniak to have picked the hard way to try to lead his company out of its predicament. The son of Ukrainian immigrants, he not only worked his way through the University of Connecticut but, saving every penny he could, had accumulated a small bank balance by the time he was graduated in 1955 with a bachelor-of-science degree in agriculture and economics. He joined Dynamics Corp. in 1961 after five years with a small Connecticut manufacturer of aircraft equipment. He signed on as sales manager for Dynamics' Fermont division, which made generators for gasoline and diesel engines, figuring that it was a big chance for him to advance with a growing company. And so it was, though hardly for the reasons he envisioned.

The company had been incorporated in 1924 as Claude Neon Lights to license the patents of the French inventor. During the Forties it acquired what is still its best-known product, the Waring blender. It moved into electronics and won some lucrative government contracts. Soon the company was producing radar gear, gyroscopes, and guided-missile controls, and it built the first commercial analog computer. Accordingly, Neon changed its name to Dynamics Corp. of America in 1955. Former Chairman Raymond F. Kelley, now seventy-nine, furnishes a sardonic explanation for the change: "We figured we were a dynamic company."

For a while, the dynamo spun smoothly, and Kelley led the company into the big time during his twelve-year tenure as chief executive. Following the fashion of the times, the company embarked on an ambitious acquisition program in the Sixties, picking up fifteen other companies. Dynamics spread out into air-conditioning systems, heat-dissipating devices, farm equipment, and textile machinery. Its stock was listed on the New York Stock Exchange. The company even ventured abroad, setting up an English electronics subsidiary, Dynamco.

But as an empire builder, Dynamics was not very discriminating. Some of its acquisitions proved to be high-priced lemons, and the company had trouble managing its new diversity. By 1969, the year Dynamics' sales reached a record $148 million, its profits had begun to slip. In fact, much of the company's $5.8-million reported pretax earnings that year were illusory. The company included in its profits some $2.2 million of "unbilled estimated earnings" on government business. Those profits never materialized. When the Department of Defense cut back on military procurement, Dynamics had to keep rolling over bank loans to stay afloat.

"The outstanding man"

One division that remained conspicuously profitable was Fermont, the generator division headed by Lozyniak. But he began to get complaints from his suppliers that they weren't being paid. Sensing serious trouble, Lozyniak moved to protect his own operation. The company had just established a central paying office at its Manhattan headquarters. "I'd go in with checks from our customers in my hand," he said, "and I'd agree to split with headquarters if they'd let me keep half to pay my bills myself."

He rarely saw "Mr. Kelley" on those visits, so he was surprised when the boss summoned him one day in May, 1970, and promoted him to group vice president, in charge of half the company's divisions. Lozyniak was even more astonished in August when, without forewarning, he heard Kelley tell the board of directors: I'm making Andy executive vice president."

After the meeting, Lozyniak asked Kelley, "What shall I do?" Kelley replied, "Collect more receivables"—and Lozyniak did. On September 24, Kelley, then seventy-four, retired to Palm Beach and his yacht *Eden,* bequeathing the presidency to Lozyniak. "Andy was the outstanding man among all our people," Kelley explained recently. "He ran his division well. He was young. He had a lot of spark and vitality and good common sense."

Kelley had wanted to retire for some years, but when he did, he left a floundering enterprise—and no suggestions to his successor about how to run it. For years a consortium of banks headed by Marine Midland had allowed Kelley to borrow large sums for Dynamics' acquisitions. But after the stock market turned down, foreclosing on Kelley's hope of floating more common stock to repay some of those loans, Marine Midland had begun putting pressure on Kelley to reduce his company's huge debt, then $64 million. In July the bankers had joined in imposing a common thirty-day maturity date. (After that, the company had to persuade the banks to extend the loans once a month.)

Well aware that the company was in precarious financial condition, the new chief executive moved immediately to tackle the problems created by those illusory profits After reviewing all the government contracts, he wrote down assets by $6 million, accounting for most of the company's $9.9-million deficit in 1970. It was Dynamics' first report loss in twenty-nine years.

More write-offs led to a $6.3-million loss in 1971. But Lozyniak was beginning, he says, to turn the company around. By mid-1972, he had managed to pay off $9 million in bank loans and $1 million in long-term debt to insurance companies. For the first time in ten years, according to Lozyniak, the company enjoyed two consecutive quarters of positive cash flow.

Oddly enough, though, Lozyniak's moves may have aggravated Dynamics' difficulties. Worried over the company's two years of losses and its remaining burden of debt, executives at Marine Midland shifted the company's account from the uptown Park Avenue branch to the Wall Street area office and put a new man, Senior Vice President H. Everett Smith, in charge. Smith, now sixty-six, headed the loan-workout section (the bank's euphemism for the bum-loan department).

The blow fell at 10:29 on the morning of that July 28, when Smith "offset" the loan, applying the company's entire commercial account against its debt. Dynamics' other bankers, Chase Manhattan,

First Pennsylvania of Philadelphia, Northeastern of Scranton, and United Bank & Trust of Hartford, followed the leader.   Chase, however, honored the executive payroll before Seizing Dynamics' deposits.   So the company's headquarters staff, at least, got paid that day.

No money for groceries

Still bitter about the episode, Lozyniak insists that "Midland pulled the rug out from under us" without warning. The first word of disaster reached him at 11:00 A.M., when an executive at Waring phoned to report that its payroll checks were bouncing. ("Some people had no money to buy their groceries that weekend," Lozyniak recalls.)   At first, he was incredulous.   It all must be a mistake. In the twenty-three years that Dynamics had done business with Marine Midland, the company had never missed an interest payment. Perhaps somebody at corporate had blundered, forgetting to authorize the Waring payroll.

Unable to reach Smith by telephone, Lozyniak took a taxi to the banker's office.   He tried pleading, then he offered his resignation if Smith would rescind the offset.   Finally, struggling to control his rage, Lozyniak fumed at Smith: "What the hell do you think you're doing?   Midland has been our banker for years.   You're our transfer agent.   You're in charge of our pension fund."

Smith was adamant—and he argues today that his action should have come as no surprise.   He retired to Fort Lauderdale last March and joined a local bank as a senior vice president, but he still gets worked up when talking about Dynamics and Lozyniak.   He insists he warned Lozyniak that Marine Midland would not roll over the note again.   "I called him on the telephone," says Smith, "and told him.   No way.   I wrote him a letter.   No way.   I sent him a wire. No way."   Lozyniak denies that he received a telephone call, a letter, or a wire.

At last convinced that he could not renew the note. Lozyniak headed for Cravath, Swaine & Moore, the company's lawyers, where he advised the New York Stock Exchange to halt trading in the company's stock.   He spent the rest of the day boning up on bankruptcy proceedings and taking emergency steps to raise funds. He needed at least $1 million to meet the payroll and cover checks already in the mail.   He phoned all his division presidents and ordered them to ask customers who had sent checks directly to Dynamics' "lockbox" at Marine Midland to cancel them, write new ones, and send them directly to Dynamics. Shaken and exhausted, Lozyniak finally headed for Westport. "It was the first time in my married life that I didn't want to go home," he says.

The champagne tasted flat

Lozyniak was angry, bewildered, and bitter. He had worked hard, sacrificed his family life, and now he felt he had been publicly humiliated. He was also two hours late for his forty-first birthday party. One of his wife's sisters was flying in from Europe. Another would be there, some neighbors too, and all five Lozyniak children were to stay up late for the festivities.

Trying to keep up a front for the family, he drank some of the champagne his wife, Florence, had ordered, but it tasted flat. He blew out the candles on his birthday cake with the first breath but he didn't make a wish. He believes a man gets what he wants by working hard. When Lozyniak is troubled, he is quiet. His mood was contagious, and the birthday guests remained solemn. Frequently he left the party to answer incessant phone calls from worried stockholders. Then he turned to the voluminous paperwork required for bankruptcy petitions.

The creditors set up a fifteen-member committee that included representatives of banks, insurance companies, and suppliers—and acted in behalf of 5,000 others. Right from the start of the proceedings, Lozyniak and the committee were at loggerheads because their objectives conflicted. Lozyniak was determined to preserve assets so the company would have a base for future growth. "My job was to protect the stockholders, to keep the company from going down the drain," he says. The chairman of the creditors' committee, Alex Ardrey, a vice president of Chase Manhattan, felt that his job was "to maximize recovery for all the creditors."

The Princeton banker and the immigrant's son never were able to establish a rapport that might have helped smooth the bumpy road. The creditors demanded 90 percent of Dynamics' stock. Their idea was to unload unprofitable divisions, get the company in the black, and sell stock to satisfy a large part of their claims. With that kind of arrangement, Lozyniak—and the shareholders—would be out in the cold. Lozyniak flatly refused. When the committee came down to 75 percent, he still wouldn't budge, even though Ardrey threatened to push the company into Chapter Ten proceedings or liquidation.

Playing for survival

In fact, the threats contained more rhetoric than substance. Lozyniak was convinced that the creditors would get only about 15 cents on the dollar from a forced sale of assets, and a Chapter Ten proceeding would be more costly and time consuming than one under Chapter Eleven. Marine Midland's Smith explained recently: "In Chapter Ten the trustee is a political hack who spends six months trying to find his way to the men's room. And the expenses are horrendous." Besides, a number of the company's major suppliers had told the committee they would refuse to ship their products to the company if the creditors forced it into Chapter Ten. If the manufacturing divisions had to suspend production, the company would obviously be worth less than ever.

From the beginning, Lozyniak struggled to arrange a cash settlement, which would get the creditors off his back and give him a chance to turn Dynamics around. He had no idea where he could get the money—certainly not from the creditor banks—but he thought he could find funds somehow. So he played for time and survival.

Lozyniak also faced threats to his own survival as Dynamics' boss. The first came when the committee suggested hiring Worden & Risberg, a Philadelphia management-consultant firm, to help in the reorganization. Lozyniak regarded this as a move to get rid of him. He saw no need for management consultants, and particularly not one picked by the committee. He concedes now that it might have been naive to expect the committee to give him carte blanche, but at the time he was too deeply hurt to be conciliatory. He felt that the committee was bullying him, treating him as if he were an upstart and a failure when it should have respected his own efforts to straighten out a mess that originated under the previous management. In the company's straitened circumstances, he especially resented spending money for advice when he was convinced he already *knew* what had to be done.

The committee, to judge from the comments of some of its members, considered Lozyniak stubborn and abrasive. After much bickering, both parties settled on the Manhattan consulting firm of A. T. Kearney, Inc. Kearney cost Dynamics $221,000. "I hated spending that money," says Lozyniak.

At the outset, the committee insisted on bringing in the accounting firm of S. D. Leidesdorf to be sure the books were in order. The committee's subsequent meetings were held in one of the Leidesdorf offices, every two or three weeks. They were a source of irritation and frustration to Lozyniak. He never knew when he would be called in to answer questions, or what the questions would be, and he often spent hours waiting in an anteroom for a chance to appear. A couple of times he was even summarily dismissed when the committee broke for lunch.

Still, he felt he had to be there because "nobody protects your interests like you do yourself, and that goes for your own high-priced lawyers too." The size of the legal bills for the Chapter Eleven proceedings pained him. Dynamics paid its own special bankruptcy counsel $450,000 (for 2,973 hours of work at $151 per hour). In addition, the company had to pay the creditors' committee lawyers $200,000. But what galled Lozyniak most of all was that his company had to pick up a tab of $4,695 for those lunches, labeled an "administrative expense."

The long days and nights took their toll. Lozyniak ate a lot; he always does when he's frustrated. He did lose twenty-five pounds to win a $200 bet with a friend, but gained it back promptly. When his wife insisted that he needed a vacation, the family spent a week together on the island of Jamaica. After three days of enforced leisure, Lozyniak could stand no more. Thereafter he spent more time on the telephone than on the beach. Except for his annual attack of flu, however, Lozyniak remained in surprisingly good shape. Perhaps the tennis he took up—"because it's fast"—was a help.

"They want you to sell your winners"

One of Lozyniak's biggest fights with the creditors' committee was over how to shrink his company enough to make it profitable. "They always want you to sell your winners," he complains. "That's a mistake. The winners are the ones that can support the new debt you need to carry you." The committee constantly nagged him about his progress. At one point it suggested that he sell Waring, the company's largest division, which accounted for more than half of its revenues. Though Waring was losing money, Lozyniak refused to sell it because he needed its cash flow, and besides, he was certain he could turn it around.

Lozyniak became the company's busiest traveling salesman; his territory was the whole country and his bag of wares those money-losing divisions. He was quite willing to part with past glory and glamor—for example, the once profitable Electronic Systems Division, at that stage losing $7 million a year. Unable to find a buyer, he wrote down its assets from $28 million to $6 million. Finally, Lozyniak sold the division to Frederick Pro, a Palm Beach manufacturer of antique-auto replicas, who bargained the price down from $16 million to $8.3 million.

When he couldn't sell losers, Lozyniak closed them and auctioned off their assets. By the end of 1973, he had reduced the number of divisions from twenty to seven, cutting the company's work force from 5,500 to 2,600. At that point, he figured the company could afford the interest charges on some $15 million of debt. The big problem was to find the money. What bank would be willing to lend to a company in Chapter Eleven? Fortunately, at this time Lozyniak found his David.

Morton David, thirty-eight, a self-assured and urbane financial expert, had made his first million when he was thirty-two—and lost a lot of it by the time he was thirty-six. He had once been counsel to deal maker Martin Ackerman before the latter's brief fling with the *Saturday Evening Post*, but now he was running a struggling company that operated a chain of sperm banks. So David was looking for another opportunity when an acquaintance piqued his curiosity with a tale of a man with "a massive financial problem." A four-hour talk with Lozyniak just before Thanksgiving in 1973 convinced David that the tale was no exaggeration. After ten days of looking over Dynamics' receivables—"They were quality receivables, and that's the key to refinancing," says David—he joined the company as financial vice president.

A high price for favor

Curiously enough, it was the recession that finally came to the rescue of Dynamics Corp. The creditors worried with each falling economic indicator, and the stock market's plunge particularly jarred them. "The committee started to see the pitfalls of owning equity in this company in the bottom of a recession," says Ardrey. "So many problems were developing that we figured a lot of creditors could ill afford to be speculating in the stock of a company that had been sick. We decided to take what cash we could get and run."

After talking to a dozen banks, Lozyniak, with David's help, finally found one bold enough to lend them the money. But Chemical Bank exacted an interesting price for its favor. The loan had to be cross-collateralized by all fixed assets and all receivables, and the interest rate was a stiff 4½ percent over prime. Chemical insisted that other lenders advance $7 million of the total $17-million loan

($15 million to pay off creditors; $2 million for working capital). Usually the lead bank lines up participants, but Lozyniak and David were in no position to be finicky. Once again they made the rounds, pleading the company's case. In February, Hartford National consented to come in for $2 million. In mid-March, Manufacturers Hanover Commercial Corp. signed up for $5 million.

At last Ardrey and his group agreed to Lozyniak's proposal to pay the creditors off in cash, but soon they were haggling over the amount. The committee wanted 50 cents on the dollar, or a total cash package of $25 million. Lozyniak knew he couldn't afford that. At one point he offered to go as high as 37.8 cents on the dollar, spread out over six years, for a total face value of $19.5 million.

On May 15, 1974—twenty-one months after the first meeting—Ardrey and Lozyniak came to terms. In satisfaction of Dynamics' $51.5-million debt, the creditors accepted a cash payment of $15 million or 28½ cents on the dollar, whichever turned out to be larger, and two new shares of stock (one voting and one nonvoting) for every $100 in claims. That gives the creditors about 15 percent of the outstanding shares.

Even after both shareholders and a majority of the creditors approved the arrangement, Lozyniak almost didn't make it out of Chapter Eleven last year. The night before a court hearing to confirm the plan, he was still wrestling with last-minute difficulties. Band leader Fred Waring, who had financed the company that first distributed the blender, had sued Dynamics during the Chapter Eleven proceedings to regain his trademark. It wasn't until 7:00 P.M. on November 26 that Waring's attorneys agreed on terms for the sale of the trademark to Dynamics. At 3:30 A.M. on November 27, Lozyniak began dickering by telephone to get a long-delayed ratification from the British liquidators of Dynamco. At 8:30 A.M. the necessary telegram of approval arrived from London.

At 10:05 David appeared at New York's federal court in Foley Square with a check from Chemical Bank. Dynamics' lawyers and the creditors' lawyers huddled over papers in the corridor before the judge called the court to order at 10:15. At 12:10 on November 27, 1974, Dynamics emerged from Chapter Eleven. The long ordeal was over for Lozyniak. He had beaten the odds, and Dynamics had survived. In May, Lozyniak announced that Dynamics earned nearly $1 million on $24 million in sales during the first quarter of this year.

"They picked a lot of pockets"

The stigma of bankruptcy lingers. Interest rates remain high, and there is a residue of ill will. The controller of one of Dynamics' big suppliers noted recently: "The company *should* be doing well. They picked a lot of pockets; they've got a lot of our money." Clearly, Lozyniak still has much to do. He hopes to reduce the debt, pare down interest payments, and buy in some of the company's common stock, which he considers to be bargain priced at its recent level of $3.

With some justification, Lozyniak considers himself a professional guide to the intricacies of corporate bankruptcy. Last February when Bowmar Instrument Corp. filed for a bankruptcy reorganization under Chapter Eleven, Lozyniak found himself on the other side of the table. He went to the first meeting of the creditors and volunteered to serve on the committee. Lozyniak has even offered Edward White, Bowmar's former chairman and largest stockholder, a few words of advice: "You've got to go to those creditors' meetings."

EXHIBIT 1

Dynamics Corporation of America

Balance Sheets, December 31, 1968 to December 31, 1971

(rounded thousands of dollars)

	12/31/68	12/31/69	12/31/70	12/31/71
Total cash	$ 3,462	$ 3,729	$ 2,940	$ 1,762
Accounts receivable	43,408	45,974	37,067	27,090
Tax claims	0	1,162	9,302	2,035
Inventories	23,309	30,382	29,835	20,438
Prepaid expenses	1,072	724	1,760	2,011
Other current assets *	0	0	0	10,397
Total current assets	71,252	81,970	80,904	63,734
Net property, plant, and equipment	11,973	11,777	11,982	9,402
Claims receivable	2,002	1,112	1,424	3,886
Excess acquisition cost	2,591	2,591	1,880	1,596
Patents	988	803	662	452
Deferred cost	0	0	1,438	0
Deferred charges	1,649	2,594	2,348	868
Total assets	$ 90,454	$100,846	$100,638	$ 79,938

EXHIBIT 1 (Cont'd)

Notes payable	$ 17,435	$ 21,200	$ 29,365	$ 21,299
Accounts payable	11,546	11,908	15,284	11,197
Accruals	3,473	3,644	4,215	2,829
Federal income taxes	2,220	854	206	0
Deferred federal income taxes	2,309	3,300	2,647	0
Other current liabilities	0	0	0	4,525
Total current liabilities	36,984	40,906	51,717	39,849
Long-term debt	15,234	21,409	20,545	19,000
Deferred income tax	1,381	1,387	2,165	1,201
Common stock	4,954	4,960	4,960	4,960
Capital surplus	6,132	6,077	6,077	6,079
Retained earnings	25,770	26,108	15,173	8,849
Total owners' equity	36,856	37,145	26,210	19,888
Total liabilities and owners' equity	$ 90,454	$100,846	$100,638	$ 79,938

*Businesses held for sale.

EXHIBIT 2

Dynamics Corporation of America

Income Statements, for Years Ending December 31, 1968 to December 31, 1971

(rounded thousands of dollars)

	12/31/68	*12/31/69*	*12/31/70*	*12/31/71*
Net sales	$127,917	$147,922	$ 89,658	$ 71,577
Cost of sales	92,856	116,111	75,875	52,972
Gross margin on sales	35,061	31,811	13,783	18,605
Selling, etc., expenses	21,532	23,139	18,729	16,649
Operating profit (loss)	13,530	8,672	(4,946)	1,955
Other income	686	660	485	737
Total income	14,216	9,332	(4,461)	2,693
Interest	1,792	3,075	2,816	2,162
Unamortized costs	0	0	639	0
Loss constr. claims	0	0	4,140	0
Other deductions	321	434	110	111
Income taxes	6,728	3,526	(6,038)	186
Loss disc. operations	0	0	3,104	5,241
Extraordinary charges	0	0	710	1,317
Net profit (loss)	$ 5,376	$ 2,297	$ (9,943)	$ (6,324)

Questions

1. Calculate the following ratios for Dynamics Corporation of America for the years ending December 31, 1968, December 31, 1969, and December 31, 1970. What do they indicate about the general health of the firm?

   (1.) Current ratio

   (2.) Quick ratio (use only cash and accounts receivable)

   (3.) Total debt to total assets

   (4.) Gross margin as a percent of sales

   (5.) Operating profit as a percent of sales

2. The balance sheet of a firm is sometimes taken to represent its value as a going concern. Its value in liquidation is very different. In estimating liquidation value, a common method is to multiply balance sheet values by some estimated recovery percent. A possible formulation is

Assets	Estimated Percent of Book Value in Liquidation
Cash	100%
Marketable securities	Current Market Value
Inventory	70%
Accounts receivable	70%
Prepaid expenses	70%
Other current assets	70%
All physical assets	50%
All intangible or questionable assets	0%

   Using this formulation and the December 31, 1971 balance sheet, was Mr. Lozyniak's estimate of a 15 percent recovery for creditors in liquidation reasonably accurate? Use your best judgment as to what assets are "questionable". Does the formulation provide a reasonable approximation of liquidation value for Dynamics Corporation's assets? What adjustments might you make, and how might they effect the estimated recovery percent?

3. One of the assumptions of the Modigliani and Miller theory of capital structure and cost of capital is that of perfect markets. Included in this is the assumption that bankruptcy costs are zero. What insights does Mr. Lozyniak's experience and the formulation present in Question 2 lend to this assumption?

4. Why were Mr. Lozyniak and the creditors' committee at odds? Was Mr Lozyniak's view in keeping with the goals of financial management?

5. It is sometimes said that to own something implies control of that something. We often say that the owners of a firm are the stockholders. Do the owners' representatives control the firm in a "Chapter 11" proceeding? In "Chapter 10"? What input should this possible situation have on everyday management decisions?

Case 40

W. T. GRANT COMPANY [1]

LIQUIDATION

W. T. Grant opened its first store in 1906 in Lynn, Mass. The company expanded over its 70-year history, and as of January 30, 1975 [2], based on sales volume, the firm could have been termed one of the major retail corporations in the United States. At that time, the company operated 1,152 stores, coast-to-coast, under the names of Grants and Grant City. The stores ranged in sizes from 20,000 to 180,000 square feet. Sales for fiscal 1974 were $1.8 billion, and during that year, the firm averaged 69,000 employees. The firm's stock was traded on the New York Stock Exchange; see Exhibit 5, page 238, for stock prices. The stores featured a broad assortment of wearing apparel (45 percent of sales), housewares, small appliances, and home furnishings. Grant City stores also sold major appliances, automotive accessories, garden supplies, and sporting goods. Some of this merchandise was marketed under Grant's private label, Bradford.

Despite its size, Grants faced severe problems. The 1974 annual report cited the following as the three most serious problems of the firm:

1. A serious merchandise imbalance.
2. The severe burden imposed by the accelerated store-expansion program.
3. The excessive build-up of credit receivables, financed and administered through a seemingly expensive credit program. [3]

The first problem apparently refers to an imbalance in terms of inventories between everyday merchandise and big-ticket items, such as appliances. New policies were instituted, ". . . emphasizing

---

[1] This case was prepared from public information. It is designed for educational purposes, and not for the purposes of research or to illustrate correct or incorrect handling of administrative practices.

[2] For years prior to 1974, the firm ended its fiscal year on January 31. For the 1974 fiscal, an accounting change was made resulting in the closing being on January 30. However, in this case, the period February 1, 1974 to January 30, 1975 will still be referred to as "fiscal 1974," and will be compared to other fiscal years, without adjustment.

[3] W. T. Grant Company Annual Report 1974, page 2.

the basic needs of family shoppers . . ."[4] However, it was later revealed that these policies were not fully effective. Mr. John E. Sundman (recruited from Singer to become Grant's senior vice president and controller), in a later deposition, said that, just prior to January, 1975:

> . . . he learned that Grant's buying organization was still buying and stocking big-ticket merchandise, such as furniture and appliances, in quantities that couldn't be supported by existing credit policy . . .
>
> The reason, he said, was that the buyers realized that a cutback in buying in certain areas would result in a need for fewer buyers.[5]

The accelerated store-expansion program during the recent period may have led to many of Grant's stores being loss operations (see Exhibit 1 for the number of operating stores for selected fiscal year-ends). Grants had closed some of its operations in fiscal 1974.

> During the year ending January 30, 1975, 81 stores (2,073,000 gross square feet) were closed while 44 new stores (3,124,000 gross square feet) were opened. Store space in operation on that same date was 54,770,000 gross square feet, compared with 53,719,000 gross square feet on January 31, 1974. In addition to approximately 60 stores scheduled for closing during 1975 at the termination of their leases, the company has completed the closing of 64 additional stores. The majority of the latter stores were opened in the last few years, and had consistent records of unprofitability. This store closing program will significantly reduce the burden which investment in inventory, payroll and occupancy has placed upon the Company without hope of profitable return in the near future.[6]

Past credit policy was perhaps Grant's biggest problem. Credit had been granted on a liberal basis. Robert H. Anderson, a Grant executive, once commented that, if a customer's breath would fog a mirror, he could get instant credit. Again, in a deposition

> Mr. Sundman described the credit controls as a disaster area. Before he joined Grant, customer credit was approved at the store level, he said, and the rejection rate was 20%. That responsibility was transferred to headquarters in October 1974, and the rejections of consumer applications soared to 80%.[7]

---

[4] *ibid.*, page 2.

[5] "Grant Testimony Shows it Lacked Curbs on Budget, Credit and Had Internal Woes," *Wall Street Journal*, February 4, 1977, page 6.

[6] W. T. Grant Company Annual Report 1974, *op. cit.*, page 3.

[7] "Grant Testimony Shows it Lacked Curbs on Budget, Credit, and Had Internal Woes," *op. cit.*

In fiscal 1974, Grant's took a $298 million loss before taxes, and about one half of that amount was due to credit expense (see Exhibits 2 to 4, pages 235-237, for Grant's statements of income, balance sheets, and selected notes).   During fiscal 1974, Grants had written off $92 million in accounts receivable, and had increased allowance for doubtful accounts by $63 million.   Credit policy was tightened.   The sales decline from $1,850 million in fiscal 1973 to $1,762 million in fiscal 1974 was attributed, in part, to this changed policy by the company.

> While the company experienced sales declines in each of its four fiscal quarters, the largest decline, $55 million, occurred in the fourth quarter. This decline of 9.7% was due primarily to the Company's planned contraction of the promotion of Grant credit sales.[8]

On October 2, 1975, the company sought protection from the courts by filing a petition under Chapter 11 of the bankruptcy statutes.   Although the firm had expected to take losses in the first two quarters of fiscal 1975, and to lose money for the year, losses had apparently been heavier than expected.   At the time of the petition, Grant's had 1,073 stores in operation.   Grant's management may have felt that a new, smaller Grants would be viable.   A professional liquidator, Sam Nassi Company, was hired to liquidate a substantial portion of the then-operating stores.   It was felt that the hiring of a liquidator was necessary because of Grant's lack of experience in this area.   This subsequently proved correct, as Sam Nassi Company provided a substantially higher recovery than the 16 percent realized in stores liquidated by Grant's.   Although liquidators usually buy all fixtures and inventory, in stores to be liquidated, for a flat fee, this was not possible in the Grant's case because of liens on a portion of these assets.   Instead, the contract called for the Sam Nassi Company to receive 33 percent of all gross proceeds of the liquidation sale in excess of 31.5 percent of asset value. This final percentage, after expenses, was to go to Grant, as well as the remaining portion of gross proceeds.   Management consultants had estimated recovery at 22 to 35 percent of retail value, but the Sam Nassi Company was able to liquidate over 500 stores at between 45 to 50 percent of retail value. Total proceeds from these sales netted Grants about $100 million before bonuses and fees to liquidators. Nassi received more than $6 million.

---

[8] W. T. Grant Company Annual Report 1974, *op cit.*, page 10.

Unfortunately, efforts to save the firm failed, and in early February, 1976, the firm moved out of Chapter 11 and into proceedings for an orderly liquidation of all assets. At that time, the firm had 359 units in operation, and had assets totaling $512.1 million (of which $45 million was inventory at cost), and liabilities totaling $1.11 billion.

In June, 1976, it was decided that the 50.1 percent interest held by Grant's in Zeller's Ltd. would be sold to Fields Stores Ltd., based in Vancover, B. C. Zeller's was a Canadian retailer, with 152 stores, sales of $340 million, and earnings of $10.6 million for fiscal 1974. Zeller's was considered to be a subsidiary of W. T. Grant, but W. T. Grant's financial statements were not on a consolidated basis with Zeller's. Fields Stores had bid $32.7 million. A higher bid of $35 million had been received from McLeod-Stedman, a firm based in Minneapolis. The Fields' bid was accepted, because Fields did not need permission from the Canadian government to buy Zeller's, but McLeod-Stedman, a U. S. firm, did, and this might have taken months.[9]

In November, Federal Financial bought Grant's accounts receivable for $44 million plus 5 percent of the first year's profits. Federal Financial had been the winner in an auction bid for this asset. George Duffner, credit director for the Grant estate, valued these receivables at $276.3 million as of July 26, 1976. The receivables had been appraised by a law professor and two other men. The Grant estate at one point had spent $18,000 on dunning letters, but had received payments of only $4,000 in response.[10]

---

[9] See "Judge Clears Grant to Sell Its Control of Zeller's to Fields," *Wall Street Journal,* June 24, 1976, page 12.

[10] See "Federal Financial Buys Accounts Receivable Owed to W. T. Grant," *Wall Street Journal,* November 16, 1976, page 27.

EXHIBIT 1

W. T. Grant Company

Number of Operating Stores at Fiscal Year-End, Selected Years

Year-End	Number of Stores
1/31/61	864
1/31/71	1,116
1/31/72	1,168
1/31/73	1,208
1/31/74	1,189
1/30/75	1,152

EXHIBIT 2

W. T. Grant Company

Summary of Operations, for Years Ending January 31, 1971 to January 30, 1975

(rounded millions of dollars)

	1/30/75	1/31/74	1/31/73	1/31/72	1/31/71
Sales	$1,762	$1,850	$1,645	$1,375	$1,254
Income from concessions	4	4	4	3	5
Total revenue	1,766	1,854	1,649	1,378	1,259
Cost of merchandise sold, buying, and occupancy costs	1,303	1,283	1,125	931	843
Gross margin	463	571	523	447	416
Selling, general and administrative expenses	541	540	476	411	364
Store closing expenses	24	0	0	0	0
Net credit expense (income)	161	6	(14)	(22)	(13)
Other interest expense	38	18	6	5	2
Operating income	(301)	7	55	52	64
Interest earned	1	1	1	1	1
Gain on retirement of long-term debt	2	2	0	0	0
Earnings before income taxes and equity in net earnings of unconsolidated subsidiaries	(298)	10	56	53	65
Provision for taxes	(117)	3	26	26	33
Equity in earnings of unconsolidated subsidiaries	3	5	5	4	4
Net earnings (loss)	$ (178)	$ 11	$ 35	$ 32	$ 36

EXHIBIT 3

W. T. Grant Company

Consolidated Balance Sheets for Years Ending January 30, 1975 and January 31, 1974

(rounded millions of dollars)

	1/30/75	*1/31/74*
Cash	$ 80	$ 46
Customers' installment accounts receivable— see Note 3.	518	602
Less:		
Allowance for doubtful accounts	80	16
Unearned credit insurance premiums	1	5
Deferred finance income	38	60
Net accounts receivable	400	521
Merchandise inventories	407	451
Other receivables and claims	31	19
Prepaid expenses	7	7
Total current assets	925	1,045
Investments in unconsolidated subsidiaries— see Note 2.	50	44
W. T. Grant common stock held for deferred compensation	3	3
Net properties, fixtures, land, and improvements	102	101
Unamortized debt expenses and other assets	3	3
Total assets	$1,082	$1,195
Bank loans	600	0
Short-term commercial notes	0	453
Current portion of long-term debt	1	0
Accounts payable for merchandise	50	58
Salaries, wages, and bonuses	11	15
Other accrued expenses	49	14
Taxes withheld from employees	2	4
Sales and other taxes	17	13
Federal income taxes payable	18	0
Deferred income taxes related to installment sales	2	103
Total current liabilities	750	661
Long-term debt	216	220
Deferred federal income taxes	0	15
Deferred contingent compensation and other liabilities	2	4
Cumulative preferred stock	7	7
Common stock	19	19
Paid-in capital	82	84

EXHIBIT 3 (continued)

Amounts paid in by employees under purchase contracts for common stock	2	2
Retained earnings	38	219
Less: treasury stock	(34)	(37)
Total capital	114	295
Total liabilities and owners' equity	$1,082	$1,195

EXHIBIT 4

W. T. Grant Company

Excerpts From Selected Notes to Financial Statements

Note 2—Investments in Unconsolidated Subsidiaries

Investments in unconsolidated subsidiaries are carried at cost plus equity in net earnings (loss) since acquisition. There is no significant difference between the underlying net equity and such carrying amounts.

Details of investment accounts are as follows:	*1/30/75*	*1/31/74*
	($ in thousands)	
Common stock of Zeller's Limited (cost $8,893,326)	$ 32,670	$ 30,239
Common stock of Granjewel Jewelers & Distributors, Inc. (cost $3,576,240 and $2,040,000; respectively)	1,797	2,361
5½% Convertible subordinated debentures of Zeller's Limited ($6,060,000 Cdn.)	5,951	5,951
Convertible notes of Granjewel Jewelers & Distributors, Inc.	9,346	5,700
	$ 49,764	$ 44,251

Note 3—Credit Operations

A summary of net expense of credit operations is shown below:

Finance income	$ 87,012	$ 86,677
Expenses: Interest expense	48,308	32,965
Provision for doubtful accounts	155,691	21,198
Finance income related to uncollectable accounts	(4,127)	(1,317)
Administration	48,607	39,803
	248,479	92,649
Net credit expense	$161,467	$ 5,972
Credit sales	$402,916	$451,471

EXHIBIT 5

W. T. Grant Company

Chart of Common Stock Price Ranges, 1970 to 1974

Year	High	Low	Thousands of Outstanding Shares
1970	$52.00	$26.88	13,829
1971	70.63	41.88	14,168
1972	48.75	34.75	13,993
1973	44.38	9.88	14,072
1974	12.00	1.50	14,125

Questions

1. It is sometimes said that a firm's value in liquidation is substantially different from its value as a going concern. Contrast the following three concepts for the W. T. Grant case:

   (1) Market value
   (2) Book value
   (3) Liquidation value

   Use early 1975 as a reference point, and Grant's common stock as an example.

2. In evaluating the liquidation value of a firm, book values are often adjusted by an estimated recovery percent based on past experience. For inventory and receivables, these recovery percents are sometimes estimated at 70 percent. Compare these with the actual recovery percents in the Grant case. For the purpose of argument, assume that Federal Financial will make $10 million in profit during the first year on the receivables transaction. Give reasons for any similarities or discrepancies between the "rule of thumb" and the actual recovery percents.

3. What do the circumstances regarding the sales of Zeller's tell you about the reasons for the differences between the market and liquidation value? Was the price paid for Zeller's near what the price would be in a nonliquidation situation?

4. Give some reasons why a liquidation might be preferable to reorganization, from a creditor's view, given W. T. Grant's financial position as of early February, 1976.

APPENDIX A

APPENDIX A

Present Value Interest Factors for a Single Payment
Payment received k Years from Now Discounted at i Percent

k/i	1%	2%	3%	4%	5%	6%	7%	8%	i/k
01	0.99010	0.98039	0.97087	0.96154	0.95238	0.94340	0.93458	0.92593	01
02	.98030	.96117	.94260	.92456	.90703	.89000	.87344	.85734	02
03	.97059	.94232	.91514	.88900	.86384	.83962	.81630	.79383	03
04	.96098	.92385	.88849	.85480	.82270	.79209	.76290	.73503	04
05	.95147	.90573	.86261	.82193	.78353	.74726	.71299	.68058	05
06	.94205	.88797	.83748	.79031	.74622	.70496	.66634	.63017	06
07	.93272	.87056	.81309	.75992	.71068	.66506	.62275	.58349	07
08	.92348	.85349	.78941	.73069	.67664	.62741	.58201	.54027	08
09	.91434	.83676	.76642	.70259	.64461	.59190	.54393	.50025	09
10	.90529	.82035	.74409	.67556	.61391	.55839	.50835	.46319	10
11	.89632	.80426	.72242	.64958	.58468	.52679	.47509	.42888	11
12	.88745	.78849	.70138	.62460	.55684	.49697	.44401	.39711	12
13	.87866	.77303	.68095	.60057	.53032	.46884	.41496	.36670	13
14	.86996	.75788	.66112	.57748	.50507	.44230	.38782	.34046	14
15	.86135	.74301	.64186	.55526	.48102	.41727	.36245	.31524	15
16	.85282	.72845	.62317	.53391	.45811	.39365	.33873	.29189	16
17	.84438	.71416	.60502	.51337	.43630	.37136	.31657	.27027	17
18	.83602	.70016	.58739	.49363	.41552	.35034	.29586	.25025	18
19	.82774	.68643	.57029	.47464	.39573	.33051	.27651	.23171	19
20	.81954	.67297	.55368	.45639	.37689	.31180	.25842	.21455	20
25	.77977	.60953	.47761	.37512	.29530	.23300	.18425	.14602	25
30	.74192	.55207	.41199	.30832	.23138	.17411	.13137	.09938	30
35	.70591	.50003	.35538	.25342	.18129	.13011	.09366	.06763	35
40	.67165	.45289	.30656	.20829	.14205	.09722	.06678	.04603	40
45	.63905	.41020	.26444	.17120	.11130	.07265	.04760	.03133	45

APPENDIX A (cont'd)

k/i	9%	10%	11%	12%	13%	14%	15%	16%	i/k
1	0.91743	0.90909	0.90090	0.89286	0.88496	0.87719	0.86957	0.86207	1
2	.84168	.82645	.81162	.79719	.78315	.76947	.75614	.74316	2
3	.77218	.75131	.73119	.71178	.69305	.67497	.65752	.64066	3
4	.70843	.68301	.65873	.63552	.61332	.59208	.57175	.55229	4
5	.64993	.62092	.59345	.56743	.54276	.51937	.49718	.47611	5
6	.59627	.56447	.53464	.50663	.48032	.45559	.43233	.41044	6
7	.54703	.51316	.48166	.45235	.42506	.39964	.37594	.35383	7
8	.50187	.46651	.43393	.40388	.37616	.35056	.32690	.30503	8
9	.46043	.42410	.39092	.36061	.33288	.30751	.28426	.26295	9
10	.42241	.38554	.35218	.32197	.29459	.26974	.24718	.22668	10
11	.38753	.35049	.31728	.28748	.26070	.23662	.21494	.19542	11
12	.35553	.31863	.28584	.25668	.23071	.20756	.18691	.16846	12
13	.32618	.28966	.25751	.22917	.20416	.18207	.16253	.14523	13
14	.29925	.26333	.23199	.20462	.18068	.15971	.14133	.12520	14
15	.27454	.23939	.20900	.18270	.15989	.14010	.12289	.10793	15
16	.25187	.21763	.18829	.16312	.14150	.12289	.10686	.09304	16
17	.23107	.19784	.16963	.14564	.12522	.10780	.09293	.08021	17
18	.21199	.17986	.15282	.13004	.11081	.09456	.08081	.06914	18
19	.19449	.16351	.13768	.11611	.09806	.08295	.07027	.05961	19
20	.17843	.14864	.12403	.10367	.08678	.07276	.06110	.05139	20
25	.11597	.09230	.07361	.05882	.04710	.03779	.03038	.02447	25
30	.07537	.05731	.04368	.03338	.02557	.01963	.01510	.01165	30
35	.04899	.03558	.02592	.01894	.01388	.01019	.00751	.00555	35
40	.03184	.02209	.01538	.01075	.00753	.00529	.00373	.00264	40
45	.02069	.01372	.00913	.00610	.00409	.00275	.00186	.00126	45

APPENDIX A (cont'd)

k/i	17%	18%	19%	20%	25%	30%	35%	40%	i/k
1	0.85470	0.84746	0.84034	0.83333	0.80000	0.76923	0.74074	0.71429	1
2	.73051	.71818	.70616	.69444	.64000	.59172	.54870	.51020	2
3	.62437	.60863	.59342	.57870	.51200	.45517	.40644	.36443	3
4	.53365	.51579	.49867	.48225	.40960	.35013	.30107	.26031	4
5	.45611	.43711	.41905	.40188	.32768	.26933	.22301	.18593	5
6	.38984	.37043	.35214	.33490	.26214	.20718	.16520	.13281	6
7	.33320	.31393	.29592	.27908	.20972	.15937	.12237	.09486	7
8	.28478	.26604	.24867	.23257	.16777	.12259	.09064	.06776	8
9	.24340	.22546	.20897	.19381	.13422	.09430	.06714	.04840	9
10	.20804	.19106	.17560	.16151	.10737	.07254	.04974	.03457	10
11	.17781	.16192	.14757	.13459	.08590	.05580	.03684	.02469	11
12	.15197	.13722	.12400	.11216	.06872	.04292	.02729	.01764	12
13	.12989	.11629	.10421	.09346	.05498	.03302	.02021	.01260	13
14	.11102	.09855	.08757	.07789	.04398	.02540	.01497	.00900	14
15	.09489	.08352	.07359	.06491	.03518	.01954	.01109	.00643	15
16	.08110	.07078	.06184	.05409	.02815	.01503	.00822	.00459	16
17	.06932	.05998	.05196	.04507	.02252	.01156	.00609	.00328	17
18	.05925	.05083	.04367	.03756	.01801	.00889	.00451	.00234	18
19	.05064	.04308	.03670	.03130	.01441	.00684	.00334	.00167	19
20	.04328	.03651	.03084	.02608	.01153	.00526	.00247	.00120	20
25	.01974	.01596	.01292	.01048	.00378	.00142	.00055	.00022	25
30	.00900	.00697	.00541	.00421	.00124	.00038	.00012	.00004	30
35	.00411	.00305	.00227	.00169	.00041	.00010	.00003	.00001	35
40	.00187	.00133	.00095	.00068	.00013	.00003	.00001	.00000	40
45	.00085	.00058	.00040	.00027	.00004	.00001	.00000	.00000	45

APPENDIX B

APPENDIX B

Present Value Interest Factor for an Annuity
Payment Received Every Year for n Years and Discounted at i Percent

n/i	1%	2%	3%	4%	5%	6%	7%	8%	i/n
1	0.99010	0.98039	0.97087	0.96154	0.95238	0.94340	0.93458	0.92593	1
2	1.97040	1.94156	1.91347	1.88609	1.85941	1.83339	1.80802	1.78326	2
3	2.94099	2.88388	2.82861	2.77509	2.72325	2.67301	2.62432	2.57710	3
4	3.90197	3.80773	3.71710	3.62990	3.54595	3.46511	3.38721	3.31213	4
5	4.85343	4.71346	4.57971	4.45182	4.32948	4.21236	4.10020	3.99271	5
6	5.79548	5.60143	5.41719	5.24214	5.07569	4.91732	4.76654	4.62288	6
7	6.72819	6.47199	6.23028	6.00205	5.78637	5.58238	5.38929	5.20637	7
8	7.65168	7.32548	7.01969	6.73274	6.46321	6.20979	5.97130	5.74664	8
9	8.56602	8.16224	7.78611	7.43533	7.10782	6.80169	6.51523	6.24689	9
10	9.47130	8.98259	8.53020	8.11090	7.72173	7.36009	7.02358	6.71008	10
11	10.36763	9.78685	9.25262	8.76048	8.30641	7.88687	7.49867	7.13896	11
12	11.25508	10.57534	9.95400	9.38507	8.86325	8.38384	7.94269	7.53608	12
13	12.13374	11.34837	10.63496	9.98565	9.39357	8.85268	8.35765	7.90378	13
14	13.00370	12.10625	11.29607	10.56312	9.89864	9.29498	8.74547	8.24424	14
15	13.86505	12.84926	11.93794	11.11839	10.37966	9.71225	9.10791	8.55948	15
16	14.71787	13.57771	12.56110	11.65230	10.83777	10.10590	9.44665	8.85137	16
17	15.56225	14.29187	13.16612	12.16567	11.27407	10.47726	9.76322	9.12164	17
18	16.39827	14.99203	13.75351	12.65930	11.68959	10.82760	10.05909	9.37189	18
19	17.22601	15.67846	14.32380	13.13394	12.08532	11.15812	10.33560	9.60360	19
20	18.04555	16.35143	14.87747	13.59033	12.46221	11.46992	10.59401	9.81815	20
25	22.02316	19.52346	17.41315	15.62208	14.09394	12.78336	11.65358	10.67478	25
30	25.80771	22.39646	19.60044	17.29203	15.37245	13.76483	12.40904	11.25778	30
35	29.40858	24.99862	21.48722	18.66461	16.37419	14.49825	12.94767	11.65457	35
40	32.83469	27.35548	23.11477	19.79277	17.15909	15.04630	13.33171	11.92461	40
45	36.09451	29.49016	24.51871	20.72004	17.77407	15.45583	13.60552	12.10840	45

APPENDIX B (cont'd)

n/i	9%	10%	11%	12%	13%	14%	15%	16%	i/n
1	0.91743	0.90909	0.90090	0.89286	0.88496	0.87719	0.86957	0.86207	1
2	1.75911	1.73554	1.71252	1.69005	1.66810	1.64666	1.62571	1.60523	2
3	2.53129	2.48685	2.44371	2.40183	2.36115	2.32163	2.28323	2.24589	3
4	3.23972	3.16987	3.10245	3.03735	2.97447	2.91371	2.85498	2.79818	4
5	3.88965	3.79079	3.69590	3.60478	3.51723	3.43308	3.35216	3.27429	5
6	4.48592	4.35526	4.23054	4.11141	3.99755	3.88867	3.78448	3.68474	6
7	5.03295	4.86842	4.71220	4.56376	4.42261	4.28830	4.16042	4.03857	7
8	5.53482	5.33493	5.14612	4.96764	4.79877	4.63886	4.48732	4.34359	8
9	5.99525	5.75902	5.53705	5.32825	5.13166	4.94637	4.77158	4.60654	9
10	6.41766	6.14457	5.88923	5.65022	5.42624	5.21612	5.01877	4.83323	10
11	6.80519	6.49506	6.20652	5.93770	5.68694	5.45273	5.23371	5.02864	11
12	7.16073	6.81369	6.49236	6.19437	5.91765	5.66029	5.42062	5.19711	12
13	7.48690	7.10336	6.74987	6.42355	6.12181	5.84236	5.58315	5.34233	13
14	7.78615	7.36669	6.98187	6.62817	6.30249	6.00207	5.72448	5.46753	14
15	8.06069	7.60608	7.19087	6.81086	6.46238	6.14217	5.84737	5.57546	15
16	8.31256	7.82371	7.37916	6.97399	6.60388	6.26506	5.95423	5.66850	16
17	8.54363	8.02155	7.54879	7.11963	6.72909	6.37286	6.04716	5.74870	17
18	8.75563	8.20141	7.70162	7.24967	6.83991	6.46742	6.12797	5.81785	18
19	8.95011	8.36492	7.83929	7.36578	6.93797	6.55037	6.19823	5.87746	19
20	9.12855	8.51356	7.96333	7.46944	7.02475	6.62313	6.25933	5.92884	20
25	9.82258	9.07704	8.42174	7.84314	7.32998	6.87293	6.46415	6.09709	25
30	10.27365	9.42691	8.69379	8.05518	7.49565	7.00266	6.56598	6.17720	30
35	10.56682	9.64416	8.85524	8.17550	7.58557	7.07005	6.61661	6.21534	35
40	10.75736	9.77905	8.95105	8.24378	7.63438	7.10504	6.64178	6.23350	40
45	10.88120	9.86281	9.00791	8.28252	7.66086	7.12322	6.65429	6.24214	45

APPENDIX B (cont'd)

n/i	17%	18%	19%	20%	25%	30%	35%	40%	i/n
1	0.85470	0.84746	0.84034	0.83333	0.80000	0.76923	0.74074	0.71429	1
2	1.58521	1.56564	1.54650	1.52778	1.44000	1.36095	1.28944	1.22449	2
3	2.20958	2.17427	2.13992	2.10648	1.95200	1.81611	1.69588	1.58892	3
4	2.74324	2.69006	2.63859	2.58873	2.36160	2.16624	1.99695	1.84923	4
5	3.19935	3.12717	3.05763	2.99061	2.68928	2.43557	2.21996	2.03516	5
6	3.58918	3.49760	3.40978	3.32551	2.95142	2.64275	2.38516	2.16797	6
7	3.92238	3.81153	3.70570	3.60459	3.16114	2.80211	2.50752	2.26284	7
8	4.20716	4.07757	3.95437	3.83716	3.32891	2.92470	2.59817	2.33060	8
9	4.45057	4.30302	4.16333	4.03097	3.46313	3.01900	2.66531	2.37900	9
10	4.65860	4.49409	4.33893	4.19247	3.57050	3.09154	2.71504	2.41357	10
11	4.83641	4.65601	4.48650	4.32706	3.65640	3.14734	2.75188	2.43826	11
12	4.98839	4.79322	4.61050	4.43922	3.72512	3.19026	2.77917	2.45590	12
13	5.11828	4.90951	4.71471	4.53268	3.78010	3.22328	2.79939	2.46850	13
14	5.22930	5.00806	4.80228	4.61057	3.82408	3.24867	2.81436	2.47750	14
15	5.32419	5.09158	4.87586	4.67547	3.85926	3.26821	2.82545	2.48393	15
16	5.40529	5.16235	4.93770	4.72956	3.88741	3.28324	2.83367	2.48852	16
17	5.47461	5.22233	4.98966	4.77463	3.90993	3.29480	2.83975	2.49180	17
18	5.53385	5.27316	5.03333	4.81219	3.92794	3.30369	2.84426	2.49414	18
19	5.58449	5.31624	5.07003	4.84350	3.94235	3.31053	2.84760	2.49582	19
20	5.62777	5.35275	5.10086	4.86958	3.95388	3.31579	2.85008	2.49701	20
25	5.76623	5.46691	5.19515	4.94759	3.98489	3.32861	2.85557	2.49944	25
30	5.82939	5.51681	5.23466	4.97894	3.99505	3.33206	2.85679	2.49990	30
35	5.85820	5.53862	5.25122	4.99154	3.99838	3.33299	2.85706	2.49998	35
40	5.87133	5.54815	5.25815	4.99660	3.99947	3.33324	2.85713	2.50000	40
45	5.87733	5.55232	5.26106	4.99863	3.99983	3.33331	2.85714	2.50000	45